AARON and AHMED

a love story

VERTIGO
DC COMICS

AARON and

AHMED

a love story

Jay Cantor Writer

James Romberger Artist

José Villarrubia Colorist

Jared K. Fletcher Letterer

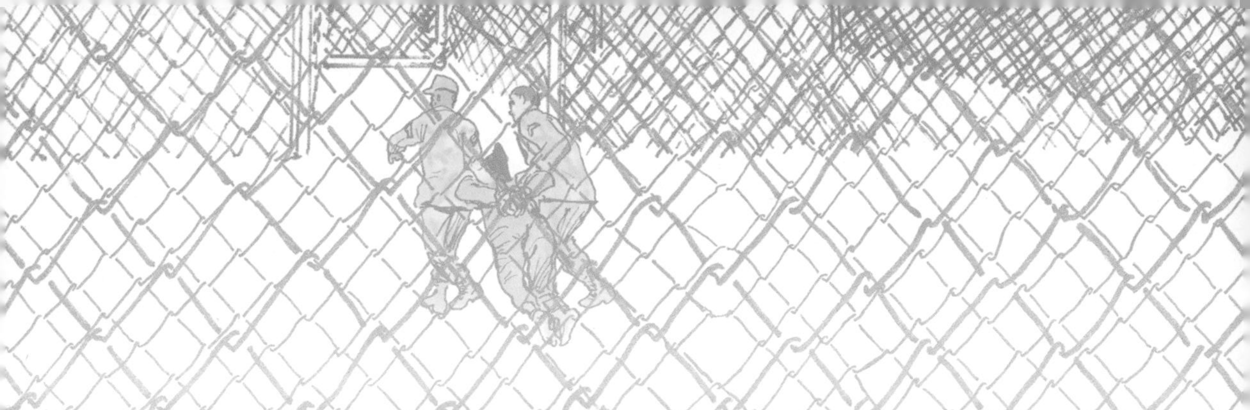

Karen Berger SVP-Executive Editor
Pornsak Pichetshote Editor
Robbin Brosterman Design Director-Books
Curtis King Jr. Senior Art Director

DC COMICS
Diane Nelson President
Dan DiDio and **Jim Lee** Co-Publishers
Geoff Johns Chief Creative Officer
Patrick Caldon EVP-Finance and Administration
John Rood EVP-Sales, Marketing and Business Development
Amy Genkins SVP-Business and Legal Affairs
Steve Rotterdam SVP-Sales and Marketing
John Cunningham VP-Marketing
Terri Cunningham VP-Managing Editor
Alison Gill VP-Manufacturing
David Hyde VP-Publicity
Sue Pohja VP-Book Trade Sales
Alysse Soll VP-Advertising and Custom Publishing
Bob Wayne VP-Sales
Mark Chiarello Art Director

AARON AND AHMED

Published by DC Comics, 1700 Broadway, New York, NY 10019.

Printed in the U.S.A. First Printing.
DC Comics, a Warner Bros. Entertainment Company.

HC ISBN: 978-1-4012-1186-8.
SC ISBN: 978-1-4012-1187-5.

SUSTAINABLE FORESTRY INITIATIVE
Certified Chain of Custody
60% Certified Fiber Sourcing and
40% Post-Consumer Recycled
www.sfiprogram.org
This label applies to the text stock
SGS-SFI/COC-US10/81072

Library of Congress Cataloging-in-Publication Data

Cantor, Jay.
Aaron and Ahmed / Jay Cantor.
p. cm.
ISBN 978-1-4012-1186-8 (hardcover)
1. Terrorism--Prevention--Comic books, strips, etc. 2. War on Terrorism, 2001-2009--Comic books, strips, etc. 3. Graphic novels. I. Title.

PN6727.C365A27 2011
741.5'973--dc22

2010050134

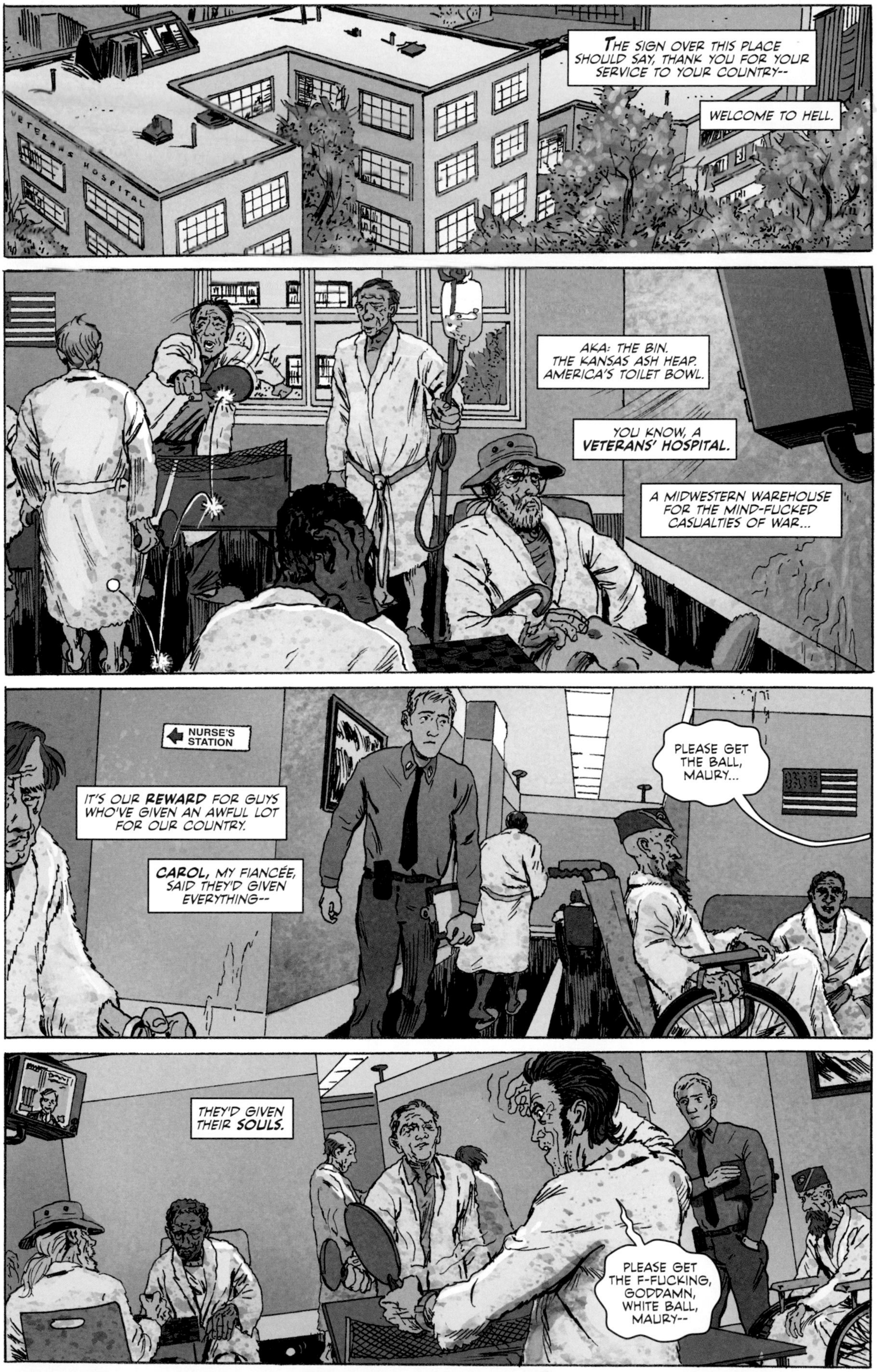
THE SIGN OVER THIS PLACE SHOULD SAY, THANK YOU FOR YOUR SERVICE TO YOUR COUNTRY--
WELCOME TO HELL.
VETERANS HOSPITAL
AKA: THE BIN. THE KANSAS ASH HEAP. AMERICA'S TOILET BOWL.
YOU KNOW, A **VETERANS' HOSPITAL.**
A MIDWESTERN WAREHOUSE FOR THE MIND-FUCKED CASUALTIES OF WAR...
NURSE'S STATION
IT'S OUR **REWARD** FOR GUYS WHO'VE GIVEN AN AWFUL LOT FOR OUR COUNTRY.
CAROL, MY FIANCÉE, SAID THEY'D GIVEN EVERYTHING--
PLEASE GET THE BALL, MAURY...
THEY'D GIVEN THEIR **SOULS.**
PLEASE GET THE F-FUCKING, GODDAMN, WHITE BALL, MAURY--

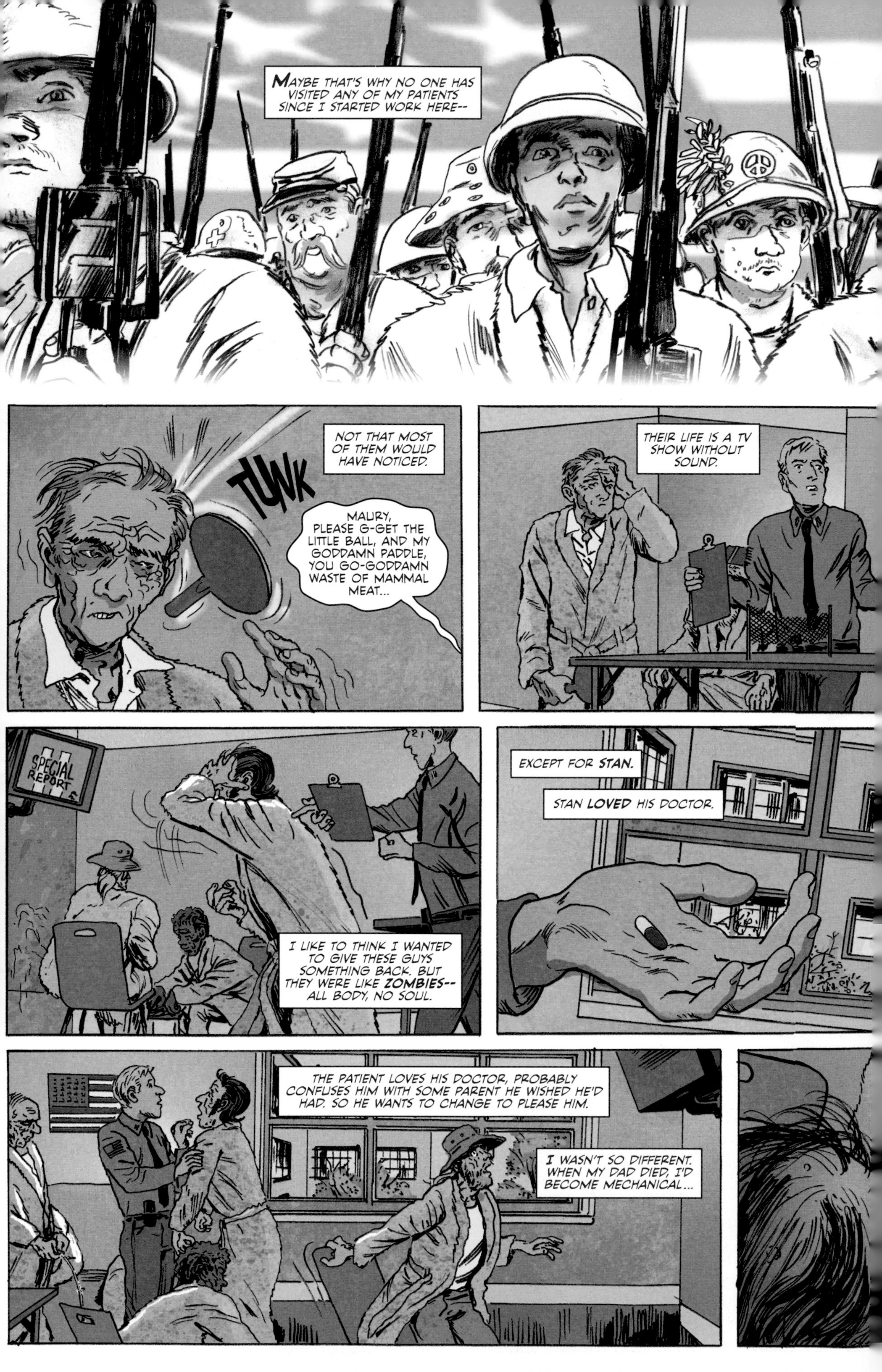
MAYBE THAT'S WHY NO ONE HAS VISITED ANY OF MY PATIENTS SINCE I STARTED WORK HERE--
NOT THAT MOST OF THEM WOULD HAVE NOTICED.
TUNK
MAURY, PLEASE G-GET THE LITTLE BALL, AND MY GODDAMN PADDLE, YOU GO-GODDAMN WASTE OF MAMMAL MEAT...
THEIR LIFE IS A TV SHOW WITHOUT SOUND.
SPECIAL REPORT
I LIKE TO THINK I WANTED TO GIVE THESE GUYS SOMETHING BACK. BUT THEY WERE LIKE ZOMBIES-- ALL BODY, NO SOUL.
EXCEPT FOR STAN.
STAN LOVED HIS DOCTOR.
THE PATIENT LOVES HIS DOCTOR, PROBABLY CONFUSES HIM WITH SOME PARENT HE WISHED HE'D HAD. SO HE WANTS TO CHANGE TO PLEASE HIM.
I WASN'T SO DIFFERENT. WHEN MY DAD DIED, I'D BECOME MECHANICAL...

I'M AARON GOODMAN, THEIR PSYCHIATRIST.

I ENDED UP HERE BECAUSE WHEN MY DAD KILLED HIMSELF, MY FAMILY WENT STONE BROKE, AND I NEEDED THE ARMY TO PAY FOR MEDICAL SCHOOL.

THAT LOVE BROUGHT HIM BACK TO LIFE.

THERAPY IS LIKE A ROMANCE--EVEN IF IT'S THE KIND OF LOVE STORY WHERE ONE PERSON GETS PAID.

...EMPTY... A TIN MAN...

HMMMM HMMMM

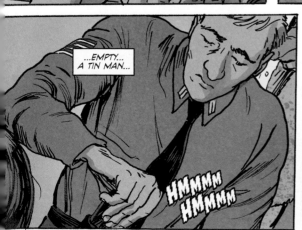

BUT THEN I MET CAROL--

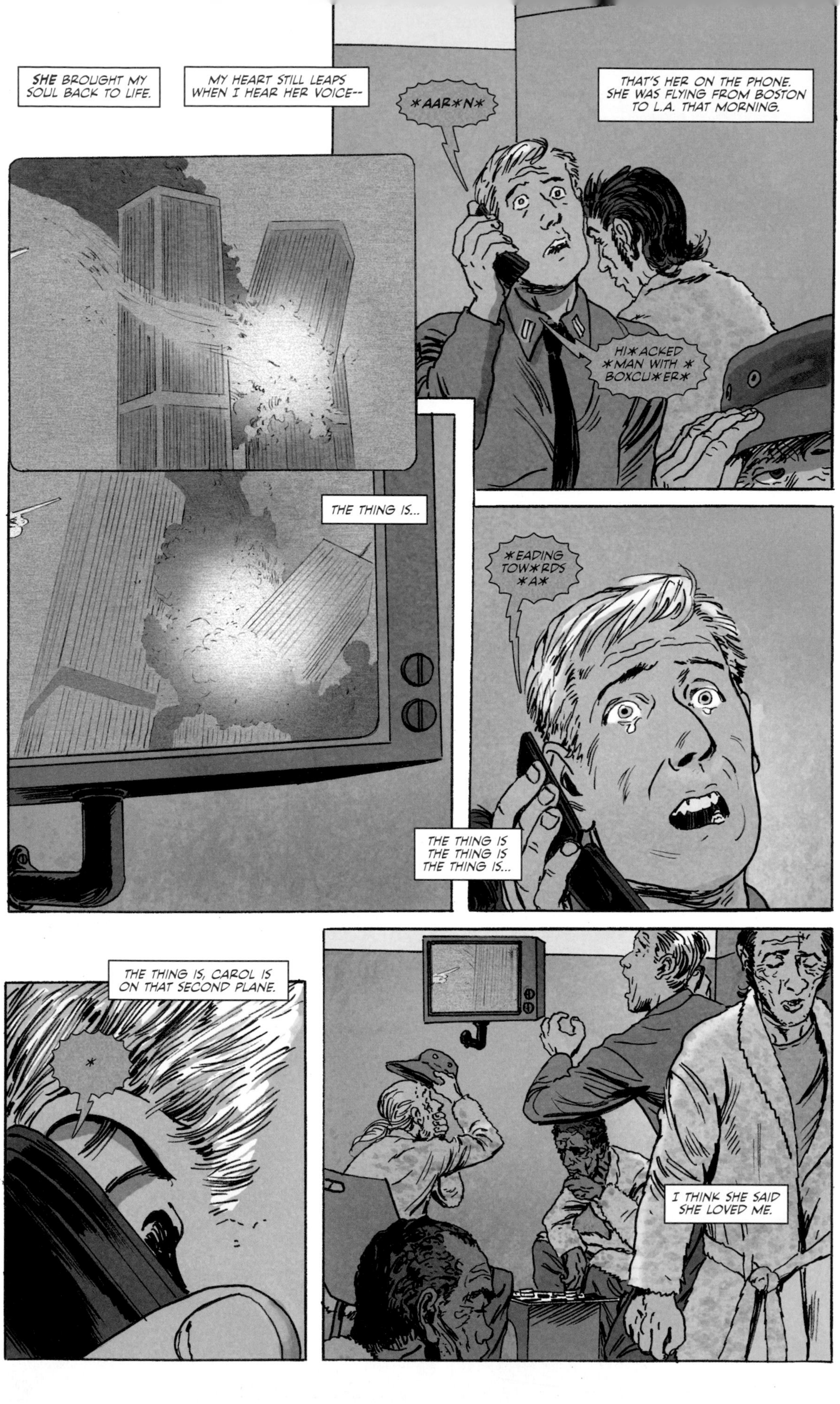
SHE BROUGHT MY SOUL BACK TO LIFE.
MY HEART STILL LEAPS WHEN I HEAR HER VOICE--
*AAR*N*
THAT'S HER ON THE PHONE. SHE WAS FLYING FROM BOSTON TO L.A. THAT MORNING.
HI*ACKED *MAN WITH * BOXCU*ER*
THE THING IS...
*EADING TOW*RDS *A*
THE THING IS THE THING IS THE THING IS...
THE THING IS, CAROL IS ON THAT SECOND PLANE.
*
I THINK SHE SAID SHE LOVED ME.

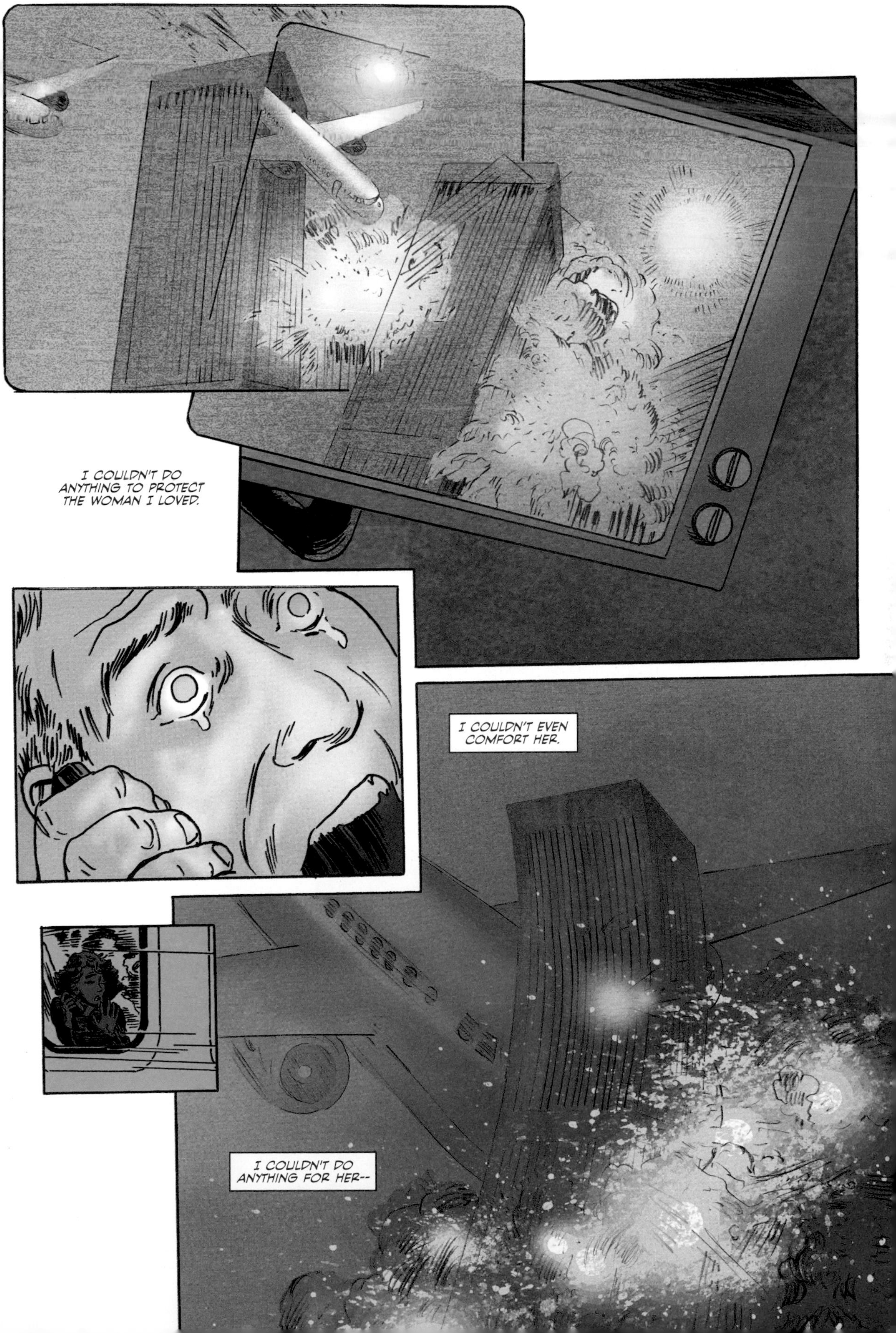
I COULDN'T DO ANYTHING TO PROTECT THE WOMAN I LOVED.
I COULDN'T EVEN COMFORT HER.
I COULDN'T DO ANYTHING FOR HER--

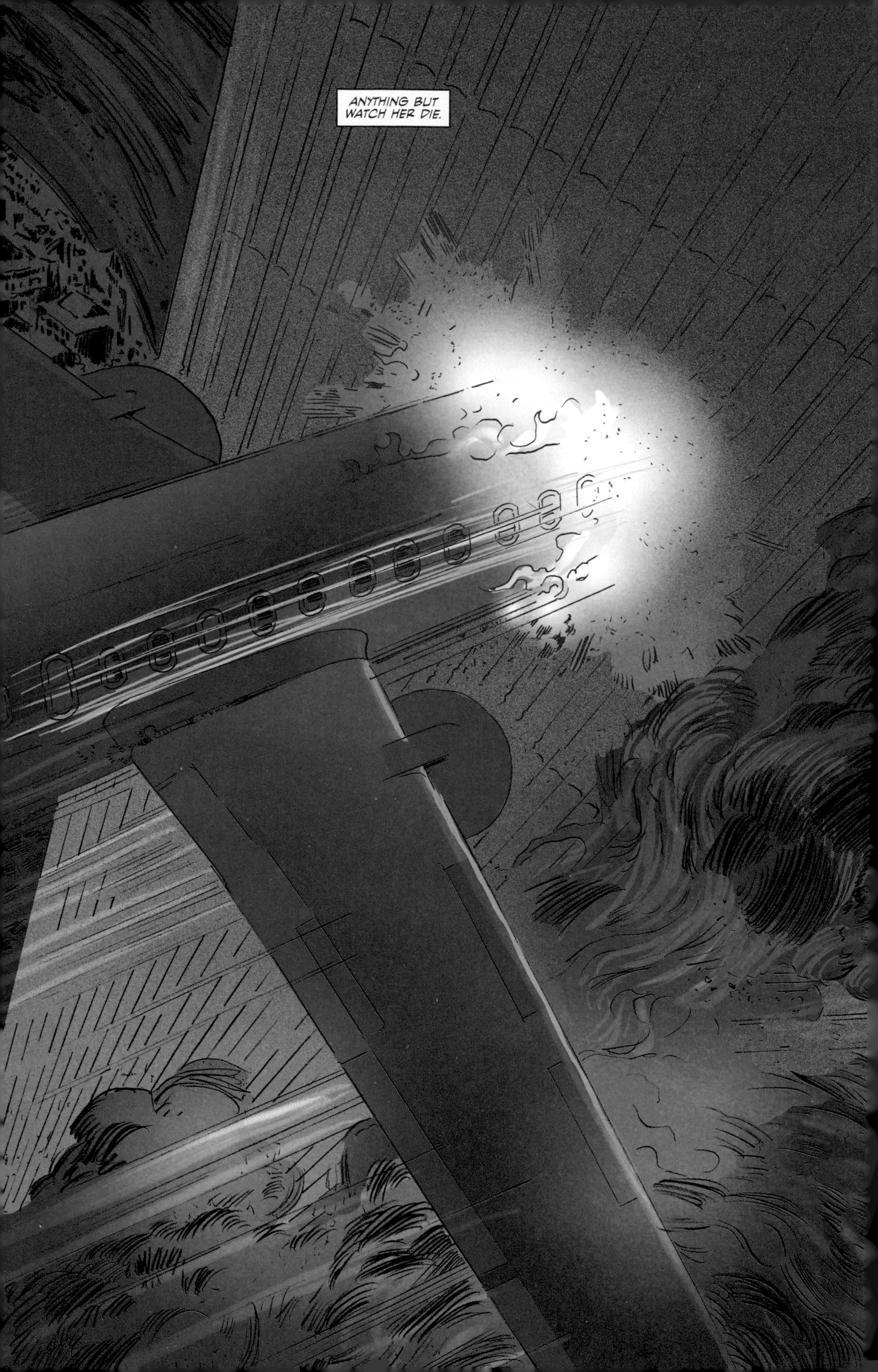
ANYTHING BUT WATCH HER DIE.

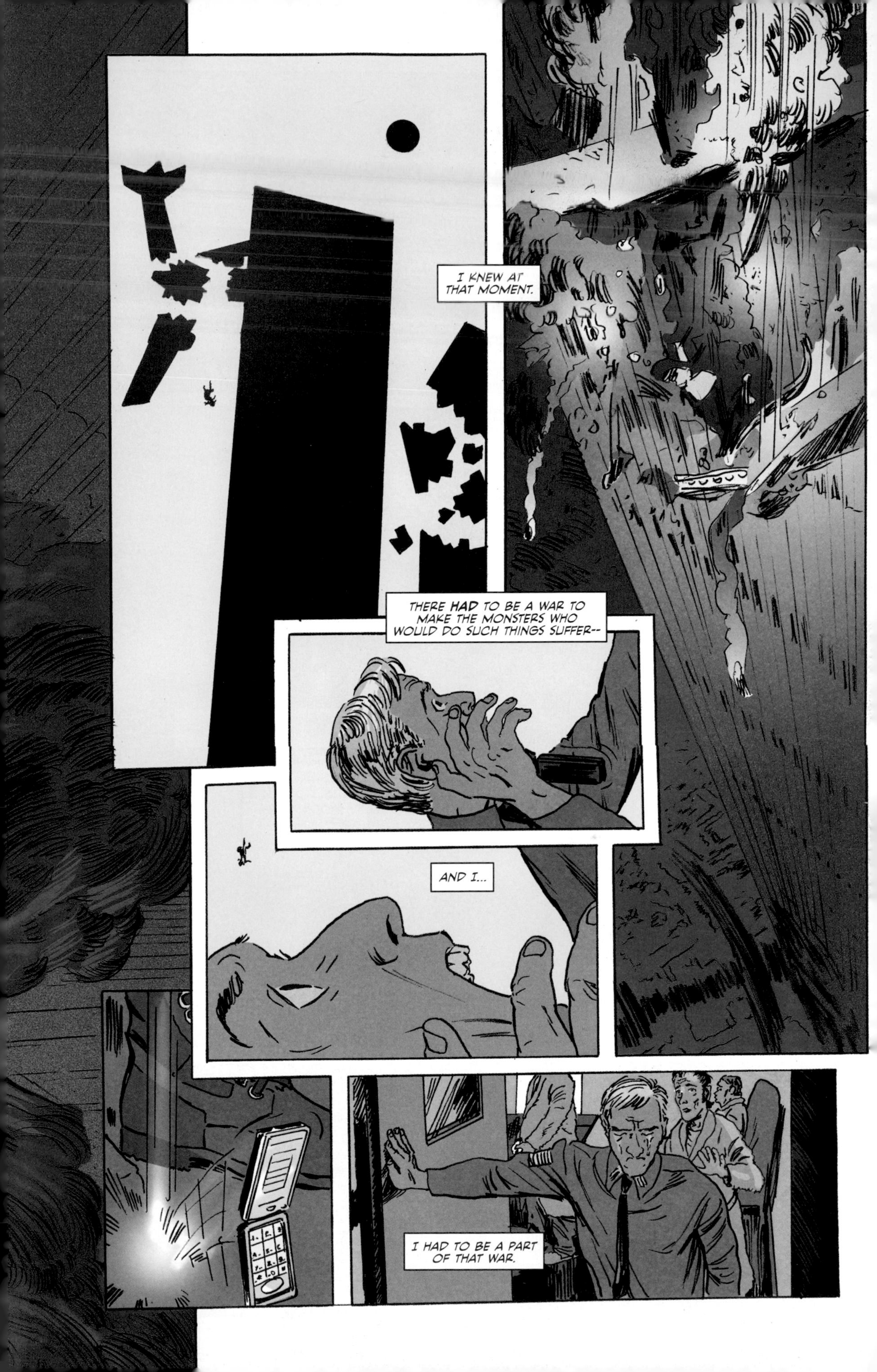
I KNEW AT THAT MOMENT.
THERE HAD TO BE A WAR TO MAKE THE MONSTERS WHO WOULD DO SUCH THINGS SUFFER--
AND I...
I HAD TO BE A PART OF THAT WAR.

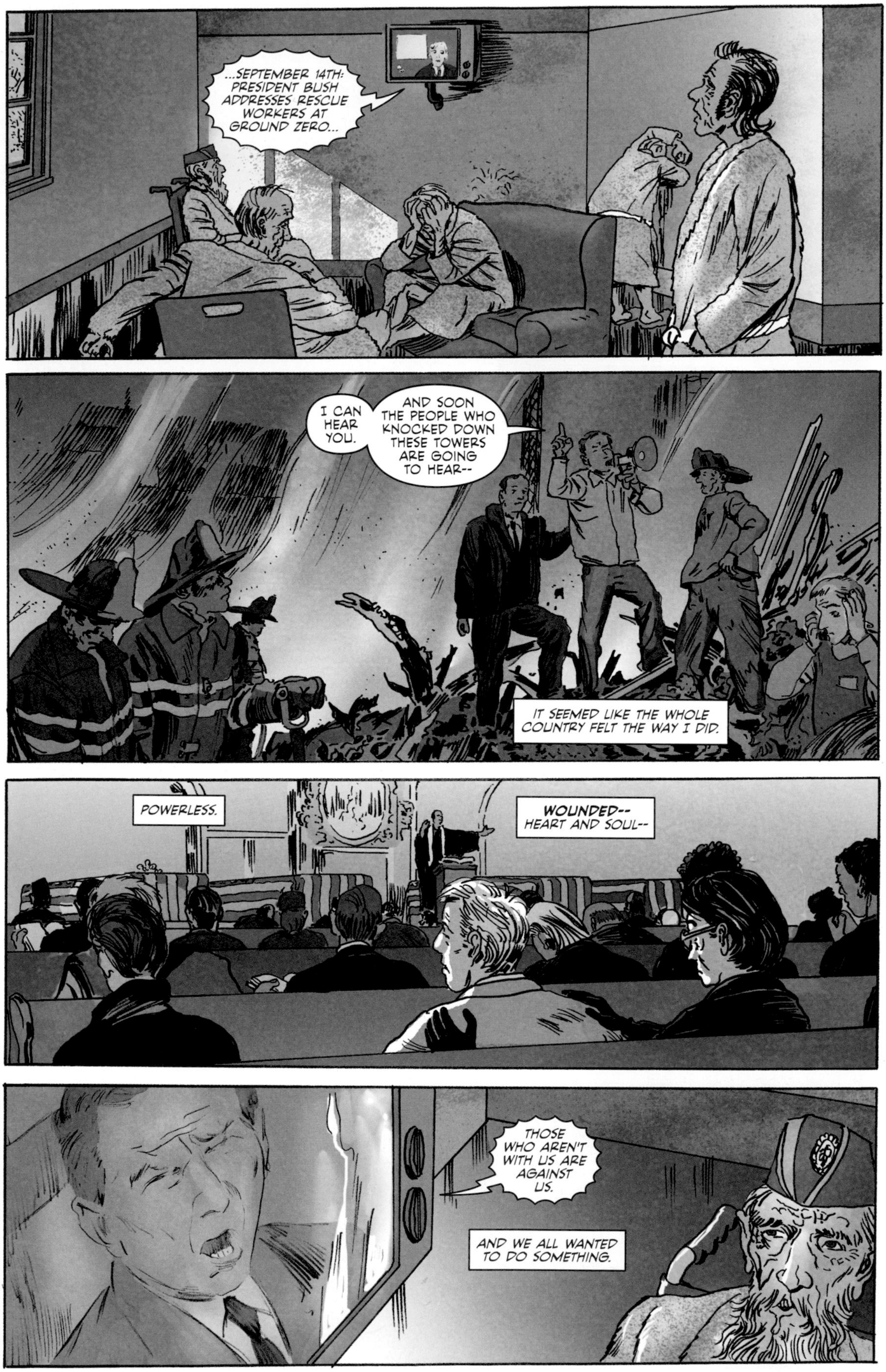
...SEPTEMBER 14TH: PRESIDENT BUSH ADDRESSES RESCUE WORKERS AT GROUND ZERO...
I CAN HEAR YOU.
AND SOON THE PEOPLE WHO KNOCKED DOWN THESE TOWERS ARE GOING TO HEAR--
IT SEEMED LIKE THE WHOLE COUNTRY FELT THE WAY I DID.
POWERLESS.
WOUNDED-- HEART AND SOUL--
THOSE WHO AREN'T WITH US ARE AGAINST US.
AND WE ALL WANTED TO DO SOMETHING.

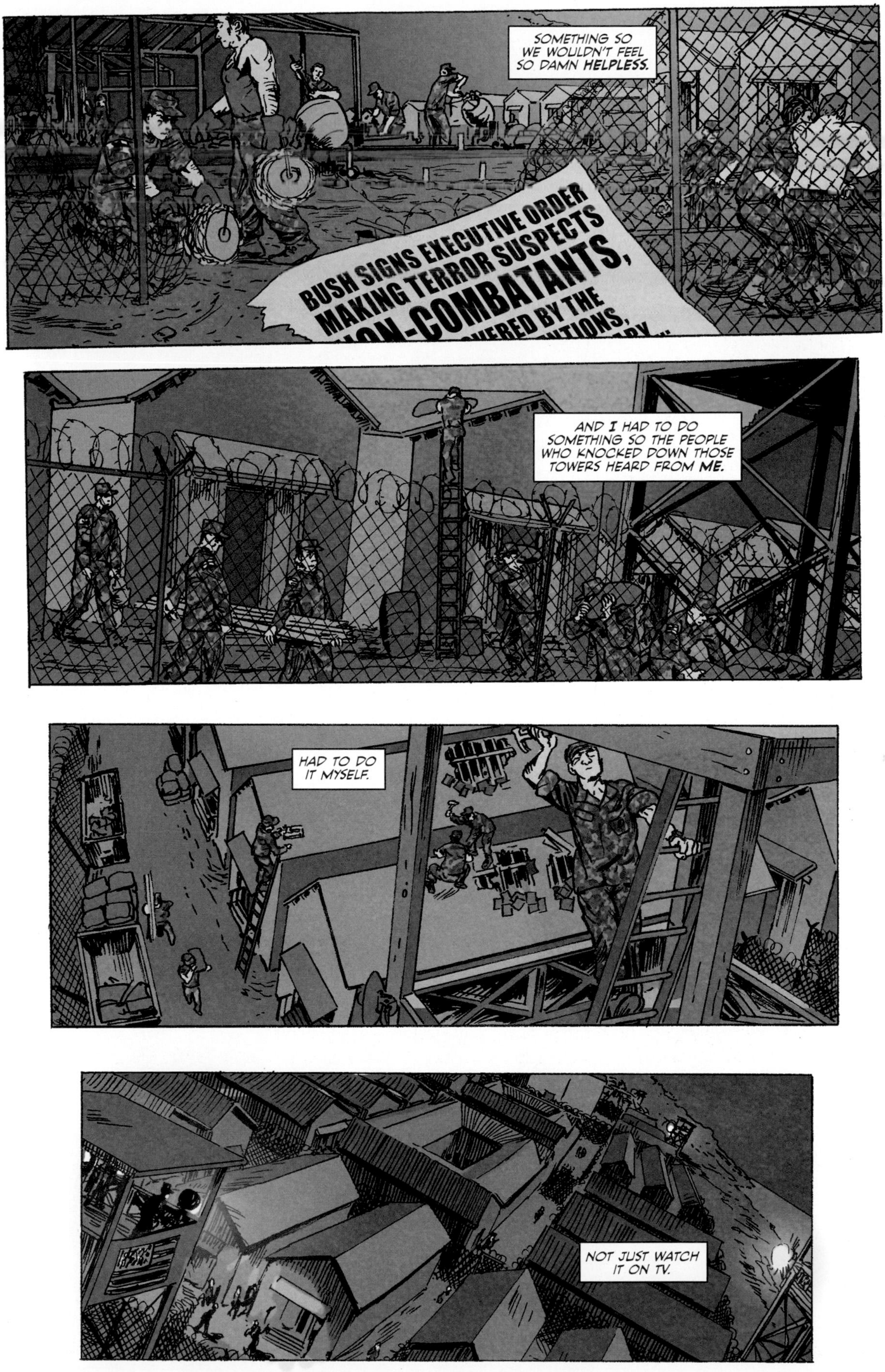
SOMETHING SO WE WOULDN'T FEEL SO DAMN HELPLESS.
BUSH SIGNS EXECUTIVE ORDER
MAKING TERROR SUSPECTS
AND I HAD TO DO SOMETHING SO THE PEOPLE WHO KNOCKED DOWN THOSE TOWERS HEARD FROM ME.
HAD TO DO IT MYSELF.
NOT JUST WATCH IT ON TV.

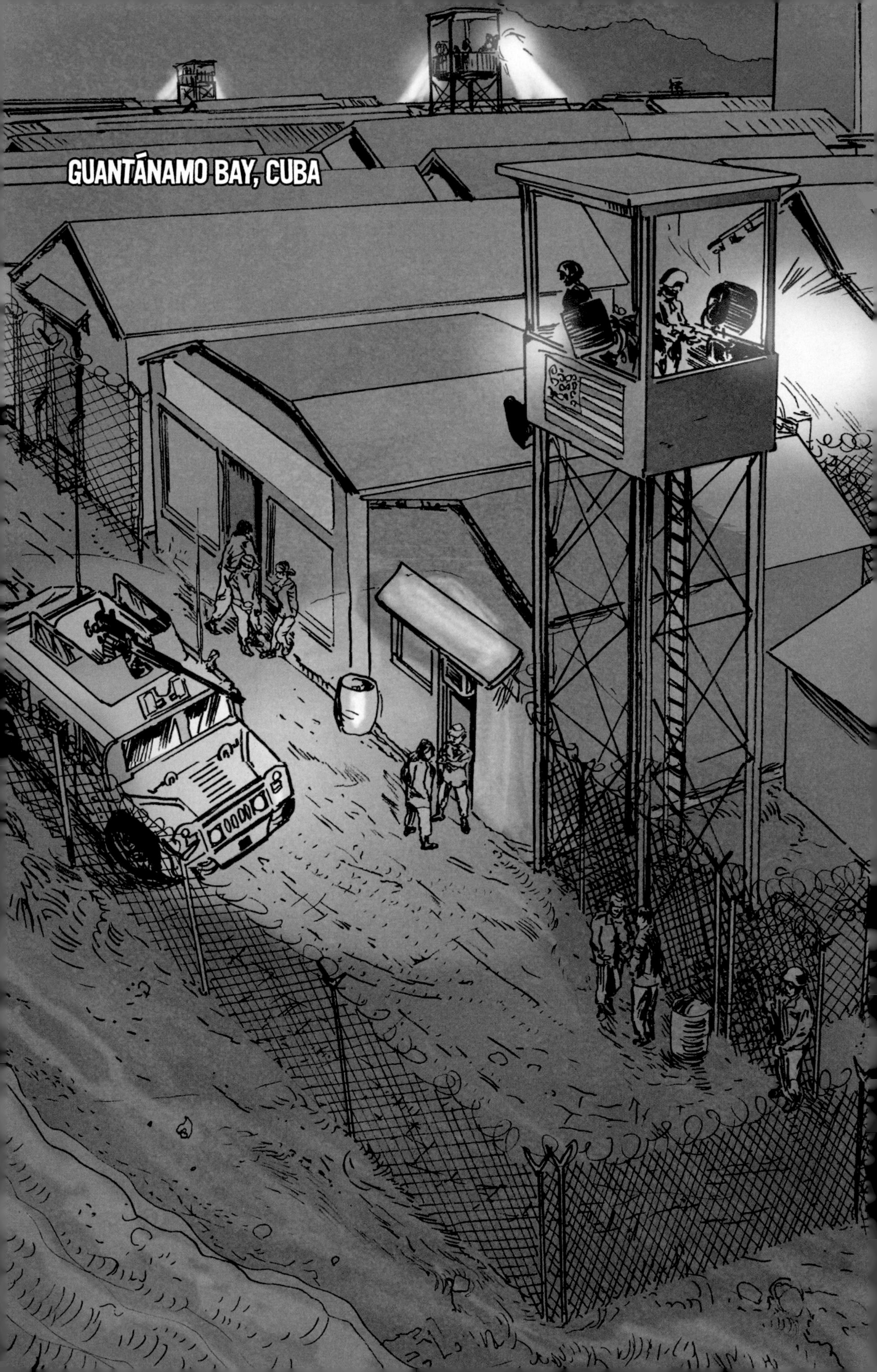
GUANTÁNAMO BAY, CUBA

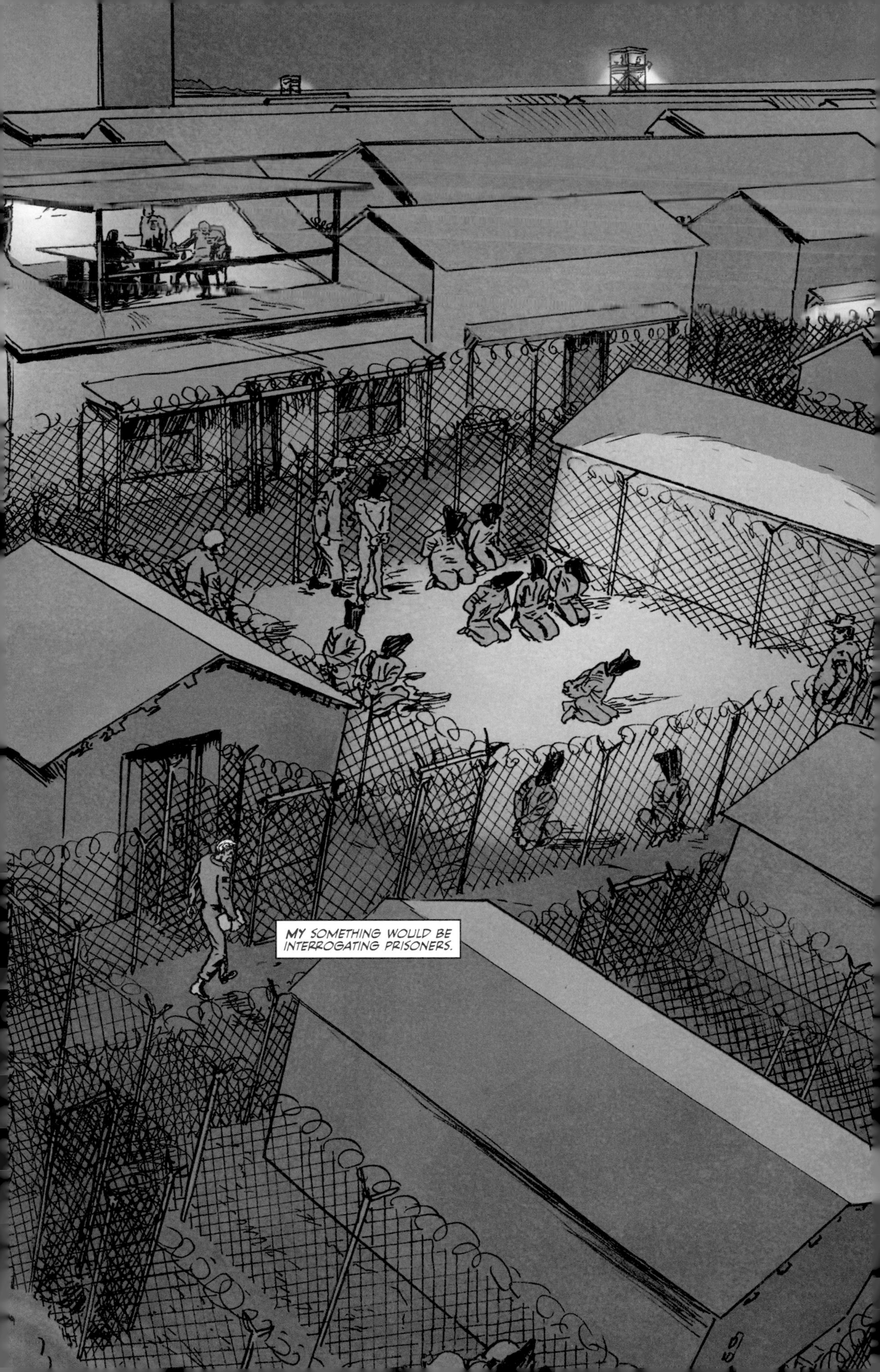
MY SOMETHING WOULD BE INTERROGATING PRISONERS.

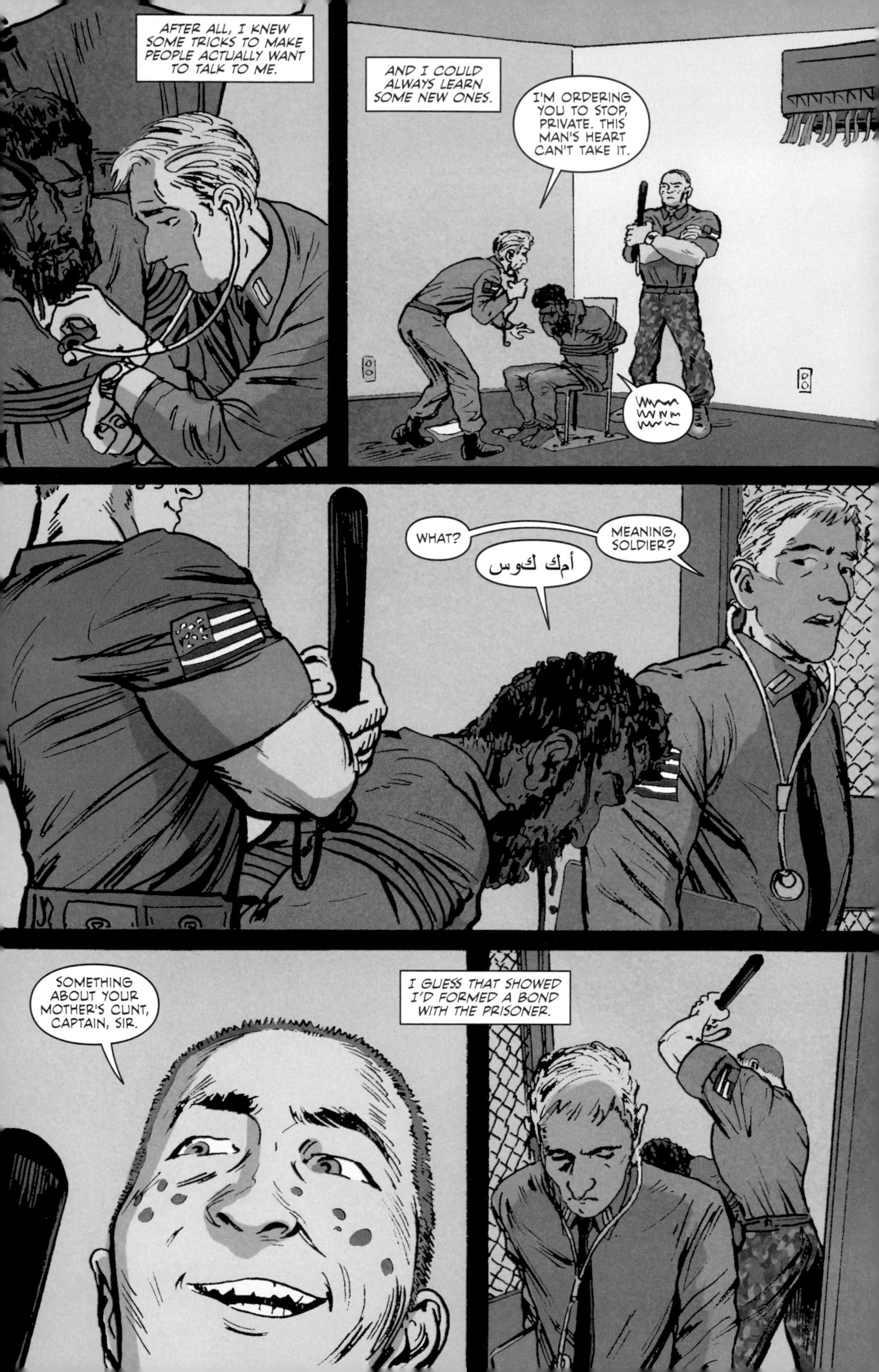
AFTER ALL, I KNEW SOME TRICKS TO MAKE PEOPLE ACTUALLY WANT TO TALK TO ME.
AND I COULD ALWAYS LEARN SOME NEW ONES.
I'M ORDERING YOU TO STOP, PRIVATE. THIS MAN'S HEART CAN'T TAKE IT.
WHAT?
MEANING, SOLDIER?
أمك كوس
SOMETHING ABOUT YOUR MOTHER'S CUNT, CAPTAIN, SIR.
I GUESS THAT SHOWED I'D FORMED A BOND WITH THE PRISONER.

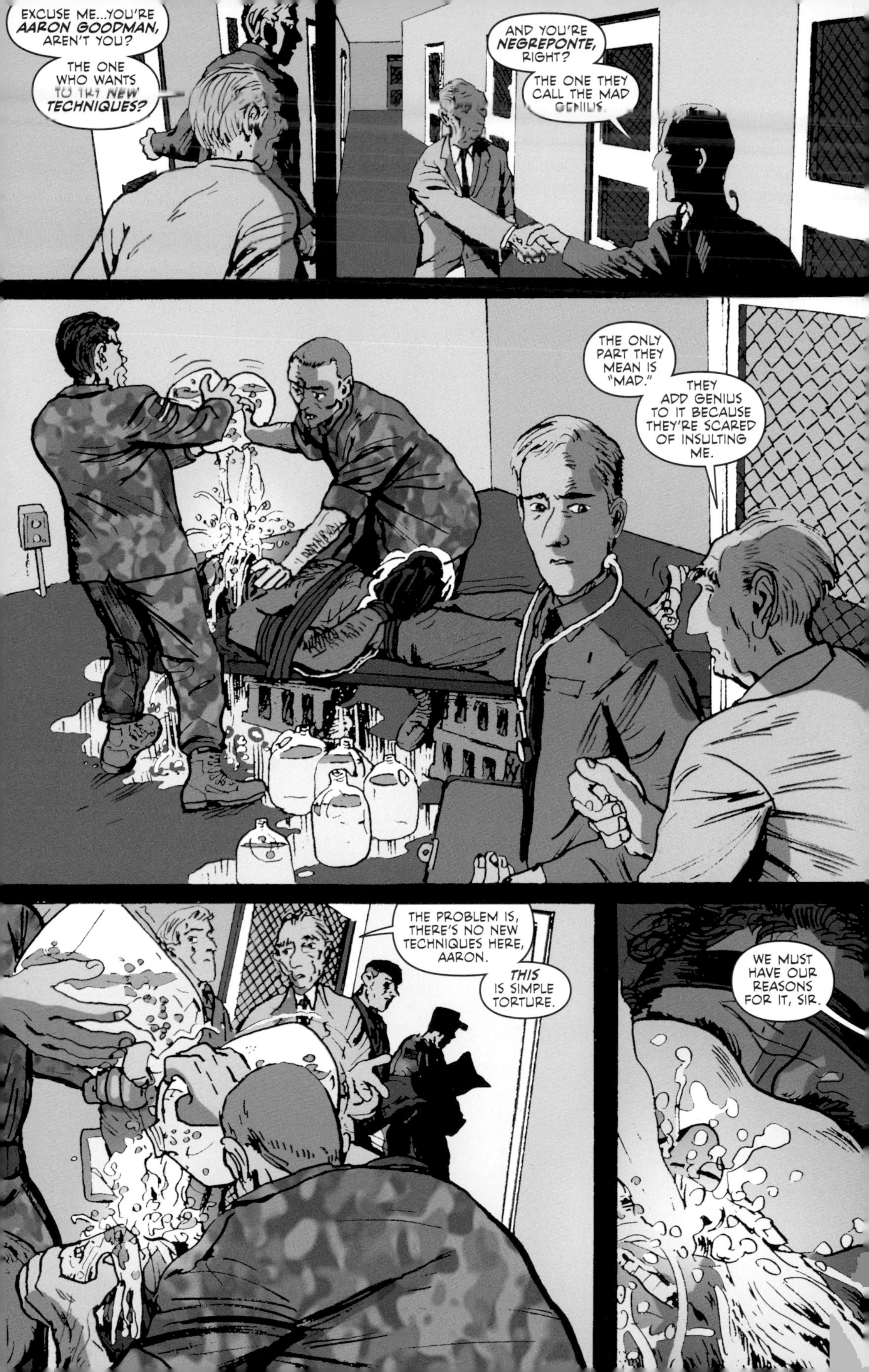
EXCUSE ME...YOU'RE AARON GOODMAN, AREN'T YOU?
THE ONE WHO WANTS TO TRY NEW TECHNIQUES?
AND YOU'RE NEGREPONTE, RIGHT?
THE ONE THEY CALL THE MAD GENIUS.
THE ONLY PART THEY MEAN IS "MAD."
THEY ADD GENIUS TO IT BECAUSE THEY'RE SCARED OF INSULTING ME.
THE PROBLEM IS, THERE'S NO NEW TECHNIQUES HERE, AARON.
THIS IS SIMPLE TORTURE.
WE MUST HAVE OUR REASONS FOR IT, SIR.

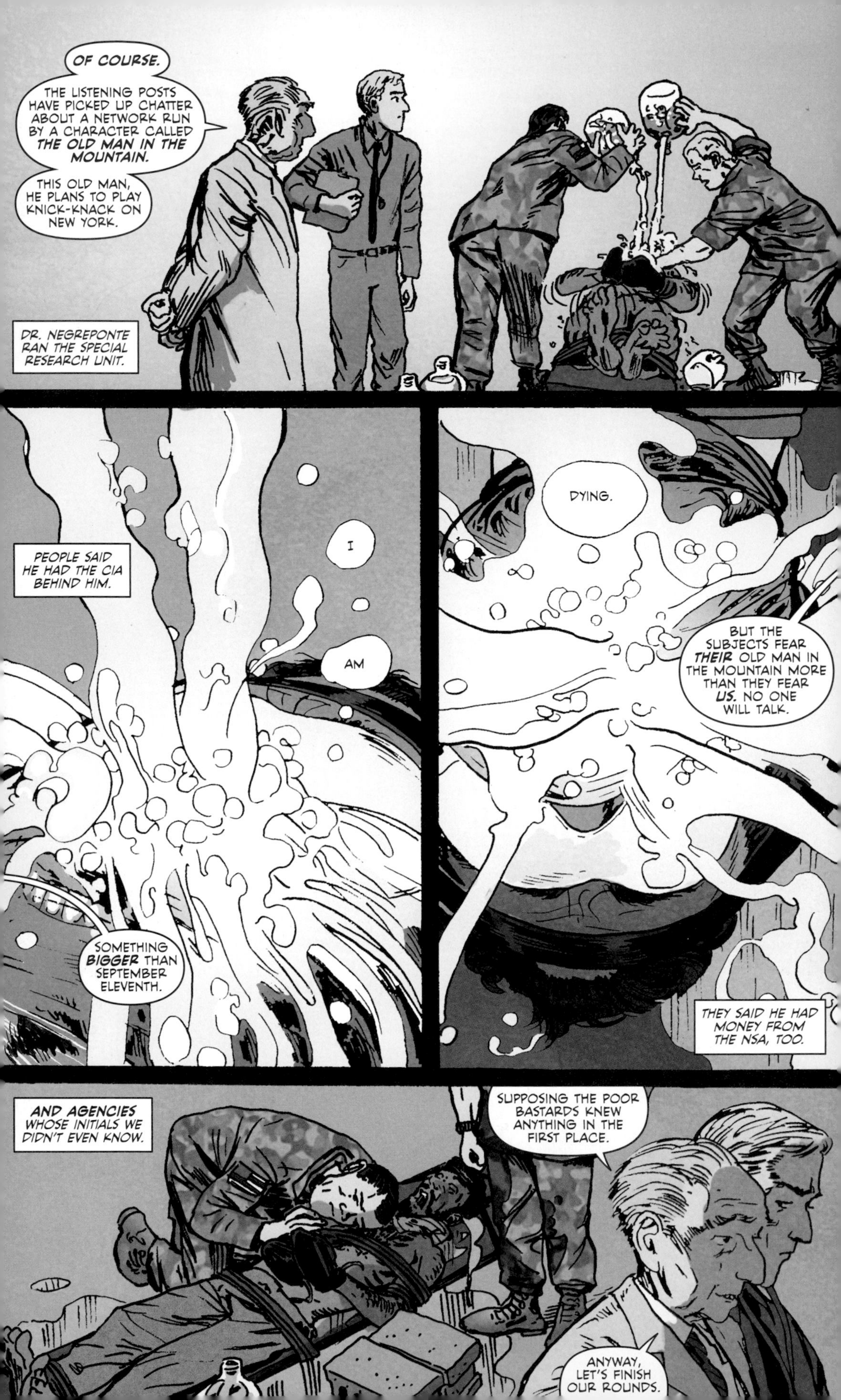
OF COURSE.
THE LISTENING POSTS HAVE PICKED UP CHATTER ABOUT A NETWORK RUN BY A CHARACTER CALLED THE OLD MAN IN THE MOUNTAIN.
THIS OLD MAN, HE PLANS TO PLAY KNICK-KNACK ON NEW YORK.
DR. NEGREPONTE RAN THE SPECIAL RESEARCH UNIT.
PEOPLE SAID HE HAD THE CIA BEHIND HIM.
I
AM
SOMETHING BIGGER THAN SEPTEMBER ELEVENTH.
DYING.
BUT THE SUBJECTS FEAR THEIR OLD MAN IN THE MOUNTAIN MORE THAN THEY FEAR US. NO ONE WILL TALK.
THEY SAID HE HAD MONEY FROM THE NSA, TOO.
AND AGENCIES WHOSE INITIALS WE DIDN'T EVEN KNOW.
SUPPOSING THE POOR BASTARDS KNEW ANYTHING IN THE FIRST PLACE.
ANYWAY, LET'S FINISH OUR ROUNDS.

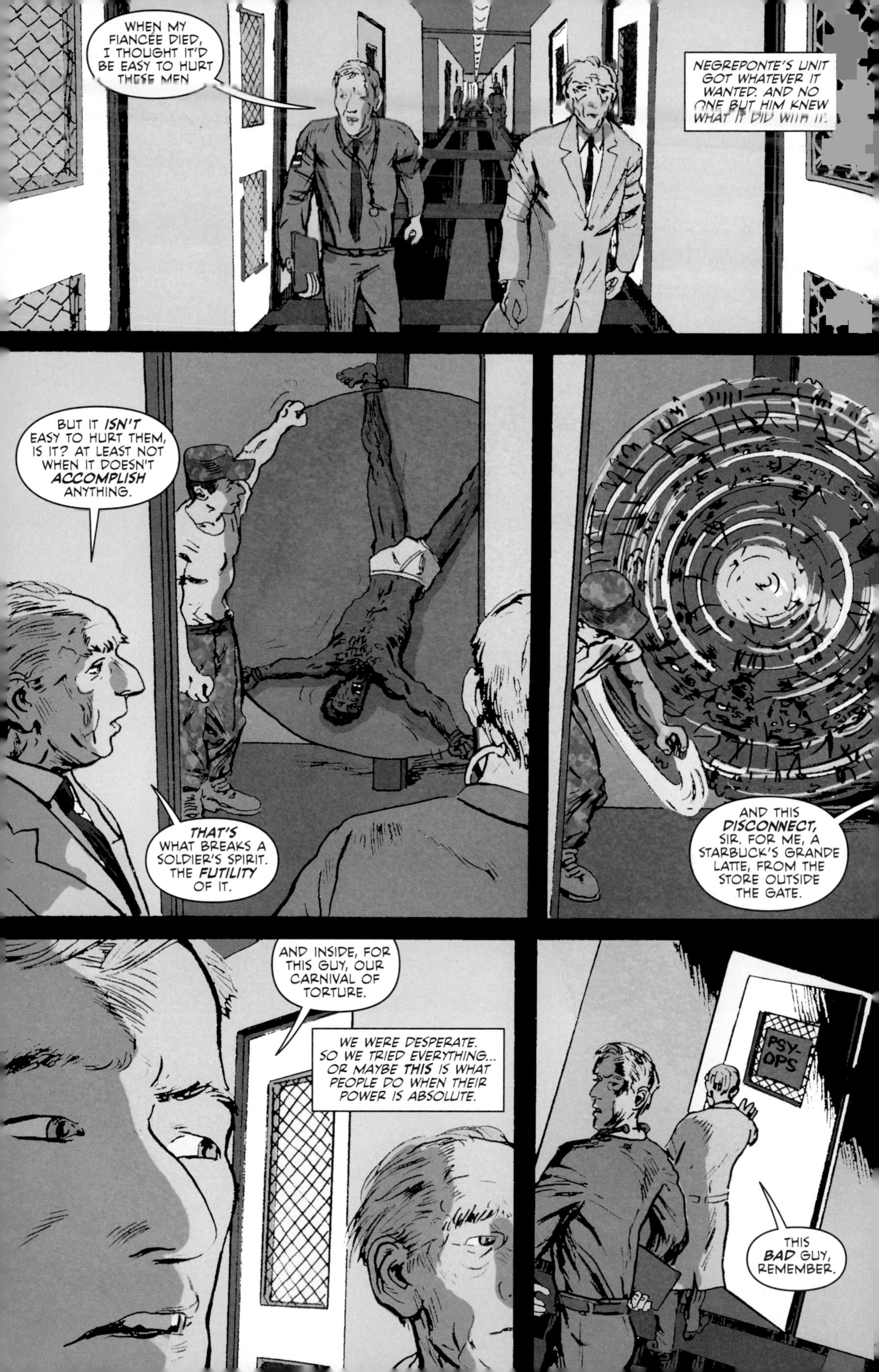
WHEN MY FIANCÉE DIED, I THOUGHT IT'D BE EASY TO HURT THESE MEN
NEGREPONTE'S UNIT GOT WHATEVER IT WANTED. AND NO ONE BUT HIM KNEW WHAT IT DID WITH IT.
BUT IT ISN'T EASY TO HURT THEM, IS IT? AT LEAST NOT WHEN IT DOESN'T ACCOMPLISH ANYTHING.
THAT'S WHAT BREAKS A SOLDIER'S SPIRIT. THE FUTILITY OF IT.
AND THIS DISCONNECT, SIR. FOR ME, A STARBUCK'S GRANDE LATTE, FROM THE STORE OUTSIDE THE GATE.
AND INSIDE, FOR THIS GUY, OUR CARNIVAL OF TORTURE.
WE WERE DESPERATE. SO WE TRIED EVERYTHING... OR MAYBE THIS IS WHAT PEOPLE DO WHEN THEIR POWER IS ABSOLUTE.
PSY-OPS
THIS BAD GUY, REMEMBER.

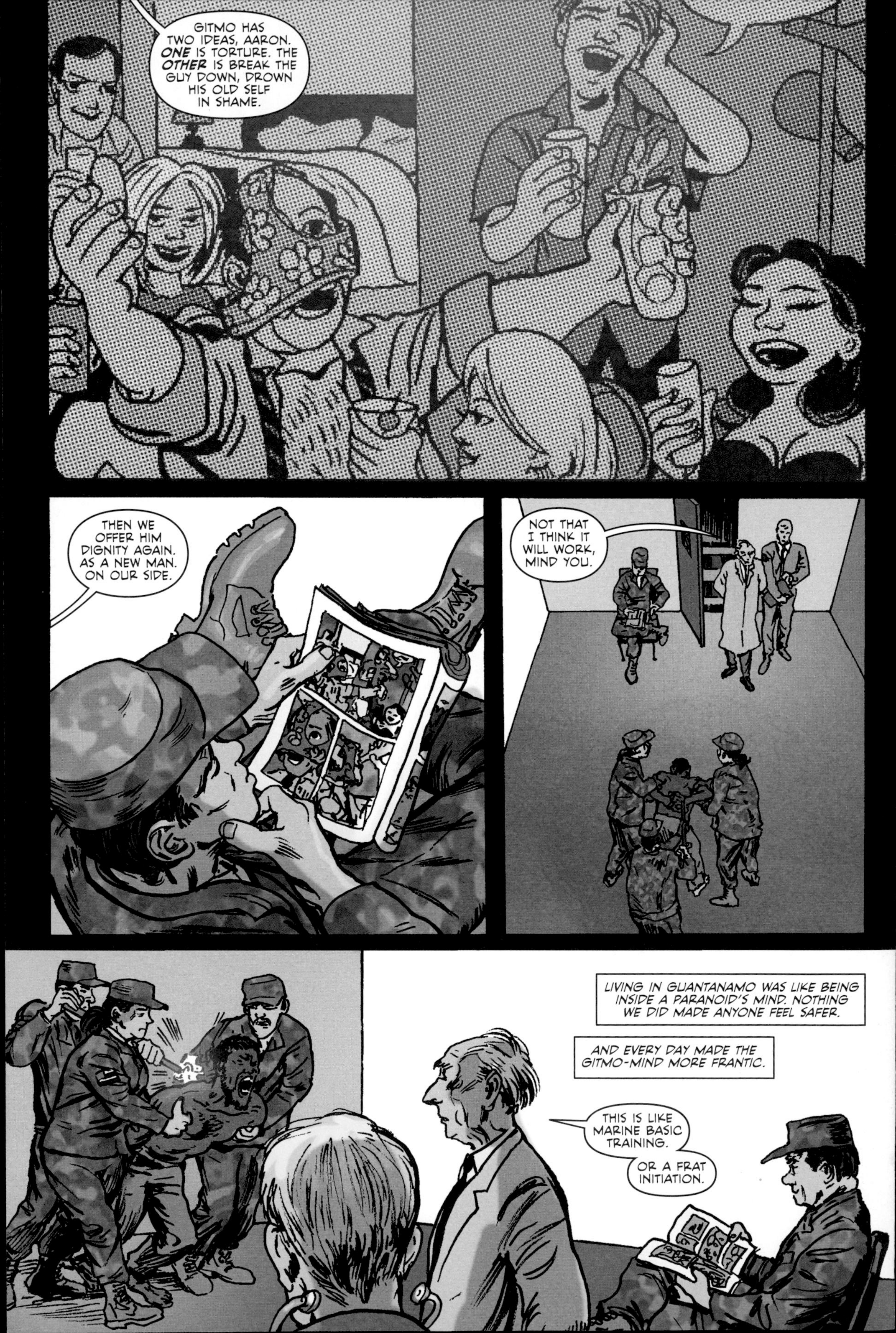

GITMO HAS TWO IDEAS, AARON. ONE IS TORTURE. THE OTHER IS BREAK THE GUY DOWN, DROWN HIS OLD SELF IN SHAME.
THEN WE OFFER HIM DIGNITY AGAIN. AS A NEW MAN. ON OUR SIDE.
NOT THAT I THINK IT WILL WORK, MIND YOU.
LIVING IN GUANTANAMO WAS LIKE BEING INSIDE A PARANOID'S MIND. NOTHING WE DID MADE ANYONE FEEL SAFER.
AND EVERY DAY MADE THE GITMO-MIND MORE FRANTIC.
THIS IS LIKE MARINE BASIC TRAINING.
OR A FRAT INITIATION.

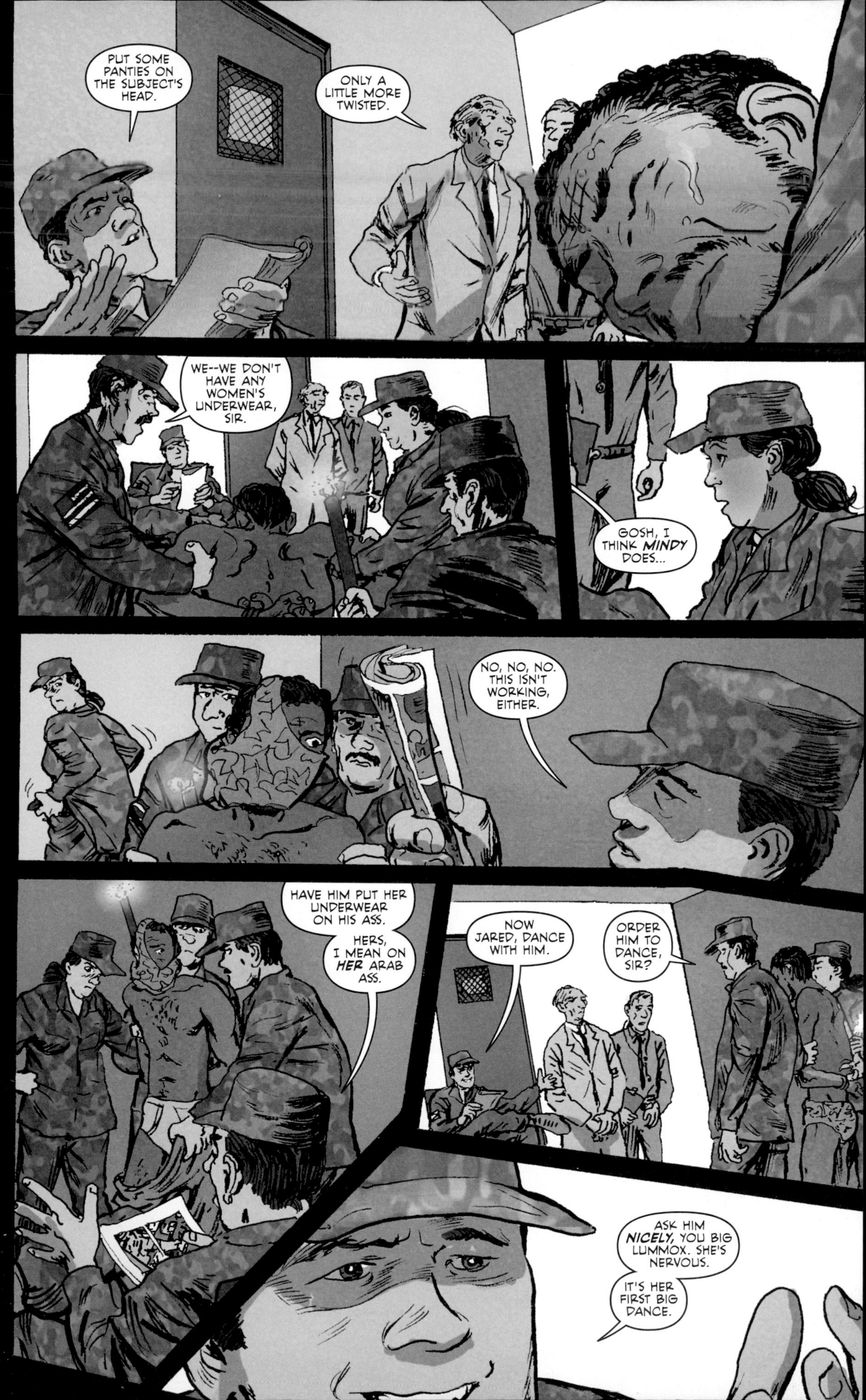
PUT SOME PANTIES ON THE SUBJECT'S HEAD.
ONLY A LITTLE MORE TWISTED.
WE--WE DON'T HAVE ANY WOMEN'S UNDERWEAR, SIR.
GOSH, I THINK MINDY DOES...
NO, NO, NO. THIS ISN'T WORKING, EITHER.
HAVE HIM PUT HER UNDERWEAR ON HIS ASS.
HERS, I MEAN ON HER ARAB ASS.
NOW JARED, DANCE WITH HIM.
ORDER HIM TO DANCE, SIR?
ASK HIM NICELY, YOU BIG LUMMOX. SHE'S NERVOUS.
IT'S HER FIRST BIG DANCE.

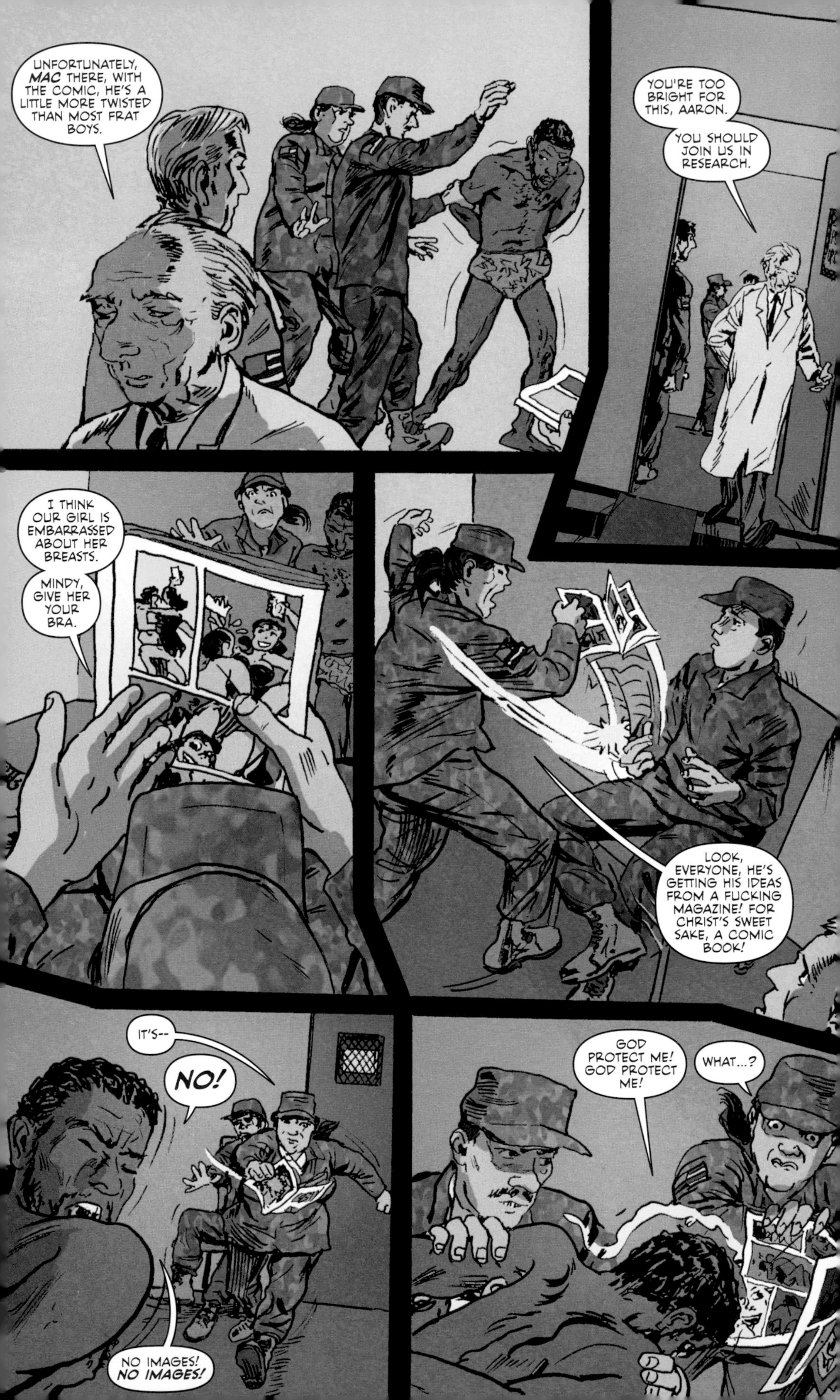
UNFORTUNATELY, MAC THERE, WITH THE COMIC, HE'S A LITTLE MORE TWISTED THAN MOST FRAT BOYS.
YOU'RE TOO BRIGHT FOR THIS, AARON.
YOU SHOULD JOIN US IN RESEARCH.
I THINK OUR GIRL IS EMBARRASSED ABOUT HER BREASTS.
MINDY, GIVE HER YOUR BRA.
LOOK, EVERYONE, HE'S GETTING HIS IDEAS FROM A FUCKING MAGAZINE! FOR CHRIST'S SWEET SAKE, A COMIC BOOK!
IT'S--
NO!
NO IMAGES! NO IMAGES!
GOD PROTECT ME! GOD PROTECT ME!
WHAT...?

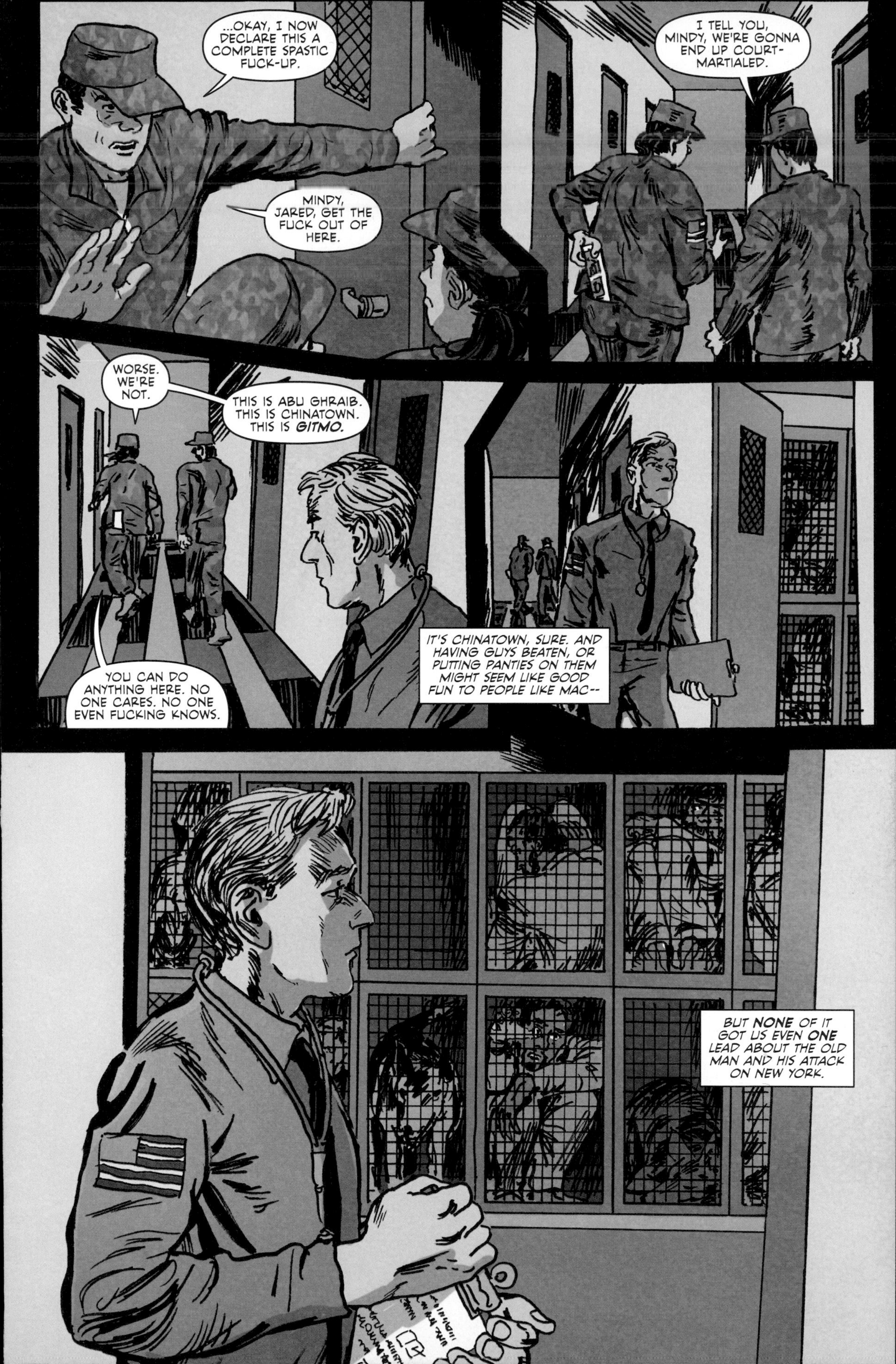

...OKAY, I NOW DECLARE THIS A COMPLETE SPASTIC FUCK-UP.
MINDY, JARED, GET THE FUCK OUT OF HERE.
I TELL YOU, MINDY, WE'RE GONNA END UP COURT-MARTIALED.
WORSE. WE'RE NOT.
THIS IS ABU GHRAIB. THIS IS CHINATOWN. THIS IS GITMO.
YOU CAN DO ANYTHING HERE. NO ONE CARES. NO ONE EVEN FUCKING KNOWS.
IT'S CHINATOWN, SURE. AND HAVING GUYS BEATEN, OR PUTTING PANTIES ON THEM MIGHT SEEM LIKE GOOD FUN TO PEOPLE LIKE MAC--
BUT NONE OF IT GOT US EVEN ONE LEAD ABOUT THE OLD MAN AND HIS ATTACK ON NEW YORK.

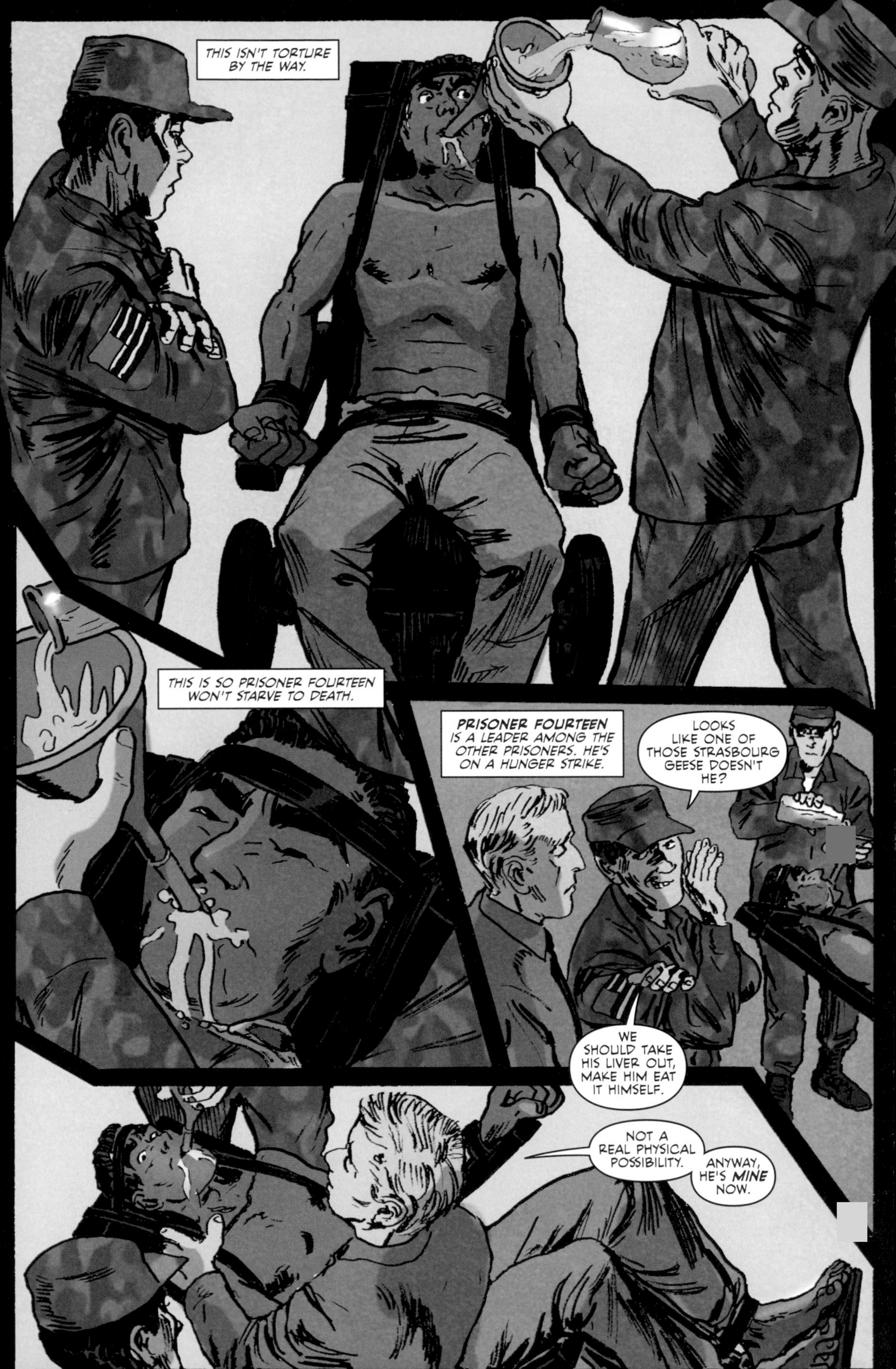
THIS ISN'T TORTURE BY THE WAY.
THIS IS SO PRISONER FOURTEEN WON'T STARVE TO DEATH.
PRISONER FOURTEEN IS A LEADER AMONG THE OTHER PRISONERS. HE'S ON A HUNGER STRIKE.
LOOKS LIKE ONE OF THOSE STRASBOURG GEESE DOESN'T HE?
WE SHOULD TAKE HIS LIVER OUT, MAKE HIM EAT IT HIMSELF.
NOT A REAL PHYSICAL POSSIBILITY.
ANYWAY, HE'S MINE NOW.

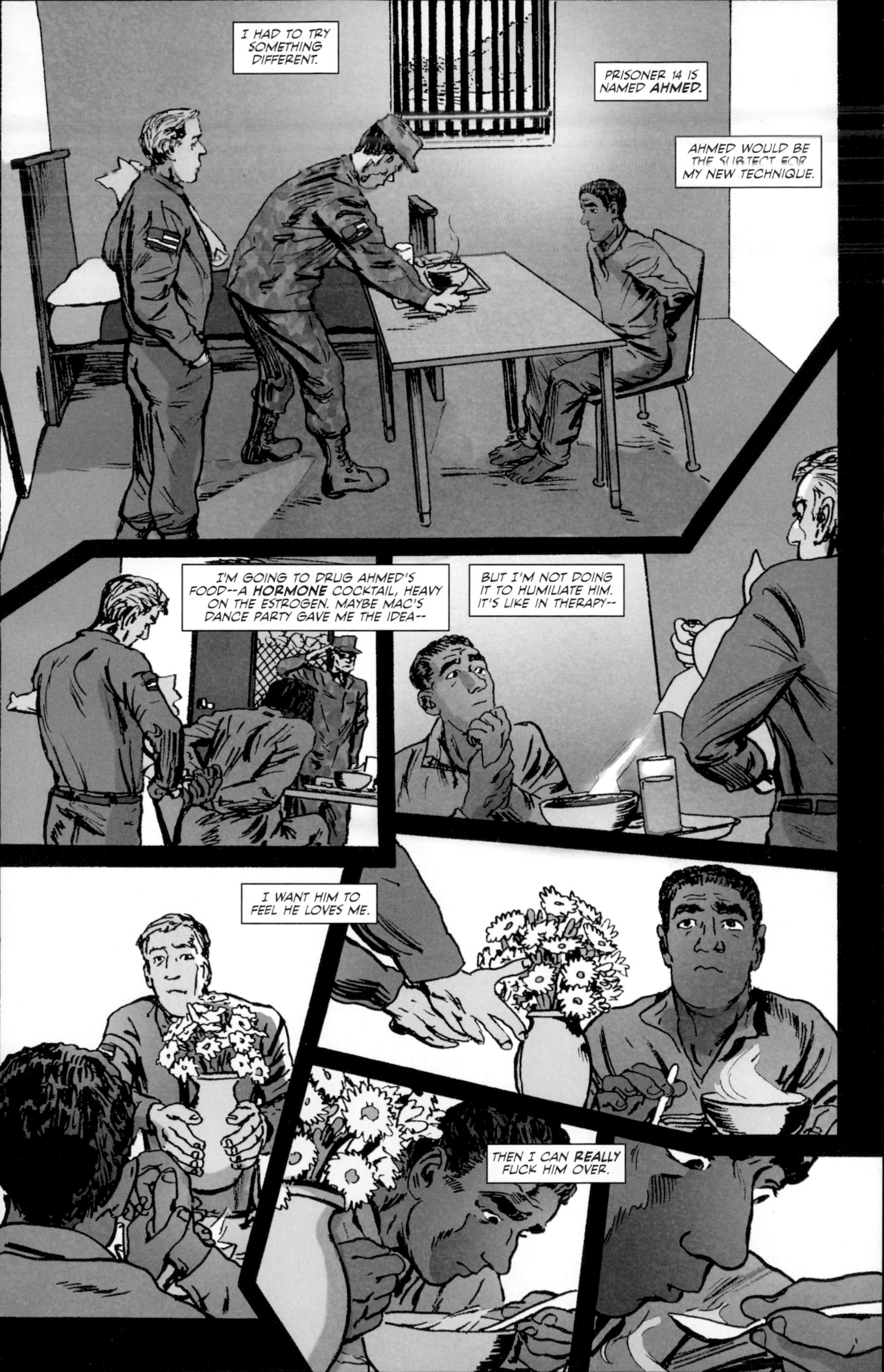
I HAD TO TRY SOMETHING DIFFERENT.
PRISONER 14 IS NAMED AHMED.
AHMED WOULD BE THE SUBJECT FOR MY NEW TECHNIQUE.
I'M GOING TO DRUG AHMED'S FOOD--A HORMONE COCKTAIL, HEAVY ON THE ESTROGEN. MAYBE MAC'S DANCE PARTY GAVE ME THE IDEA--
BUT I'M NOT DOING IT TO HUMILIATE HIM. IT'S LIKE IN THERAPY--
I WANT HIM TO FEEL HE LOVES ME.
THEN I CAN REALLY FUCK HIM OVER.

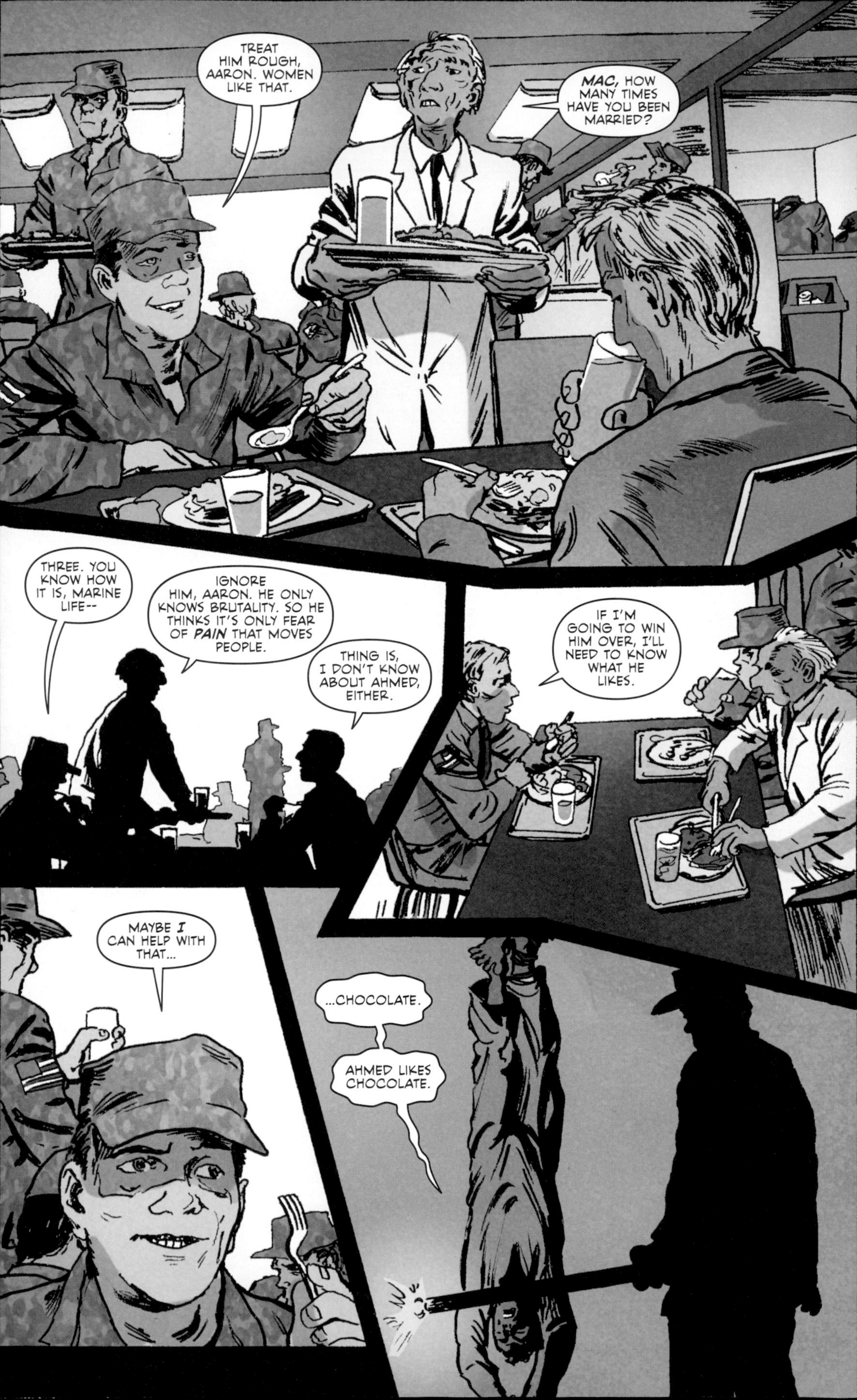
TREAT HIM ROUGH, AARON. WOMEN LIKE THAT.
MAC, HOW MANY TIMES HAVE YOU BEEN MARRIED?
THREE. YOU KNOW HOW IT IS, MARINE LIFE--
IGNORE HIM, AARON. HE ONLY KNOWS BRUTALITY. SO HE THINKS IT'S ONLY FEAR OF PAIN THAT MOVES PEOPLE.
THING IS, I DON'T KNOW ABOUT AHMED, EITHER.
IF I'M GOING TO WIN HIM OVER, I'LL NEED TO KNOW WHAT HE LIKES.
MAYBE I CAN HELP WITH THAT...
...CHOCOLATE.
AHMED LIKES CHOCOLATE.

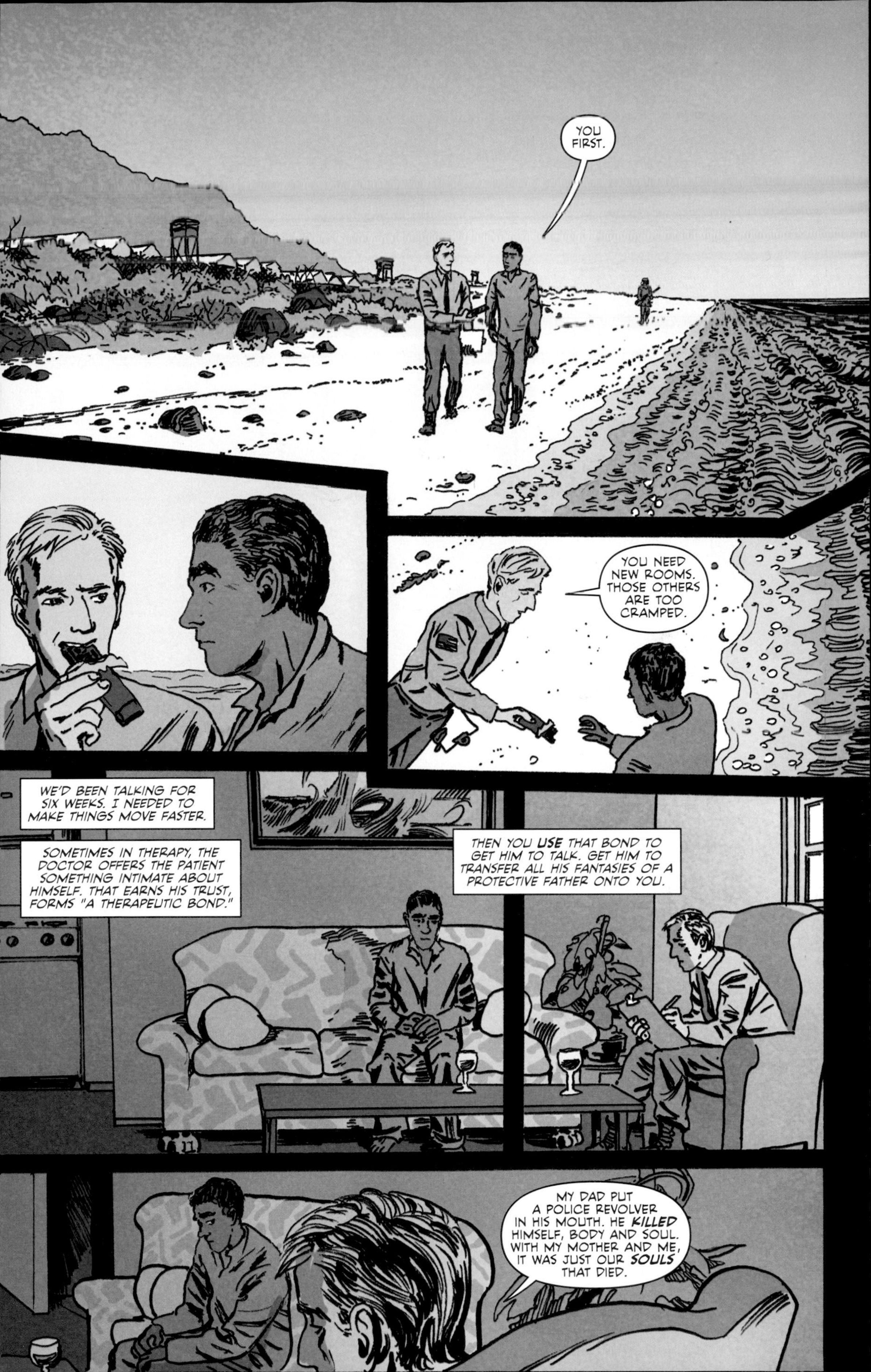
YOU FIRST.
YOU NEED NEW ROOMS. THOSE OTHERS ARE TOO CRAMPED.
WE'D BEEN TALKING FOR SIX WEEKS. I NEEDED TO MAKE THINGS MOVE FASTER.
SOMETIMES IN THERAPY, THE DOCTOR OFFERS THE PATIENT SOMETHING INTIMATE ABOUT HIMSELF. THAT EARNS HIS TRUST, FORMS "A THERAPEUTIC BOND."
THEN YOU USE THAT BOND TO GET HIM TO TALK. GET HIM TO TRANSFER ALL HIS FANTASIES OF A PROTECTIVE FATHER ONTO YOU.
MY DAD PUT A POLICE REVOLVER IN HIS MOUTH. HE KILLED HIMSELF, BODY AND SOUL. WITH MY MOTHER AND ME, IT WAS JUST OUR SOULS THAT DIED.

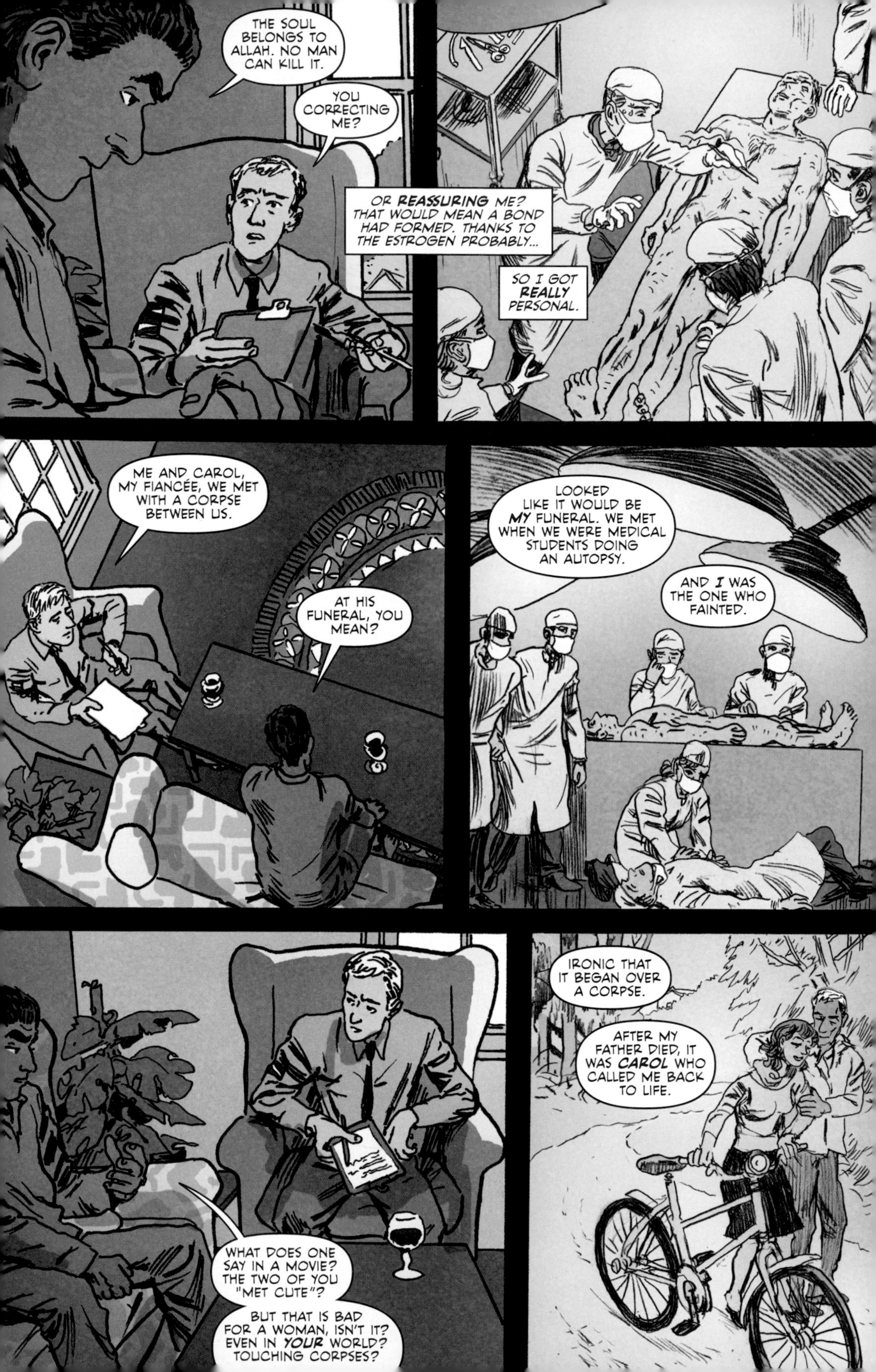
THE SOUL BELONGS TO ALLAH. NO MAN CAN KILL IT.
YOU CORRECTING ME?
OR **REASSURING** ME? THAT WOULD MEAN A BOND HAD FORMED. THANKS TO THE ESTROGEN PROBABLY...
SO I GOT **REALLY** PERSONAL.
ME AND CAROL, MY FIANCÉE, WE MET WITH A CORPSE BETWEEN US.
AT HIS FUNERAL, YOU MEAN?
LOOKED LIKE IT WOULD BE **MY** FUNERAL. WE MET WHEN WE WERE MEDICAL STUDENTS DOING AN AUTOPSY.
AND **I** WAS THE ONE WHO FAINTED.
WHAT DOES ONE SAY IN A MOVIE? THE TWO OF YOU "MET CUTE"?
BUT THAT IS BAD FOR A WOMAN, ISN'T IT? EVEN IN **YOUR** WORLD? TOUCHING CORPSES?
IRONIC THAT IT BEGAN OVER A CORPSE.
AFTER MY FATHER DIED, IT WAS **CAROL** WHO CALLED ME BACK TO LIFE.

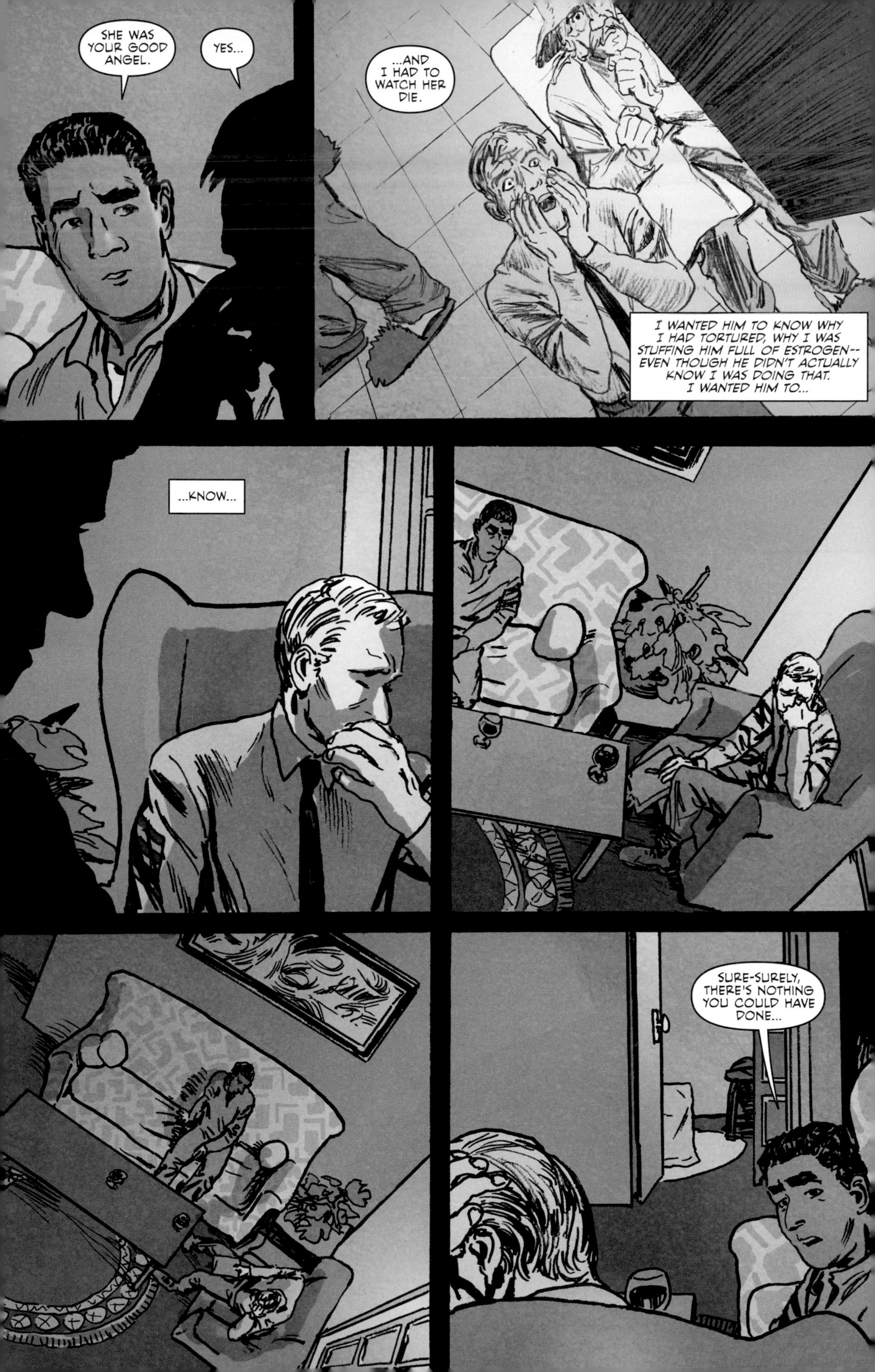
SHE WAS YOUR GOOD ANGEL.
YES...
...AND I HAD TO WATCH HER DIE.
I WANTED HIM TO KNOW WHY I HAD TORTURED, WHY I WAS STUFFING HIM FULL OF ESTROGEN-- EVEN THOUGH HE DIDN'T ACTUALLY KNOW I WAS DOING THAT. I WANTED HIM TO...
...KNOW...
SURE-SURELY, THERE'S NOTHING YOU COULD HAVE DONE...

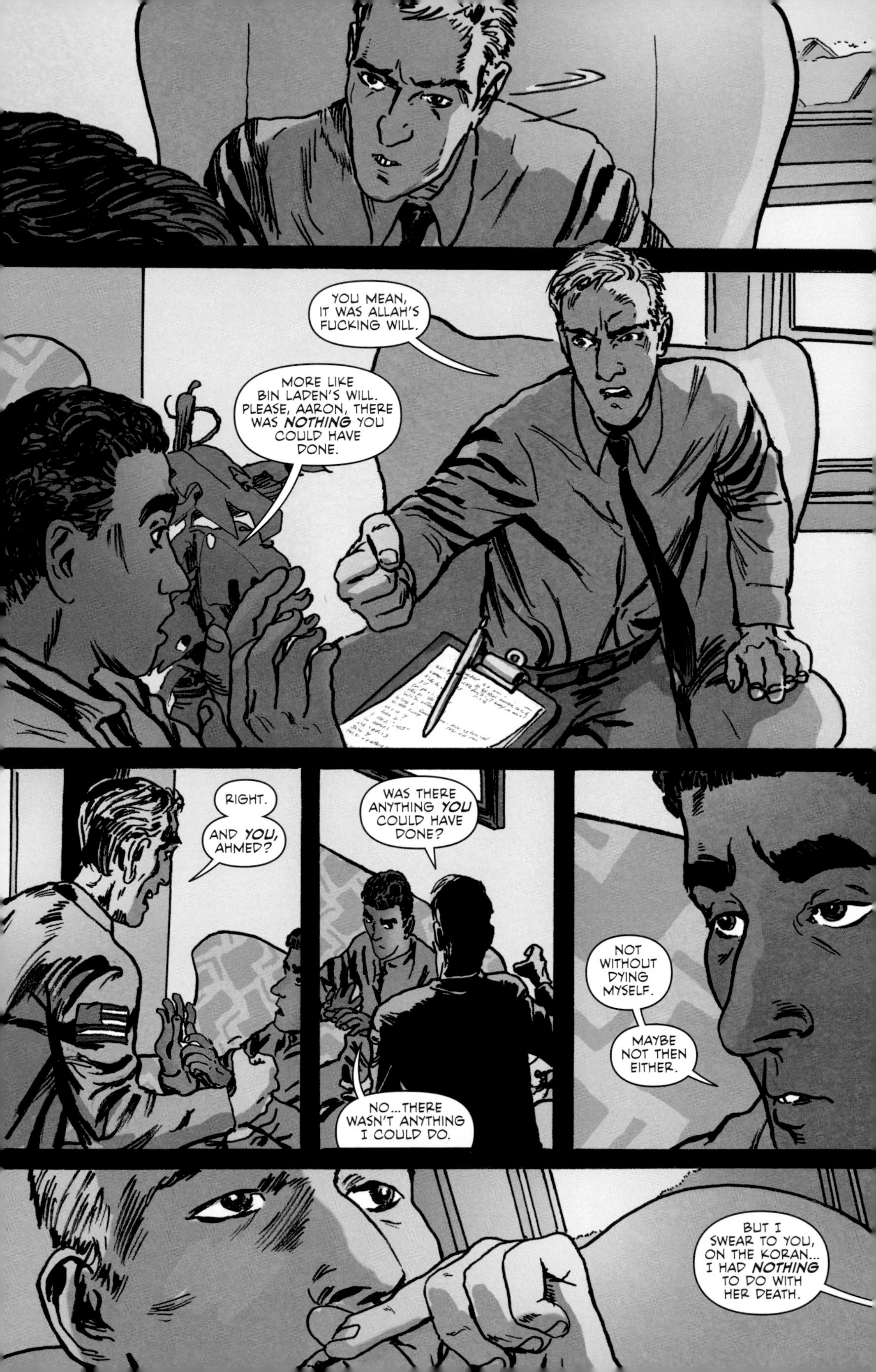
YOU MEAN, IT WAS ALLAH'S FUCKING WILL.
MORE LIKE BIN LADEN'S WILL. PLEASE, AARON, THERE WAS NOTHING YOU COULD HAVE DONE.
RIGHT.
AND YOU, AHMED?
WAS THERE ANYTHING YOU COULD HAVE DONE?
NO...THERE WASN'T ANYTHING I COULD DO.
NOT WITHOUT DYING MYSELF.
MAYBE NOT THEN EITHER.
BUT I SWEAR TO YOU, ON THE KORAN... I HAD NOTHING TO DO WITH HER DEATH.

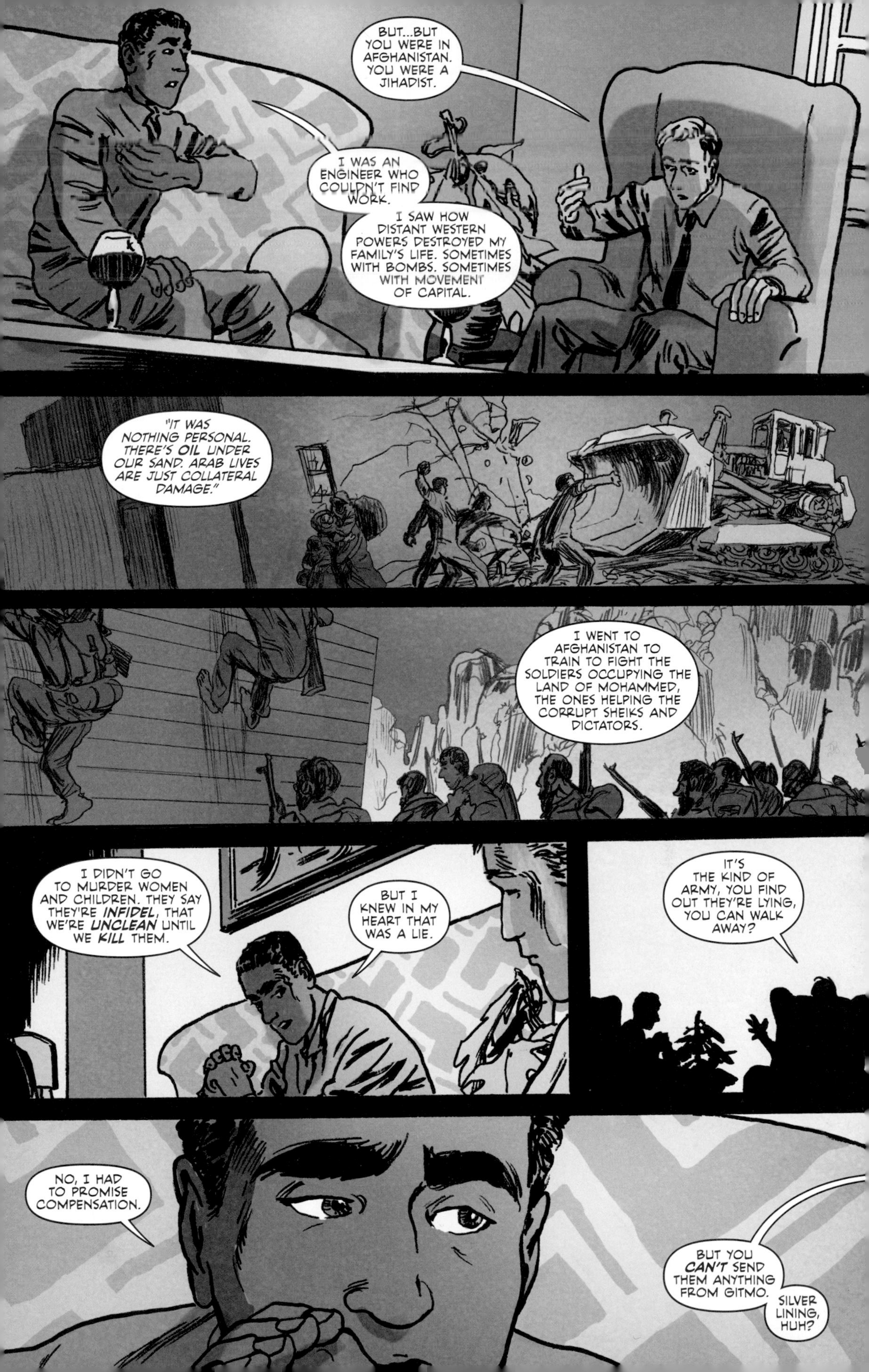
BUT...BUT YOU WERE IN AFGHANISTAN. YOU WERE A JIHADIST.
I WAS AN ENGINEER WHO COULDN'T FIND WORK.
I SAW HOW DISTANT WESTERN POWERS DESTROYED MY FAMILY'S LIFE. SOMETIMES WITH BOMBS. SOMETIMES WITH MOVEMENT OF CAPITAL.
"IT WAS NOTHING PERSONAL. THERE'S OIL UNDER OUR SAND. ARAB LIVES ARE JUST COLLATERAL DAMAGE."
I WENT TO AFGHANISTAN TO TRAIN TO FIGHT THE SOLDIERS OCCUPYING THE LAND OF MOHAMMED, THE ONES HELPING THE CORRUPT SHEIKS AND DICTATORS.
I DIDN'T GO TO MURDER WOMEN AND CHILDREN. THEY SAY THEY'RE INFIDEL, THAT WE'RE UNCLEAN UNTIL WE KILL THEM.
BUT I KNEW IN MY HEART THAT WAS A LIE.
IT'S THE KIND OF ARMY, YOU FIND OUT THEY'RE LYING, YOU CAN WALK AWAY?
NO, I HAD TO PROMISE COMPENSATION.
BUT YOU CAN'T SEND THEM ANYTHING FROM GITMO.
SILVER LINING, HUH?

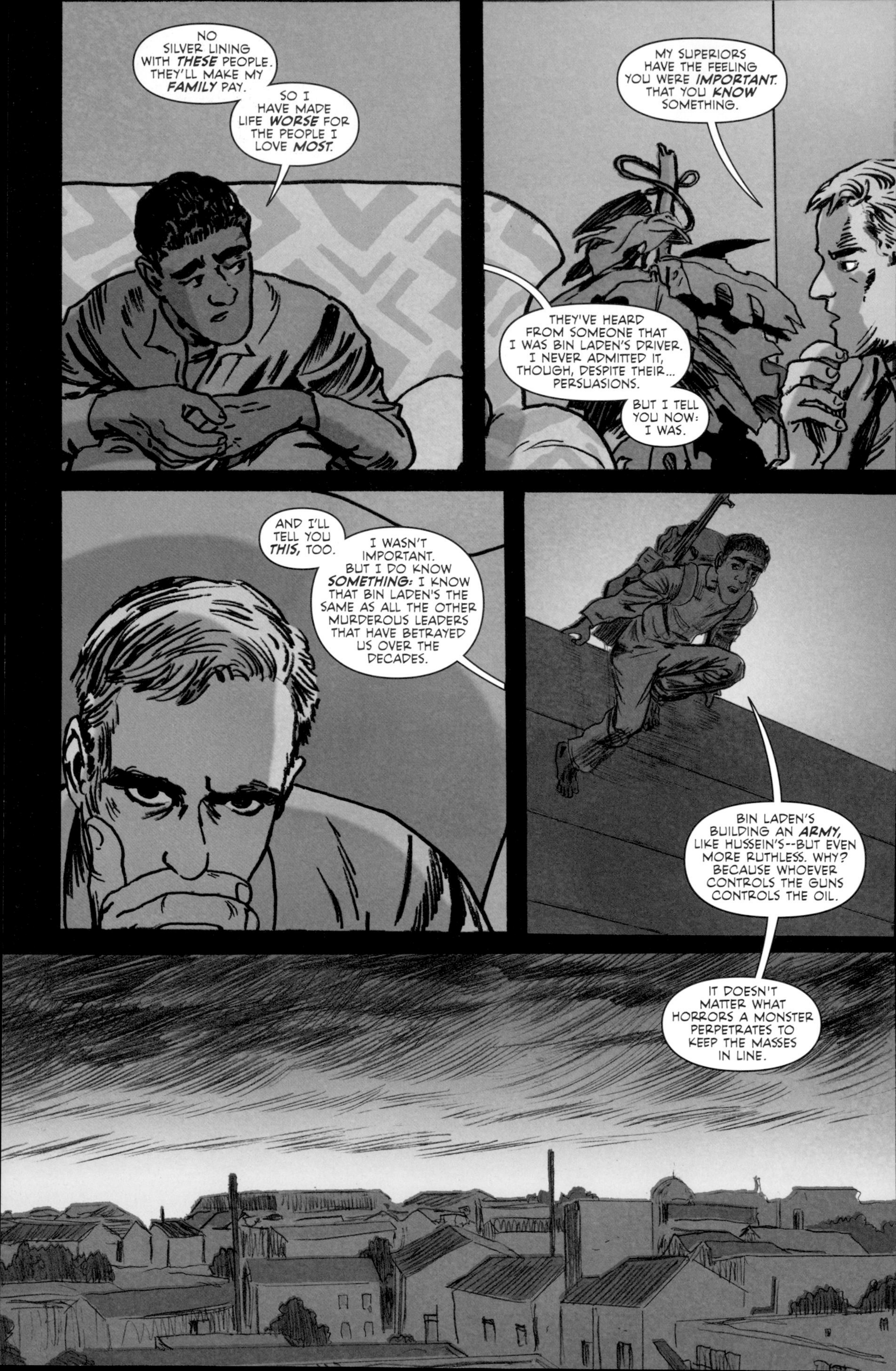

NO SILVER LINING WITH THESE PEOPLE. THEY'LL MAKE MY FAMILY PAY.
SO I HAVE MADE LIFE WORSE FOR THE PEOPLE I LOVE MOST.
MY SUPERIORS HAVE THE FEELING YOU WERE IMPORTANT. THAT YOU KNOW SOMETHING.
THEY'VE HEARD FROM SOMEONE THAT I WAS BIN LADEN'S DRIVER. I NEVER ADMITTED IT, THOUGH, DESPITE THEIR... PERSUASIONS.
BUT I TELL YOU NOW: I WAS.
AND I'LL TELL YOU THIS, TOO.
I WASN'T IMPORTANT. BUT I DO KNOW SOMETHING: I KNOW THAT BIN LADEN'S THE SAME AS ALL THE OTHER MURDEROUS LEADERS THAT HAVE BETRAYED US OVER THE DECADES.
BIN LADEN'S BUILDING AN ARMY, LIKE HUSSEIN'S--BUT EVEN MORE RUTHLESS. WHY? BECAUSE WHOEVER CONTROLS THE GUNS CONTROLS THE OIL.
IT DOESN'T MATTER WHAT HORRORS A MONSTER PERPETRATES TO KEEP THE MASSES IN LINE.

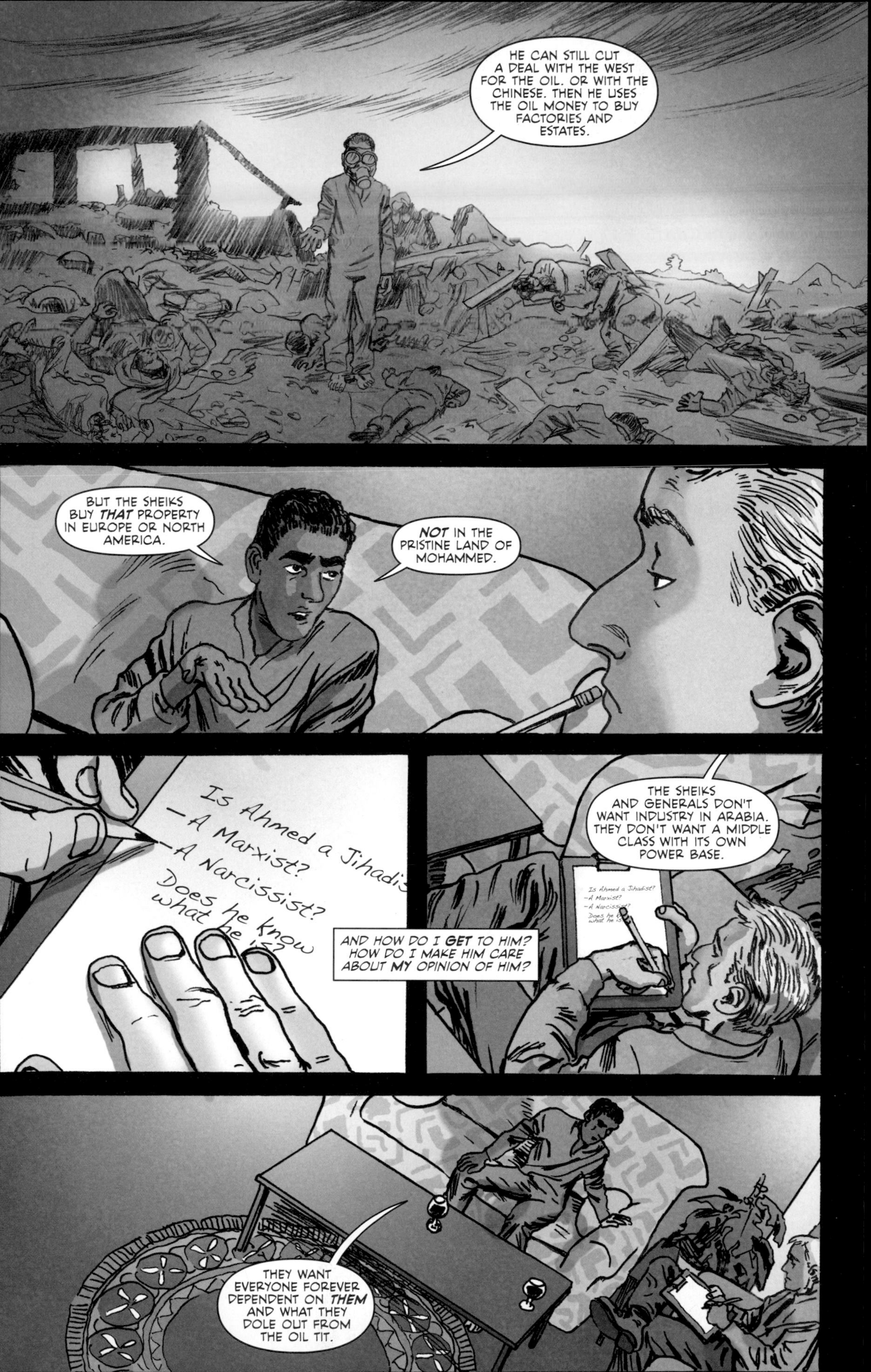
HE CAN STILL CUT A DEAL WITH THE WEST FOR THE OIL. OR WITH THE CHINESE. THEN HE USES THE OIL MONEY TO BUY FACTORIES AND ESTATES.
BUT THE SHEIKS BUY THAT PROPERTY IN EUROPE OR NORTH AMERICA.
NOT IN THE PRISTINE LAND OF MOHAMMED.
Is Ahmed a Jihadis
—A Marxist?
—A Narcissist?
Does he know what he is?
THE SHEIKS AND GENERALS DON'T WANT INDUSTRY IN ARABIA. THEY DON'T WANT A MIDDLE CLASS WITH ITS OWN POWER BASE.
Is Ahmed a Jihadist?
—A Marxist?
—A Narcissist?
AND HOW DO I GET TO HIM? HOW DO I MAKE HIM CARE ABOUT MY OPINION OF HIM?
THEY WANT EVERYONE FOREVER DEPENDENT ON THEM AND WHAT THEY DOLE OUT FROM THE OIL TIT.

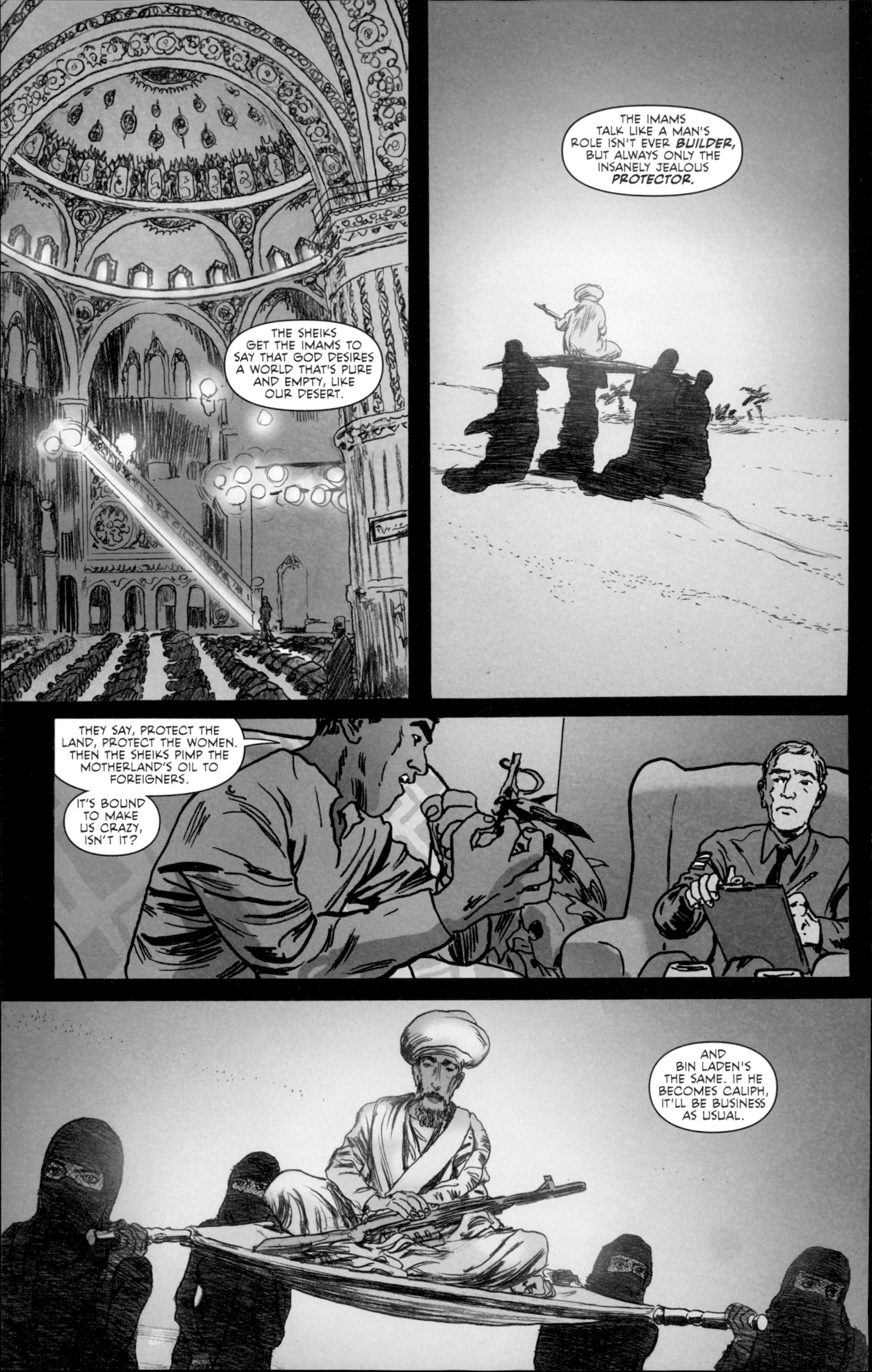
THE SHEIKS GET THE IMAMS TO SAY THAT GOD DESIRES A WORLD THAT'S PURE AND EMPTY, LIKE OUR DESERT.
THE IMAMS TALK LIKE A MAN'S ROLE ISN'T EVER BUILDER, BUT ALWAYS ONLY THE INSANELY JEALOUS PROTECTOR.
THEY SAY, PROTECT THE LAND, PROTECT THE WOMEN. THEN THE SHEIKS PIMP THE MOTHERLAND'S OIL TO FOREIGNERS.
IT'S BOUND TO MAKE US CRAZY, ISN'T IT?
AND BIN LADEN'S THE SAME. IF HE BECOMES CALIPH, IT'LL BE BUSINESS AS USUAL.

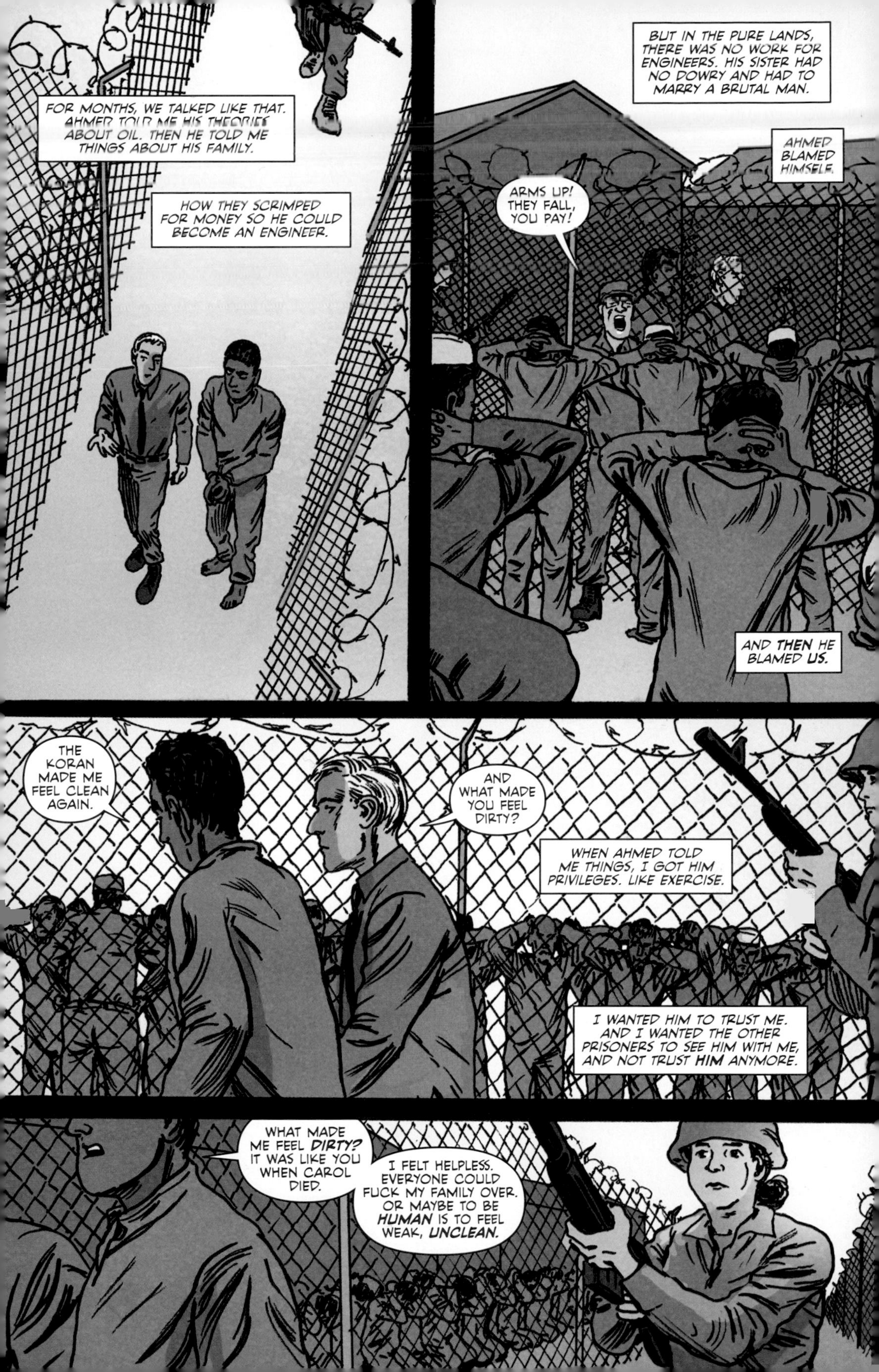
FOR MONTHS, WE TALKED LIKE THAT. AHMED TOLD ME HIS THEORIES ABOUT OIL. THEN HE TOLD ME THINGS ABOUT HIS FAMILY.
HOW THEY SCRIMPED FOR MONEY SO HE COULD BECOME AN ENGINEER.
BUT IN THE PURE LANDS, THERE WAS NO WORK FOR ENGINEERS. HIS SISTER HAD NO DOWRY AND HAD TO MARRY A BRUTAL MAN.
AHMED BLAMED HIMSELF.
ARMS UP! THEY FALL, YOU PAY!
AND THEN HE BLAMED US.
THE KORAN MADE ME FEEL CLEAN AGAIN.
AND WHAT MADE YOU FEEL DIRTY?
WHEN AHMED TOLD ME THINGS, I GOT HIM PRIVILEGES. LIKE EXERCISE.
I WANTED HIM TO TRUST ME. AND I WANTED THE OTHER PRISONERS TO SEE HIM WITH ME, AND NOT TRUST HIM ANYMORE.
WHAT MADE ME FEEL DIRTY? IT WAS LIKE YOU WHEN CAROL DIED.
I FELT HELPLESS. EVERYONE COULD FUCK MY FAMILY OVER. OR MAYBE TO BE HUMAN IS TO FEEL WEAK, UNCLEAN.

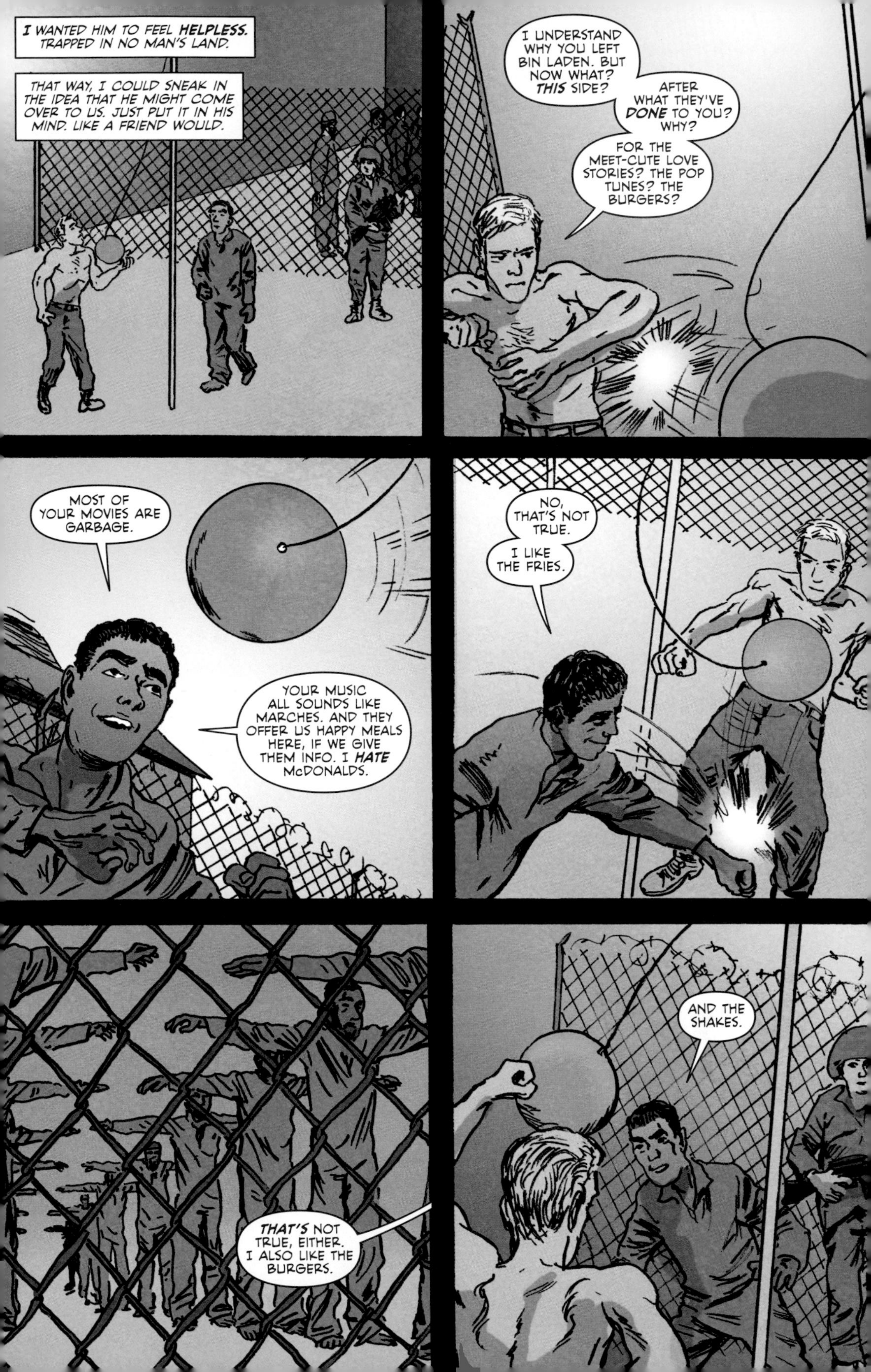
I WANTED HIM TO FEEL HELPLESS. TRAPPED IN NO MAN'S LAND.
THAT WAY, I COULD SNEAK IN THE IDEA THAT HE MIGHT COME OVER TO US. JUST PUT IT IN HIS MIND. LIKE A FRIEND WOULD.
I UNDERSTAND WHY YOU LEFT BIN LADEN. BUT NOW WHAT? THIS SIDE?
AFTER WHAT THEY'VE DONE TO YOU? WHY?
FOR THE MEET-CUTE LOVE STORIES? THE POP TUNES? THE BURGERS?
MOST OF YOUR MOVIES ARE GARBAGE.
YOUR MUSIC ALL SOUNDS LIKE MARCHES. AND THEY OFFER US HAPPY MEALS HERE, IF WE GIVE THEM INFO. I HATE McDONALDS.
NO, THAT'S NOT TRUE.
I LIKE THE FRIES.
THAT'S NOT TRUE, EITHER. I ALSO LIKE THE BURGERS.
AND THE SHAKES.

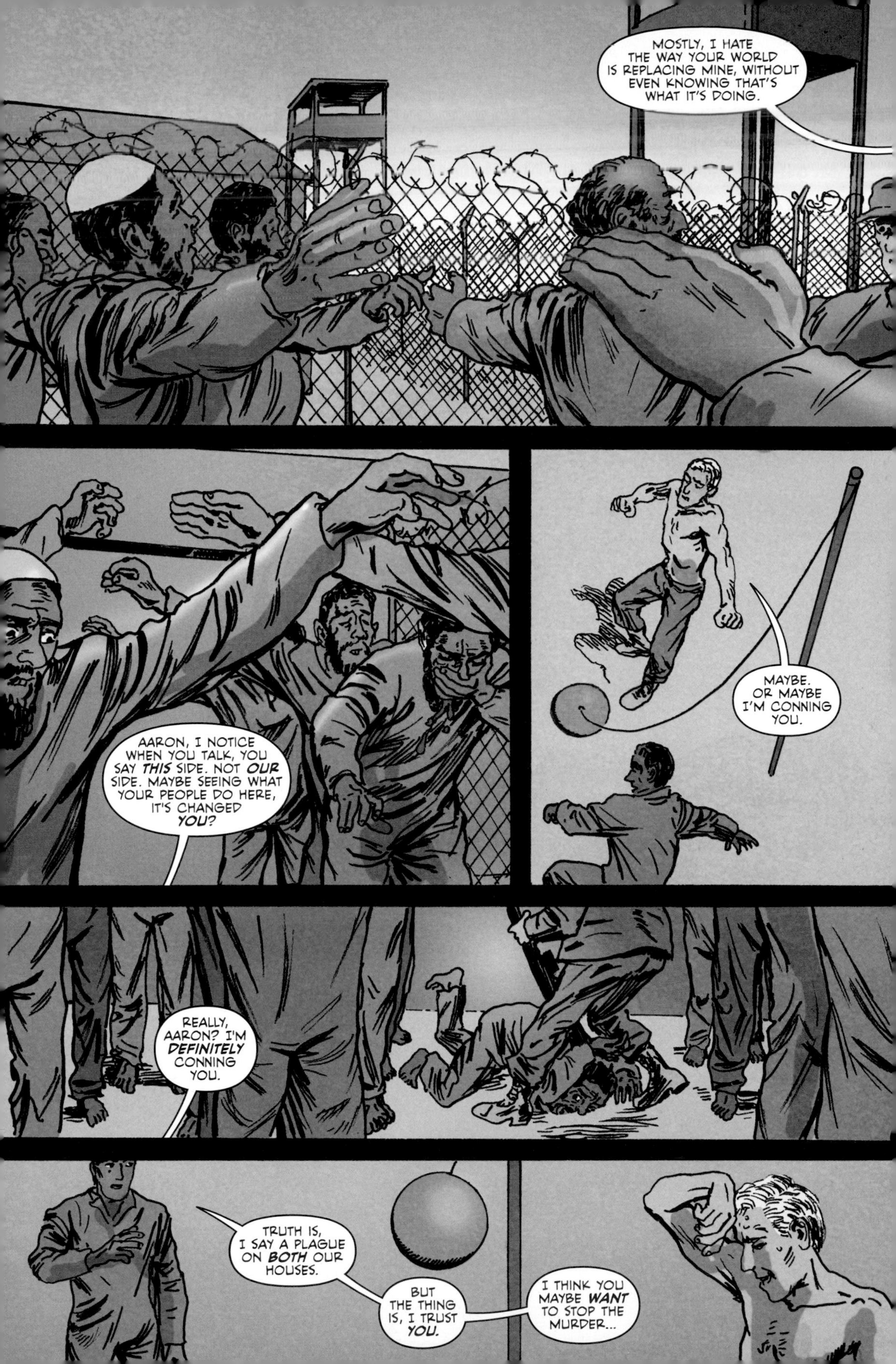
MOSTLY, I HATE THE WAY YOUR WORLD IS REPLACING MINE, WITHOUT EVEN KNOWING THAT'S WHAT IT'S DOING.
AARON, I NOTICE WHEN YOU TALK, YOU SAY THIS SIDE. NOT OUR SIDE. MAYBE SEEING WHAT YOUR PEOPLE DO HERE, IT'S CHANGED YOU?
MAYBE. OR MAYBE I'M CONNING YOU.
REALLY, AARON? I'M DEFINITELY CONNING YOU.
TRUTH IS, I SAY A PLAGUE ON BOTH OUR HOUSES.
BUT THE THING IS, I TRUST YOU.
I THINK YOU MAYBE WANT TO STOP THE MURDER...

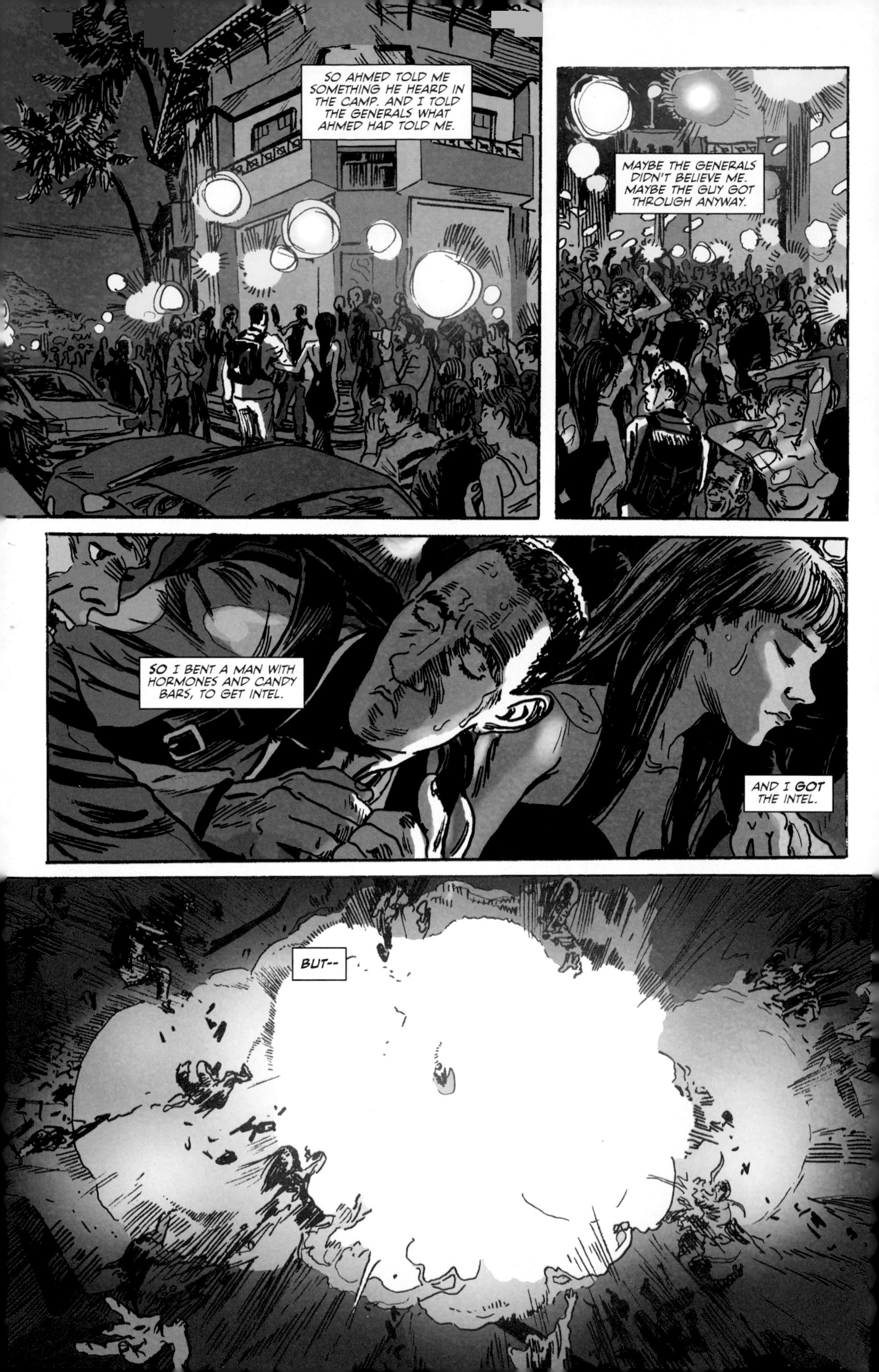
SO AHMED TOLD ME SOMETHING HE HEARD IN THE CAMP. AND I TOLD THE GENERALS WHAT AHMED HAD TOLD ME.
MAYBE THE GENERALS DIDN'T BELIEVE ME. MAYBE THE GUY GOT THROUGH ANYWAY.
SO I BENT A MAN WITH HORMONES AND CANDY BARS, TO GET INTEL.
AND I GOT THE INTEL.
BUT--

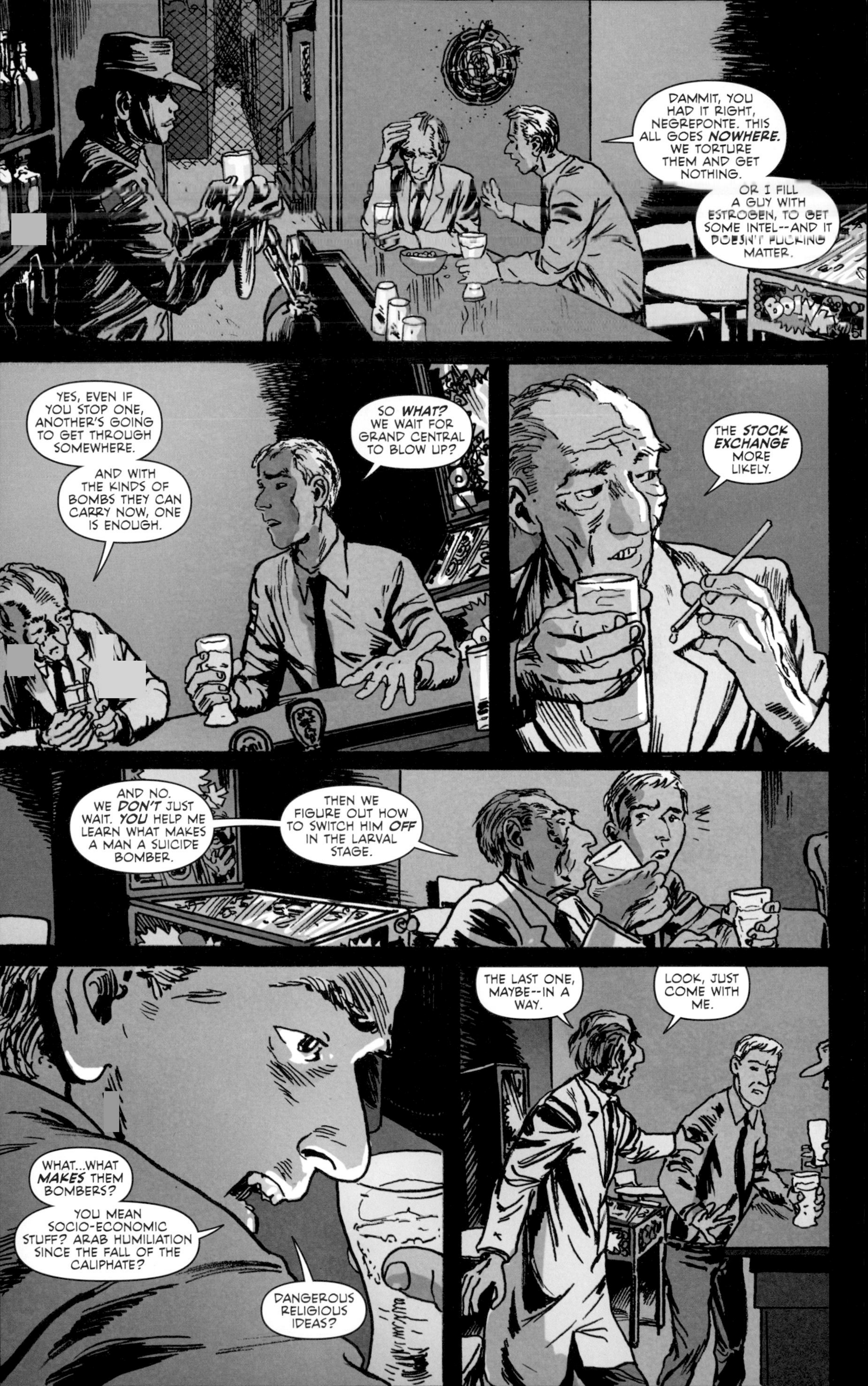
DAMMIT, YOU HAD IT RIGHT, NEGREPONTE. THIS ALL GOES NOWHERE. WE TORTURE THEM AND GET NOTHING.
OR I FILL A GUY WITH ESTROGEN, TO GET SOME INTEL--AND IT DOESN'T FUCKING MATTER.
BOING
YES, EVEN IF YOU STOP ONE, ANOTHER'S GOING TO GET THROUGH SOMEWHERE.
AND WITH THE KINDS OF BOMBS THEY CAN CARRY NOW, ONE IS ENOUGH.
SO WHAT? WE WAIT FOR GRAND CENTRAL TO BLOW UP?
THE STOCK EXCHANGE MORE LIKELY.
AND NO. WE DON'T JUST WAIT. YOU HELP ME LEARN WHAT MAKES A MAN A SUICIDE BOMBER.
THEN WE FIGURE OUT HOW TO SWITCH HIM OFF IN THE LARVAL STAGE.
WHAT...WHAT MAKES THEM BOMBERS?
YOU MEAN SOCIO-ECONOMIC STUFF? ARAB HUMILIATION SINCE THE FALL OF THE CALIPHATE?
DANGEROUS RELIGIOUS IDEAS?
THE LAST ONE, MAYBE--IN A WAY.
LOOK, JUST COME WITH ME.

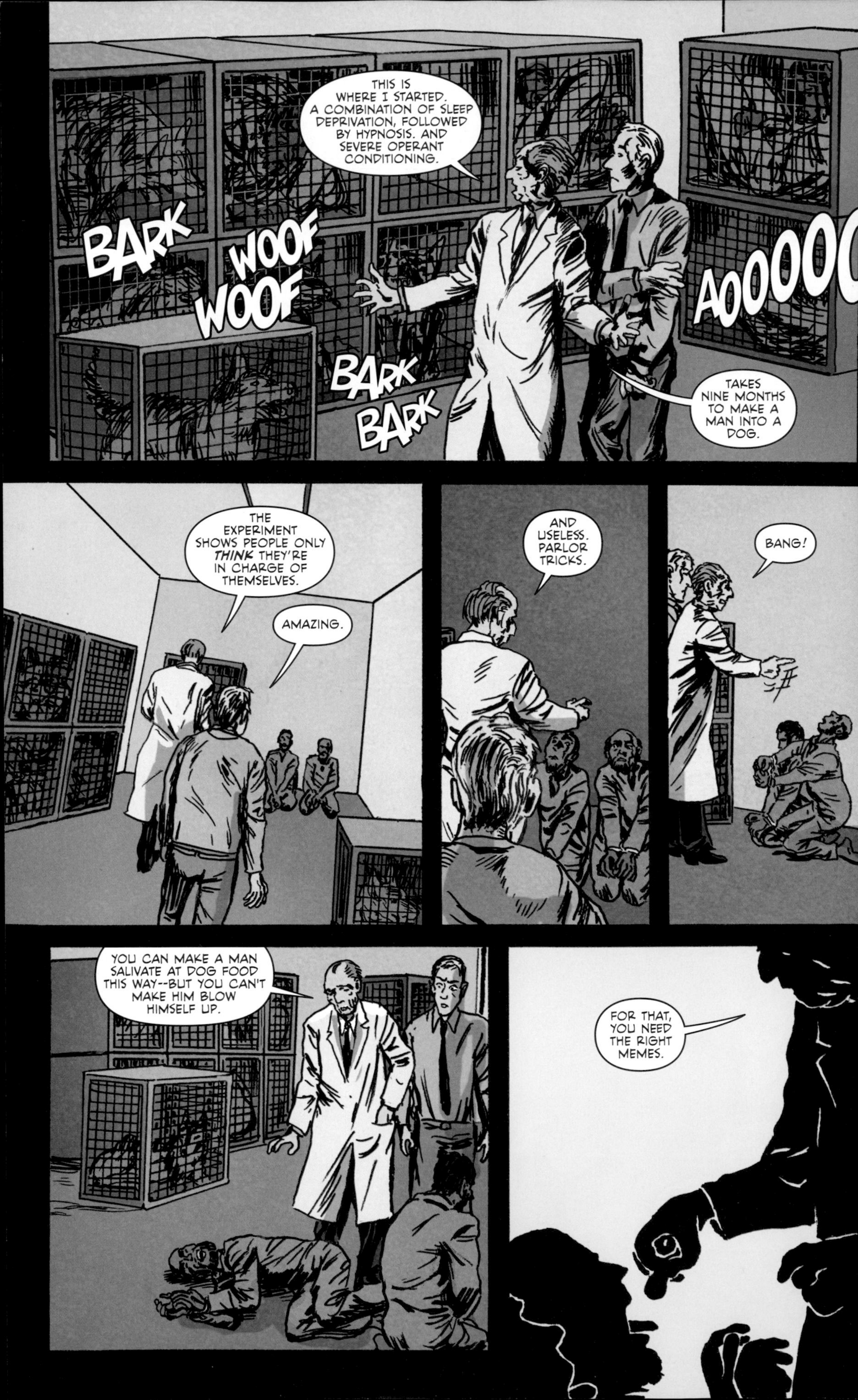
THIS IS WHERE I STARTED. A COMBINATION OF SLEEP DEPRIVATION, FOLLOWED BY HYPNOSIS. AND SEVERE OPERANT CONDITIONING.
BARK
WOOF WOOF
BARK BARK
AOOOOO
TAKES NINE MONTHS TO MAKE A MAN INTO A DOG.
THE EXPERIMENT SHOWS PEOPLE ONLY *THINK* THEY'RE IN CHARGE OF THEMSELVES.
AMAZING.
AND USELESS. PARLOR TRICKS.
BANG!
YOU CAN MAKE A MAN SALIVATE AT DOG FOOD THIS WAY--BUT YOU CAN'T MAKE HIM BLOW HIMSELF UP.
FOR THAT, YOU NEED THE RIGHT MEMES.

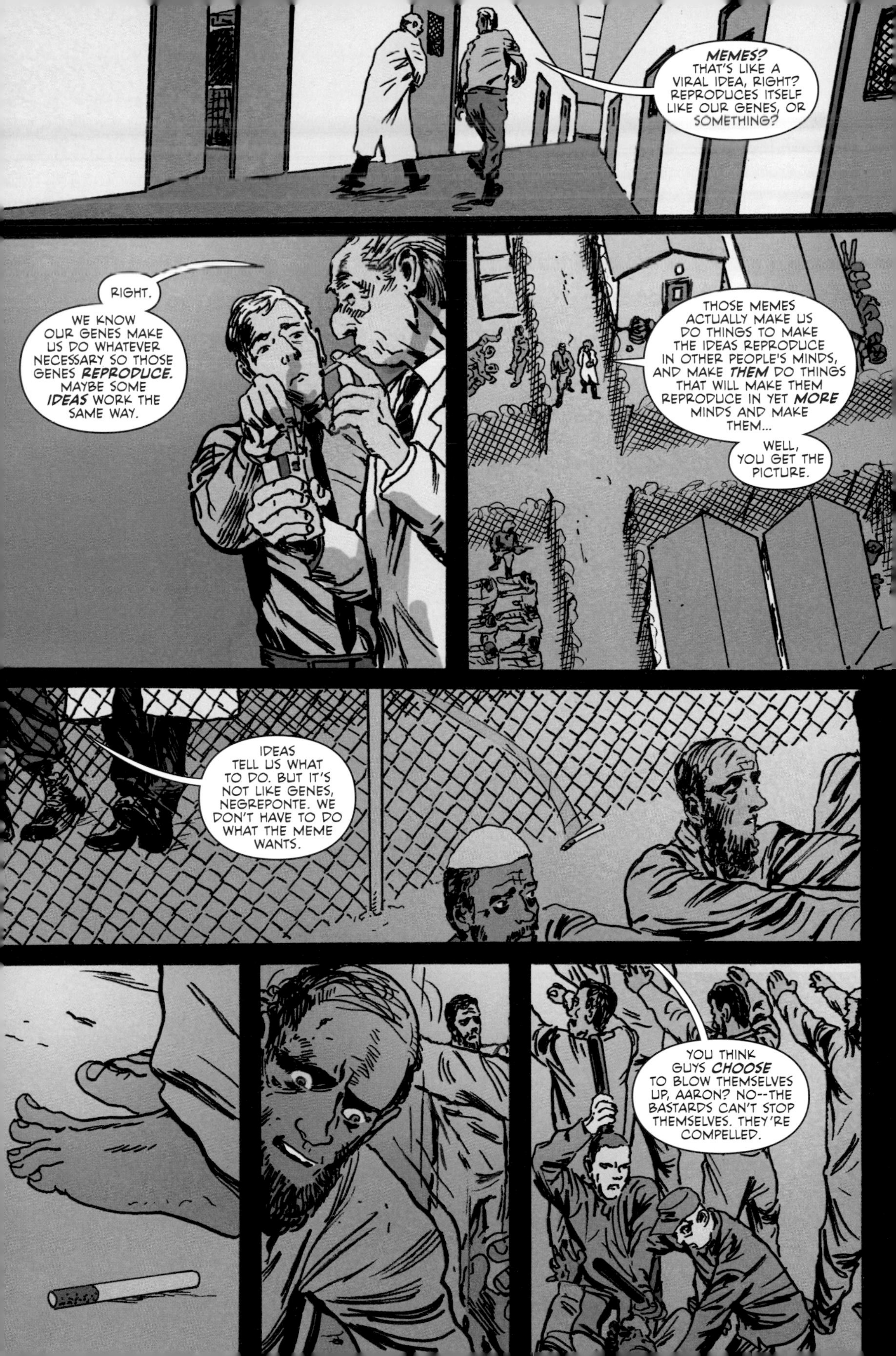
MEMES? THAT'S LIKE A VIRAL IDEA, RIGHT? REPRODUCES ITSELF LIKE OUR GENES, OR SOMETHING?
RIGHT.
WE KNOW OUR GENES MAKE US DO WHATEVER NECESSARY SO THOSE GENES REPRODUCE. MAYBE SOME IDEAS WORK THE SAME WAY.
THOSE MEMES ACTUALLY MAKE US DO THINGS TO MAKE THE IDEAS REPRODUCE IN OTHER PEOPLE'S MINDS, AND MAKE THEM DO THINGS THAT WILL MAKE THEM REPRODUCE IN YET MORE MINDS AND MAKE THEM...
WELL, YOU GET THE PICTURE.
IDEAS TELL US WHAT TO DO. BUT IT'S NOT LIKE GENES, NEGREPONTE. WE DON'T HAVE TO DO WHAT THE MEME WANTS.
YOU THINK GUYS CHOOSE TO BLOW THEMSELVES UP, AARON? NO--THE BASTARDS CAN'T STOP THEMSELVES. THEY'RE COMPELLED.

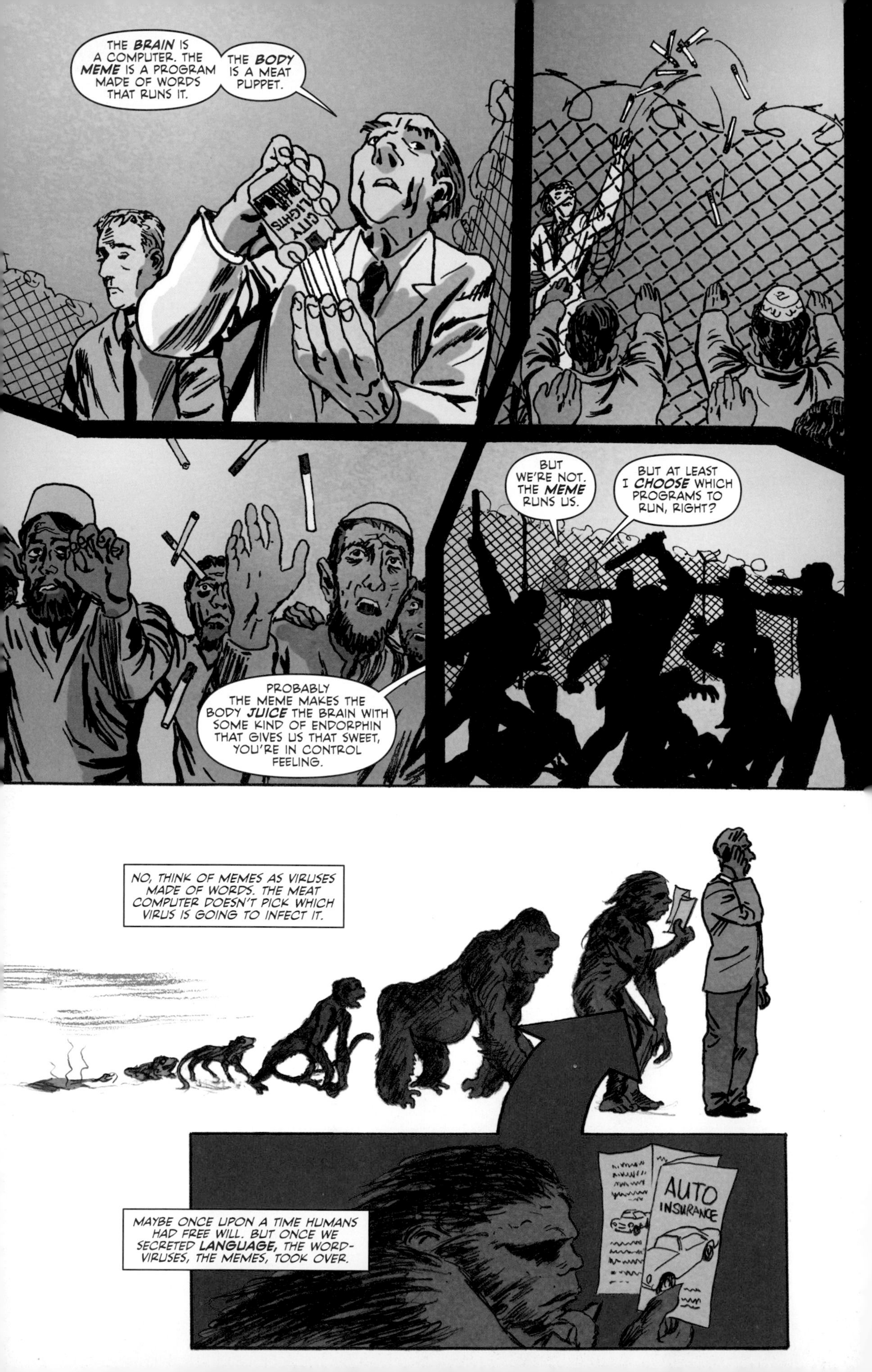
THE BRAIN IS A COMPUTER. THE MEME IS A PROGRAM MADE OF WORDS THAT RUNS IT.
THE BODY IS A MEAT PUPPET.
CITY LIGHTS
PROBABLY THE MEME MAKES THE BODY JUICE THE BRAIN WITH SOME KIND OF ENDORPHIN THAT GIVES US THAT SWEET, YOU'RE IN CONTROL FEELING.
BUT AT LEAST I CHOOSE WHICH PROGRAMS TO RUN, RIGHT?
BUT WE'RE NOT. THE MEME RUNS US.
NO, THINK OF MEMES AS VIRUSES MADE OF WORDS. THE MEAT COMPUTER DOESN'T PICK WHICH VIRUS IS GOING TO INFECT IT.
MAYBE ONCE UPON A TIME HUMANS HAD FREE WILL. BUT ONCE WE SECRETED LANGUAGE, THE WORD-VIRUSES, THE MEMES, TOOK OVER.
AUTO INSURANCE

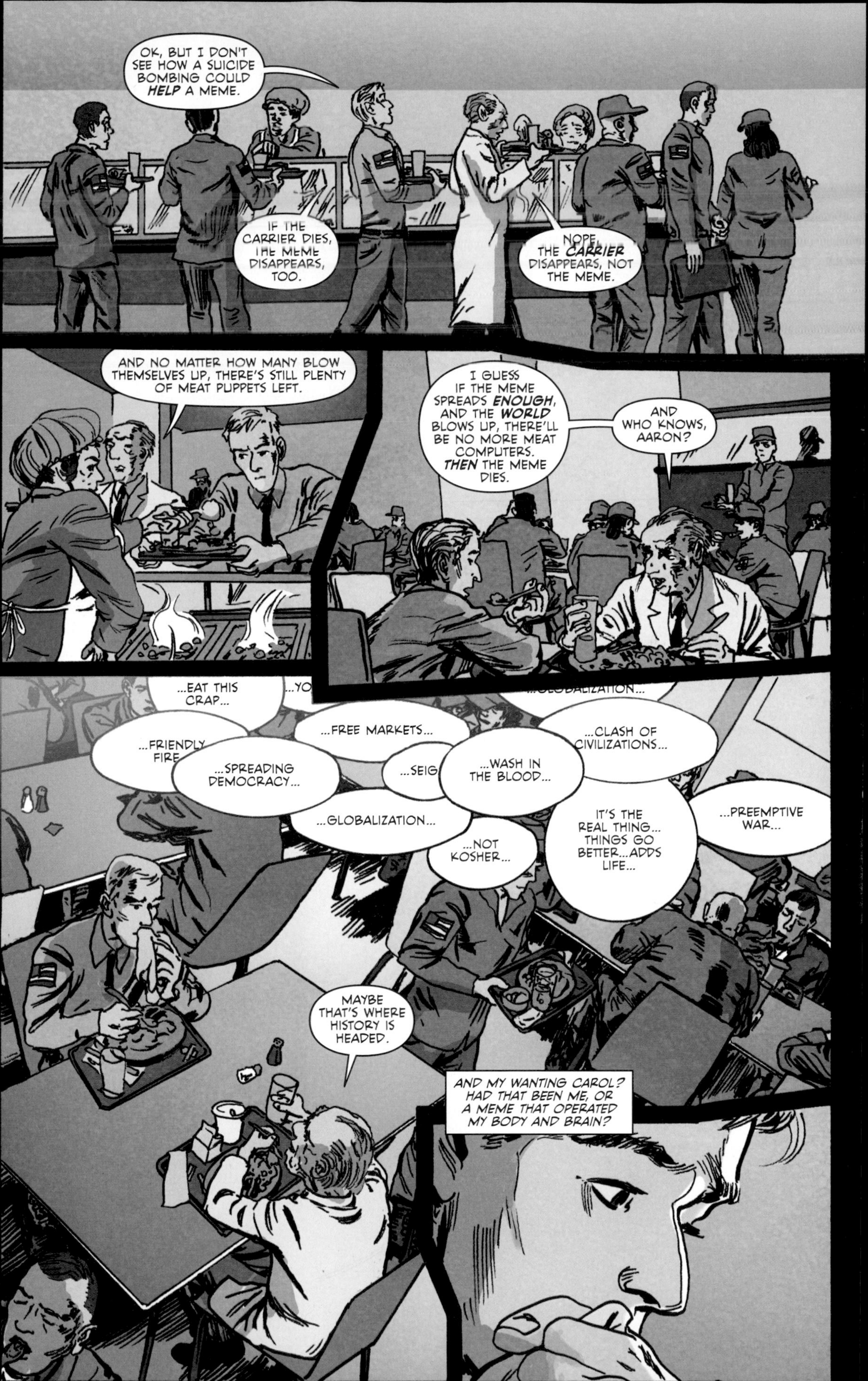

OK, BUT I DON'T SEE HOW A SUICIDE BOMBING COULD HELP A MEME.
IF THE CARRIER DIES, THE MEME DISAPPEARS, TOO.
NOPE. THE CARRIER DISAPPEARS, NOT THE MEME.
AND NO MATTER HOW MANY BLOW THEMSELVES UP, THERE'S STILL PLENTY OF MEAT PUPPETS LEFT.
I GUESS IF THE MEME SPREADS ENOUGH, AND THE WORLD BLOWS UP, THERE'LL BE NO MORE MEAT COMPUTERS. THEN THE MEME DIES.
AND WHO KNOWS, AARON?
...EAT THIS CRAP...
...FREE MARKETS...
...CLASH OF CIVILIZATIONS...
...SPREADING DEMOCRACY...
...WASH IN THE BLOOD...
...GLOBALIZATION...
...NOT KOSHER...
IT'S THE REAL THING... THINGS GO BETTER...ADDS LIFE...
...PREEMPTIVE WAR...
MAYBE THAT'S WHERE HISTORY IS HEADED.
AND MY WANTING CAROL? HAD THAT BEEN ME, OR A MEME THAT OPERATED MY BODY AND BRAIN?

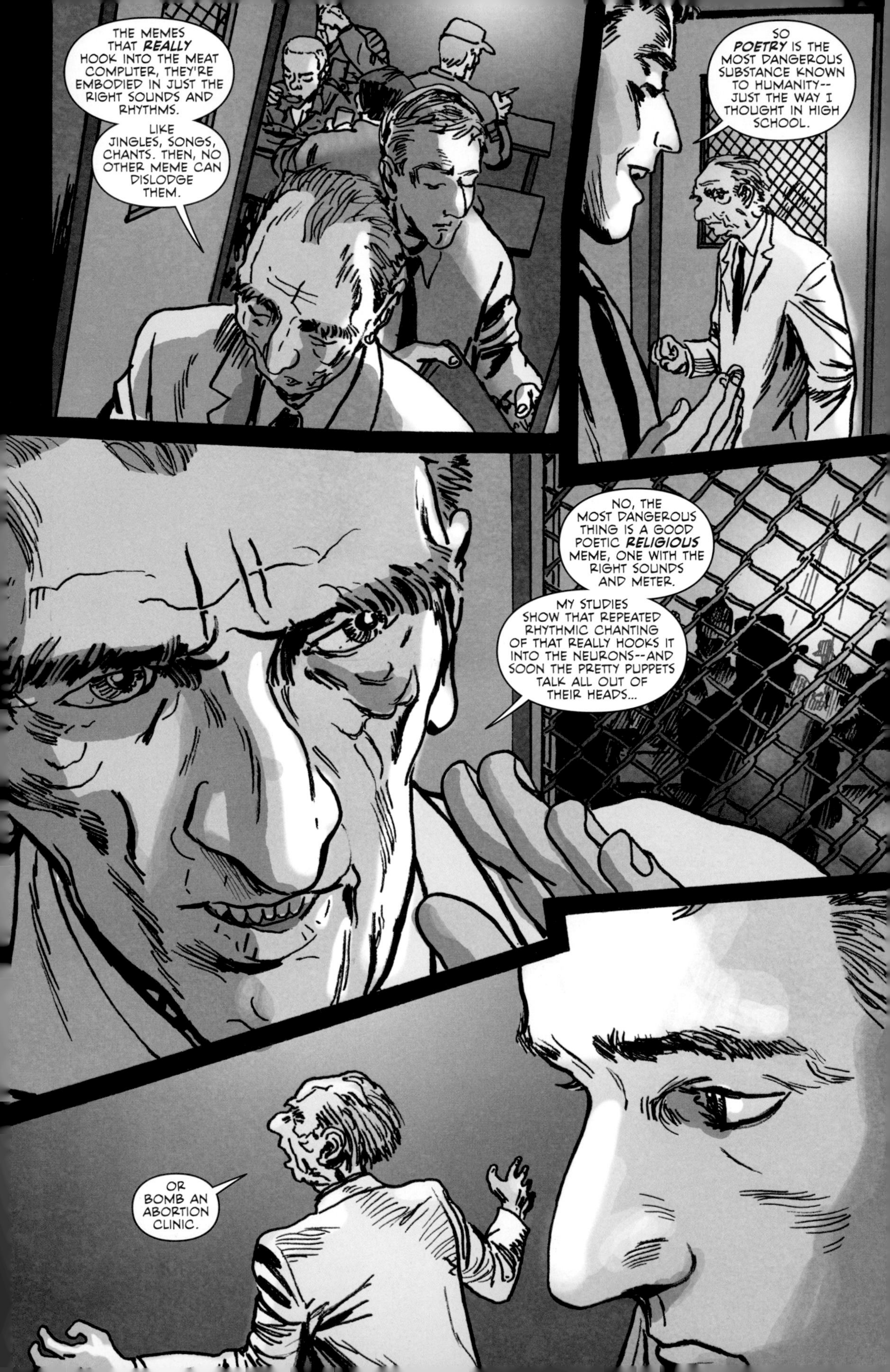
THE MEMES THAT REALLY HOOK INTO THE MEAT COMPUTER, THEY'RE EMBODIED IN JUST THE RIGHT SOUNDS AND RHYTHMS.
LIKE JINGLES, SONGS, CHANTS. THEN, NO OTHER MEME CAN DISLODGE THEM.
SO POETRY IS THE MOST DANGEROUS SUBSTANCE KNOWN TO HUMANITY--JUST THE WAY I THOUGHT IN HIGH SCHOOL.
NO, THE MOST DANGEROUS THING IS A GOOD POETIC RELIGIOUS MEME, ONE WITH THE RIGHT SOUNDS AND METER.
MY STUDIES SHOW THAT REPEATED RHYTHMIC CHANTING OF THAT REALLY HOOKS IT INTO THE NEURONS--AND SOON THE PRETTY PUPPETS TALK ALL OUT OF THEIR HEADS...
OR BOMB AN ABORTION CLINIC.

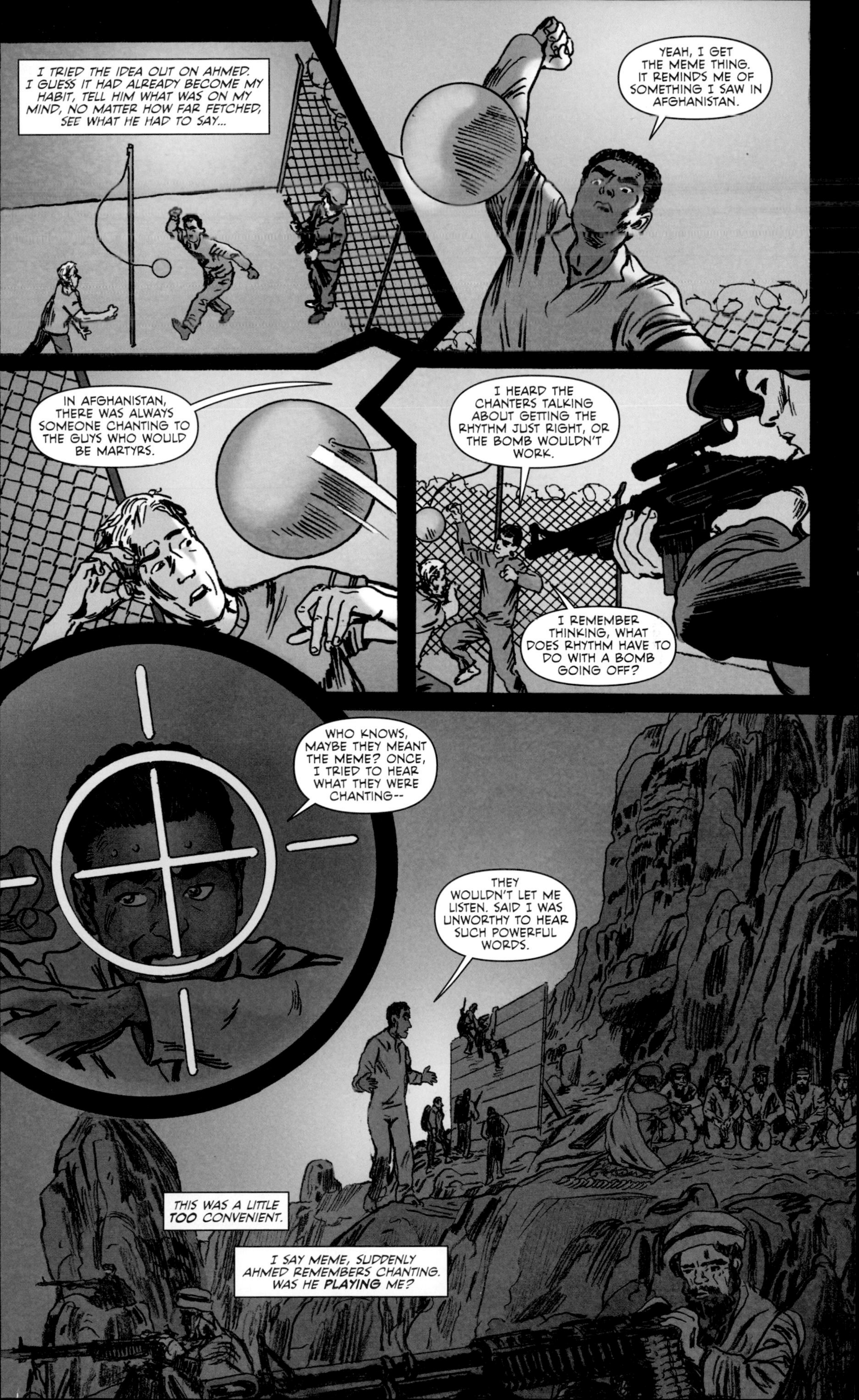
I TRIED THE IDEA OUT ON AHMED. I GUESS IT HAD ALREADY BECOME MY HABIT, TELL HIM WHAT WAS ON MY MIND, NO MATTER HOW FAR FETCHED, SEE WHAT HE HAD TO SAY...
YEAH, I GET THE MEME THING. IT REMINDS ME OF SOMETHING I SAW IN AFGHANISTAN.
IN AFGHANISTAN, THERE WAS ALWAYS SOMEONE CHANTING TO THE GUYS WHO WOULD BE MARTYRS.
I HEARD THE CHANTERS TALKING ABOUT GETTING THE RHYTHM JUST RIGHT, OR THE BOMB WOULDN'T WORK.
I REMEMBER THINKING, WHAT DOES RHYTHM HAVE TO DO WITH A BOMB GOING OFF?
WHO KNOWS, MAYBE THEY MEANT THE MEME? ONCE, I TRIED TO HEAR WHAT THEY WERE CHANTING--
THEY WOULDN'T LET ME LISTEN. SAID I WAS UNWORTHY TO HEAR SUCH POWERFUL WORDS.
THIS WAS A LITTLE TOO CONVENIENT.
I SAY MEME, SUDDENLY AHMED REMEMBERS CHANTING. WAS HE PLAYING ME?

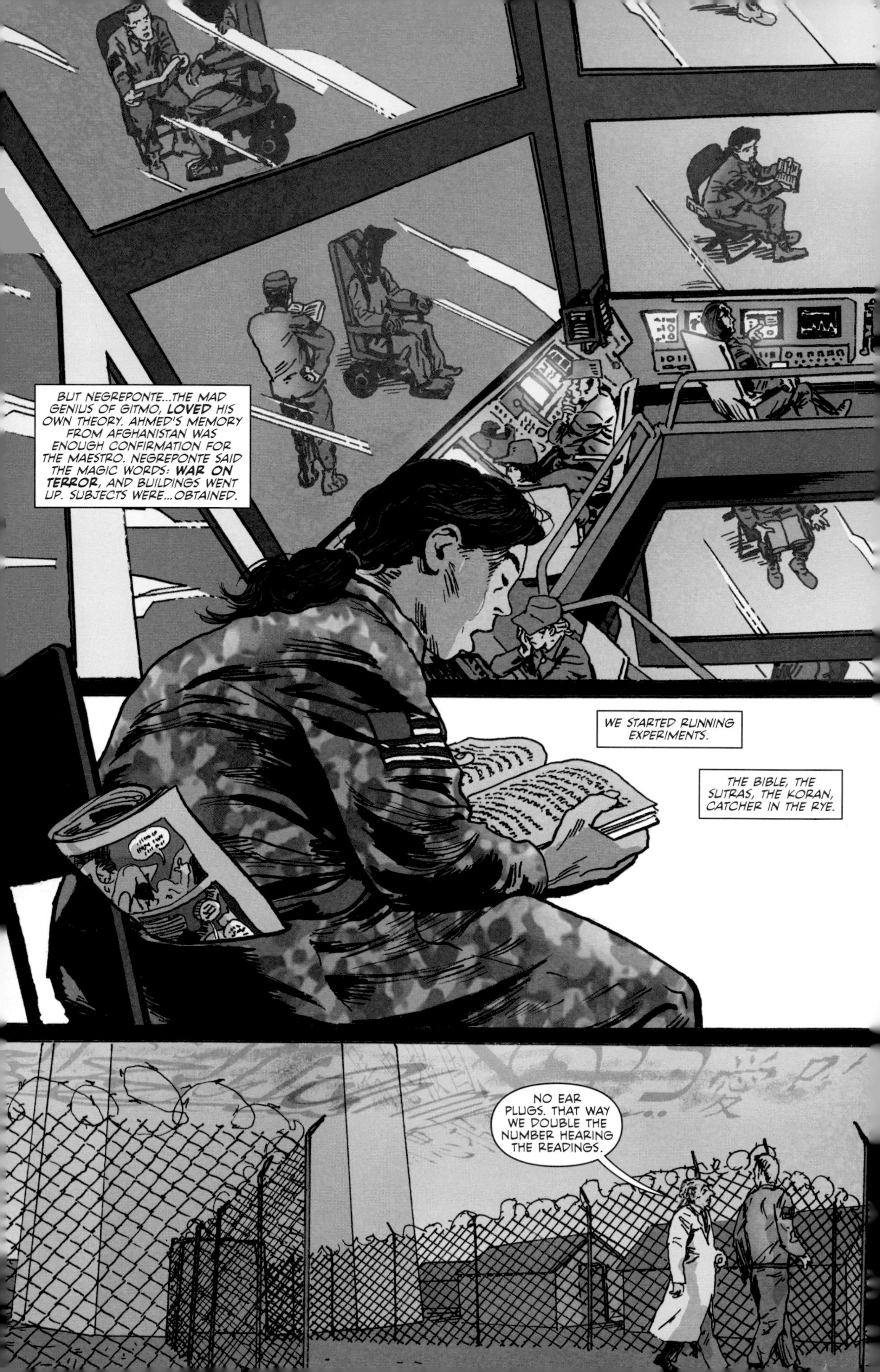
BUT NEGREPONTE...THE MAD GENIUS OF GITMO, **LOVED** HIS OWN THEORY. AHMED'S MEMORY FROM AFGHANISTAN WAS ENOUGH CONFIRMATION FOR THE MAESTRO. NEGREPONTE SAID THE MAGIC WORDS: **WAR ON TERROR**, AND BUILDINGS WENT UP. SUBJECTS WERE...OBTAINED.
WE STARTED RUNNING EXPERIMENTS.
THE BIBLE, THE SUTRAS, THE KORAN, CATCHER IN THE RYE.
NO EAR PLUGS. THAT WAY WE DOUBLE THE NUMBER HEARING THE READINGS.

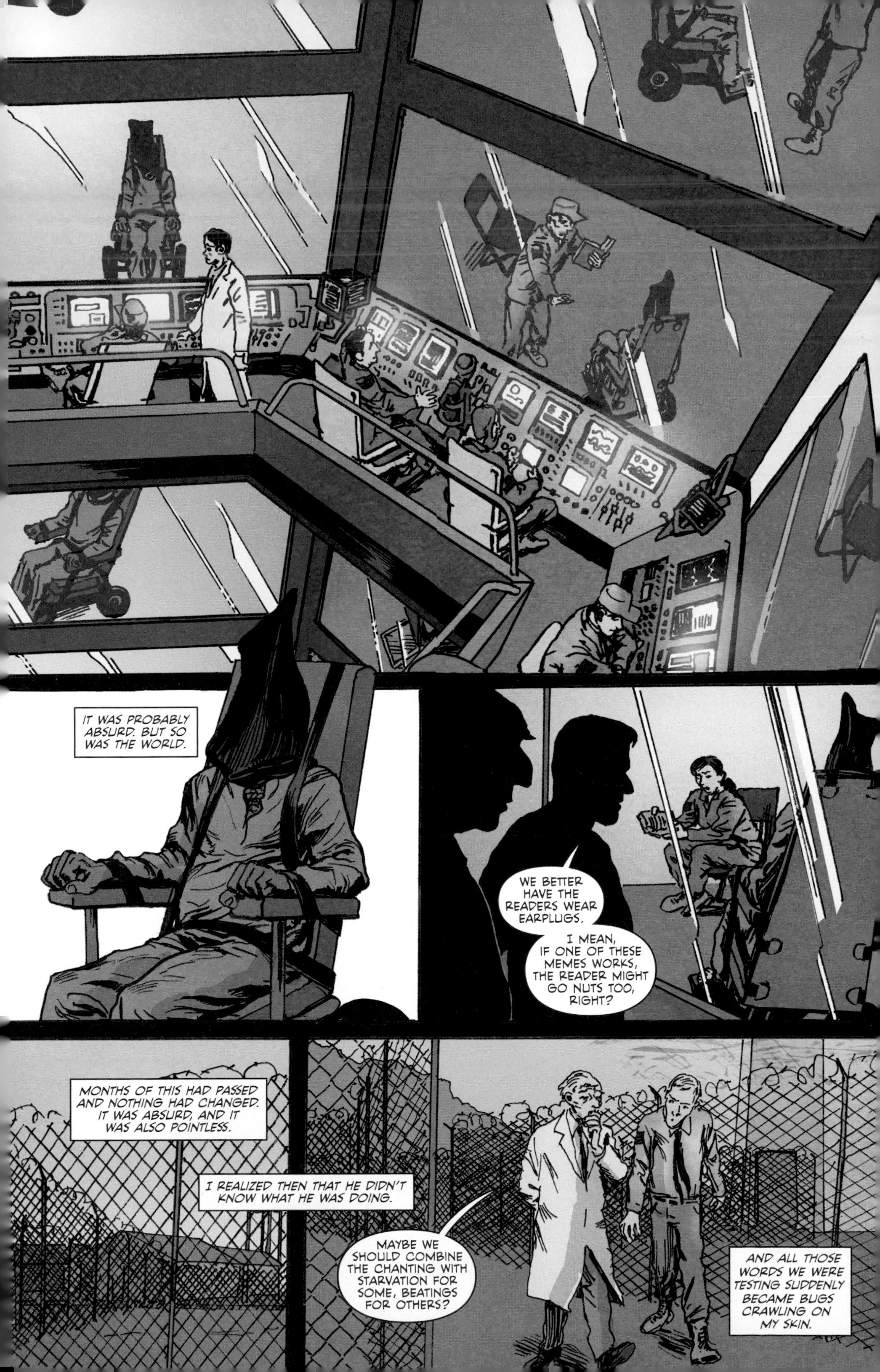
IT WAS PROBABLY ABSURD. BUT SO WAS THE WORLD.
WE BETTER HAVE THE READERS WEAR EARPLUGS.
I MEAN, IF ONE OF THESE MEMES WORKS, THE READER MIGHT GO NUTS TOO, RIGHT?
MONTHS OF THIS HAD PASSED AND NOTHING HAD CHANGED. IT WAS ABSURD, AND IT WAS ALSO POINTLESS.
I REALIZED THEN THAT HE DIDN'T KNOW WHAT HE WAS DOING.
MAYBE WE SHOULD COMBINE THE CHANTING WITH STARVATION FOR SOME, BEATINGS FOR OTHERS?
AND ALL THOSE WORDS WE WERE TESTING SUDDENLY BECAME BUGS CRAWLING ON MY SKIN.

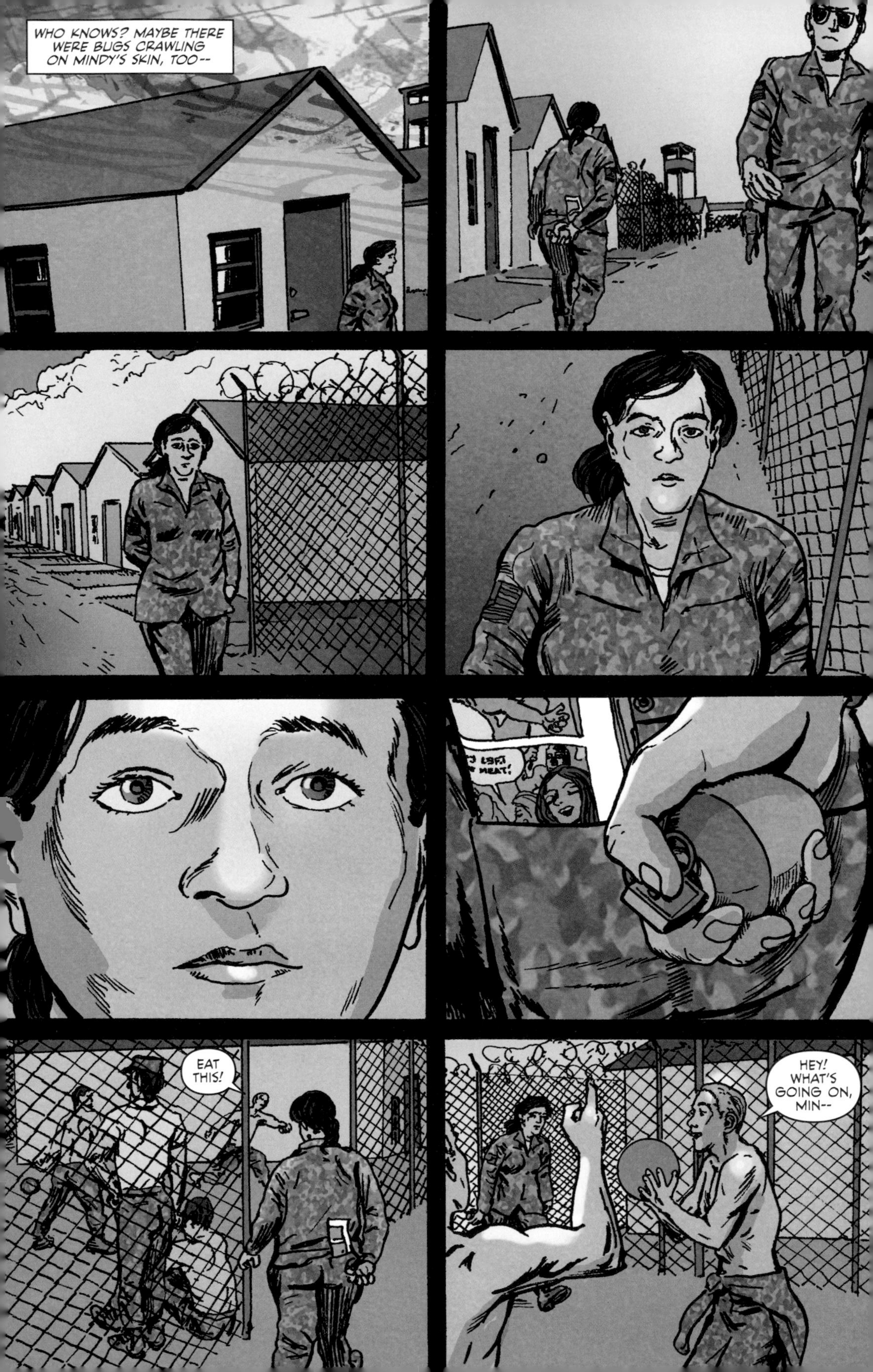
WHO KNOWS? MAYBE THERE WERE BUGS CRAWLING ON MINDY'S SKIN, TOO--
EAT THIS!
HEY! WHAT'S GOING ON, MIN--

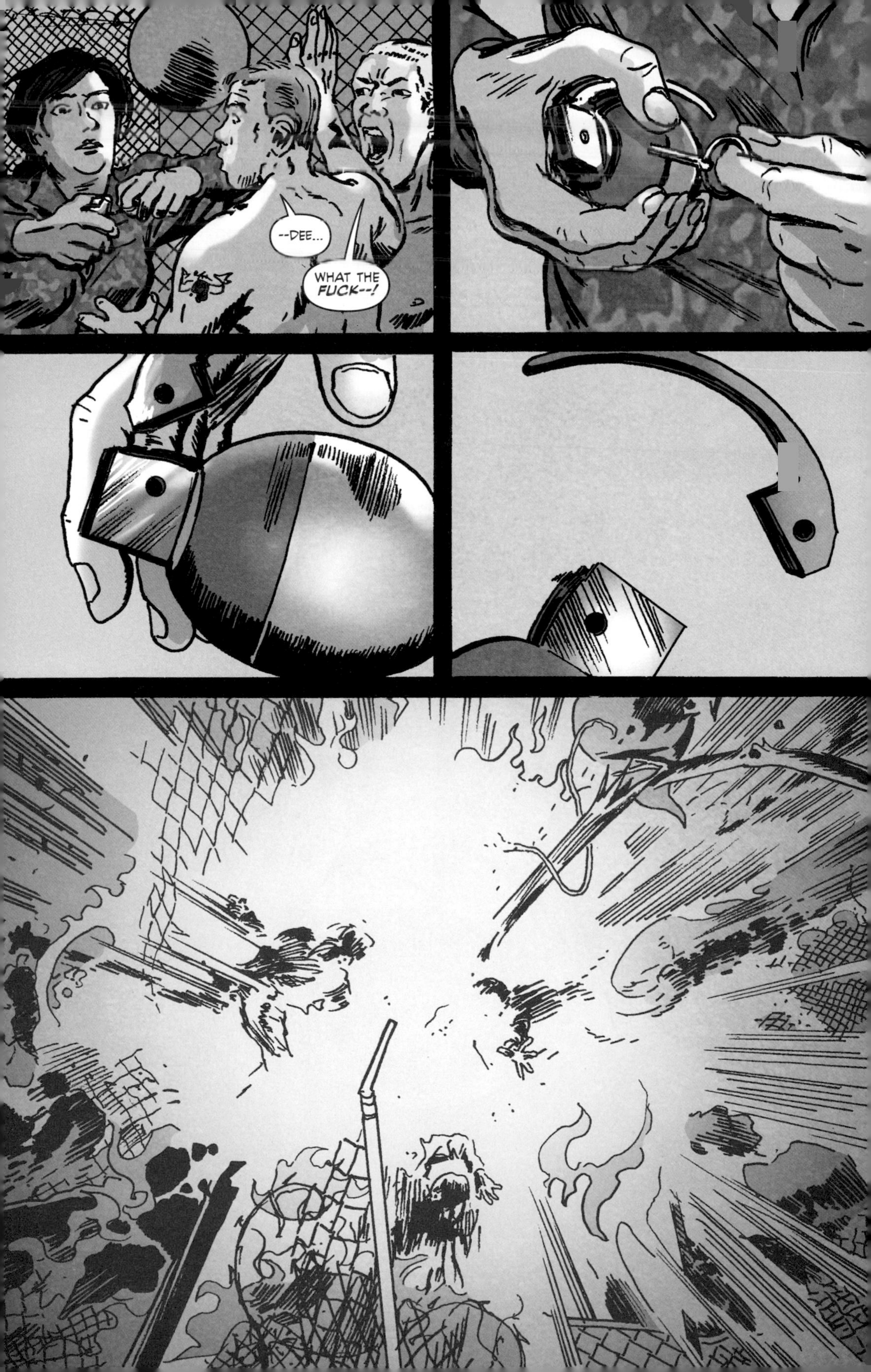
--DEE...
WHAT THE FUCK--!

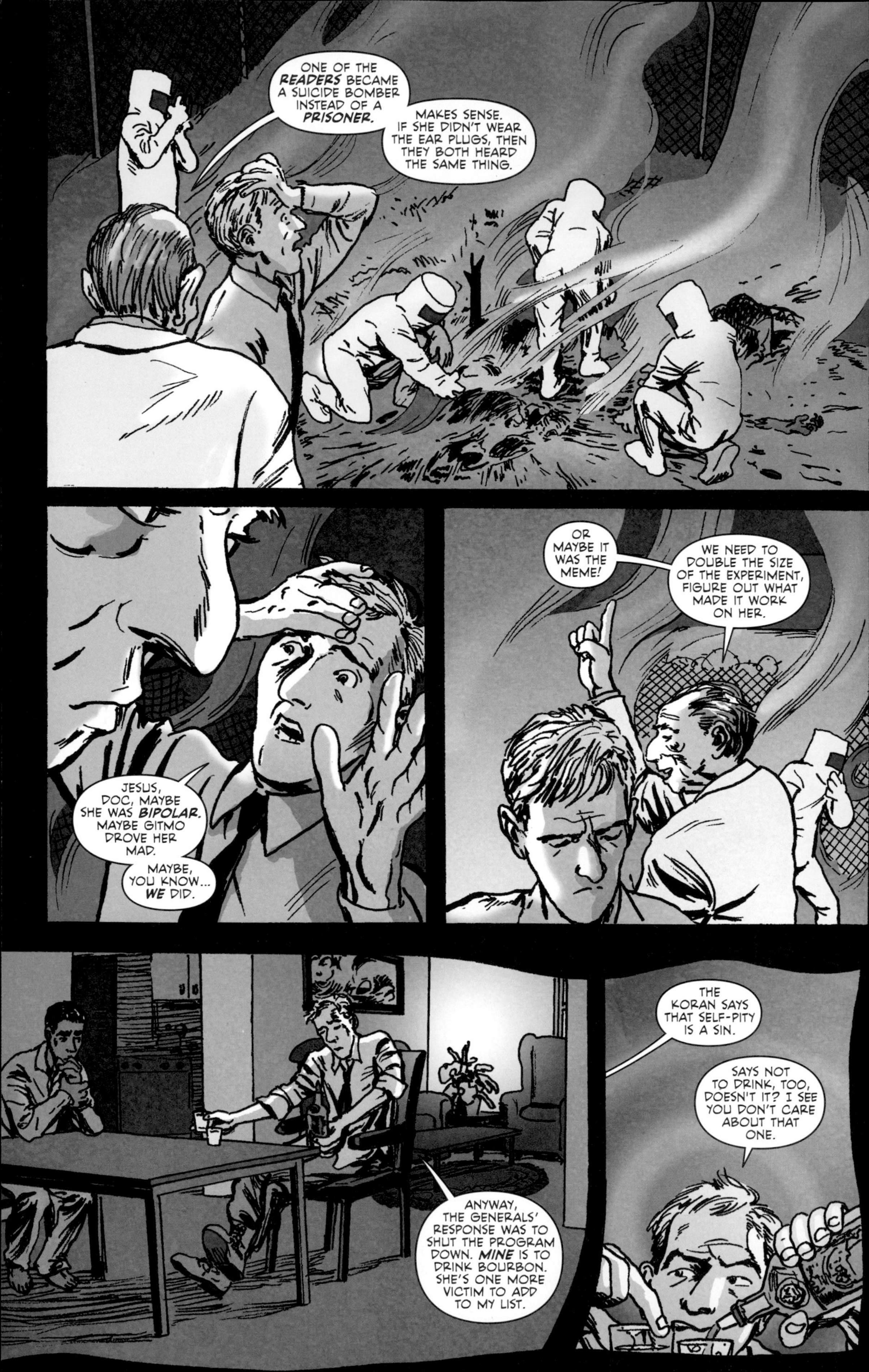
ONE OF THE *READERS* BECAME A SUICIDE BOMBER INSTEAD OF A *PRISONER.*
MAKES SENSE. IF SHE DIDN'T WEAR THE EAR PLUGS, THEN THEY BOTH HEARD THE SAME THING.
JESUS, DOC, MAYBE SHE WAS *BIPOLAR.* MAYBE GITMO DROVE HER MAD.
MAYBE, YOU KNOW... *WE* DID.
OR MAYBE IT WAS THE MEME!
WE NEED TO DOUBLE THE SIZE OF THE EXPERIMENT, FIGURE OUT WHAT MADE IT WORK ON HER.
ANYWAY, THE GENERALS' RESPONSE WAS TO SHUT THE PROGRAM DOWN. *MINE* IS TO DRINK BOURBON. SHE'S ONE MORE VICTIM TO ADD TO MY LIST.
THE KORAN SAYS THAT SELF-PITY IS A SIN.
SAYS NOT TO DRINK, TOO, DOESN'T IT? I SEE YOU DON'T CARE ABOUT THAT ONE.

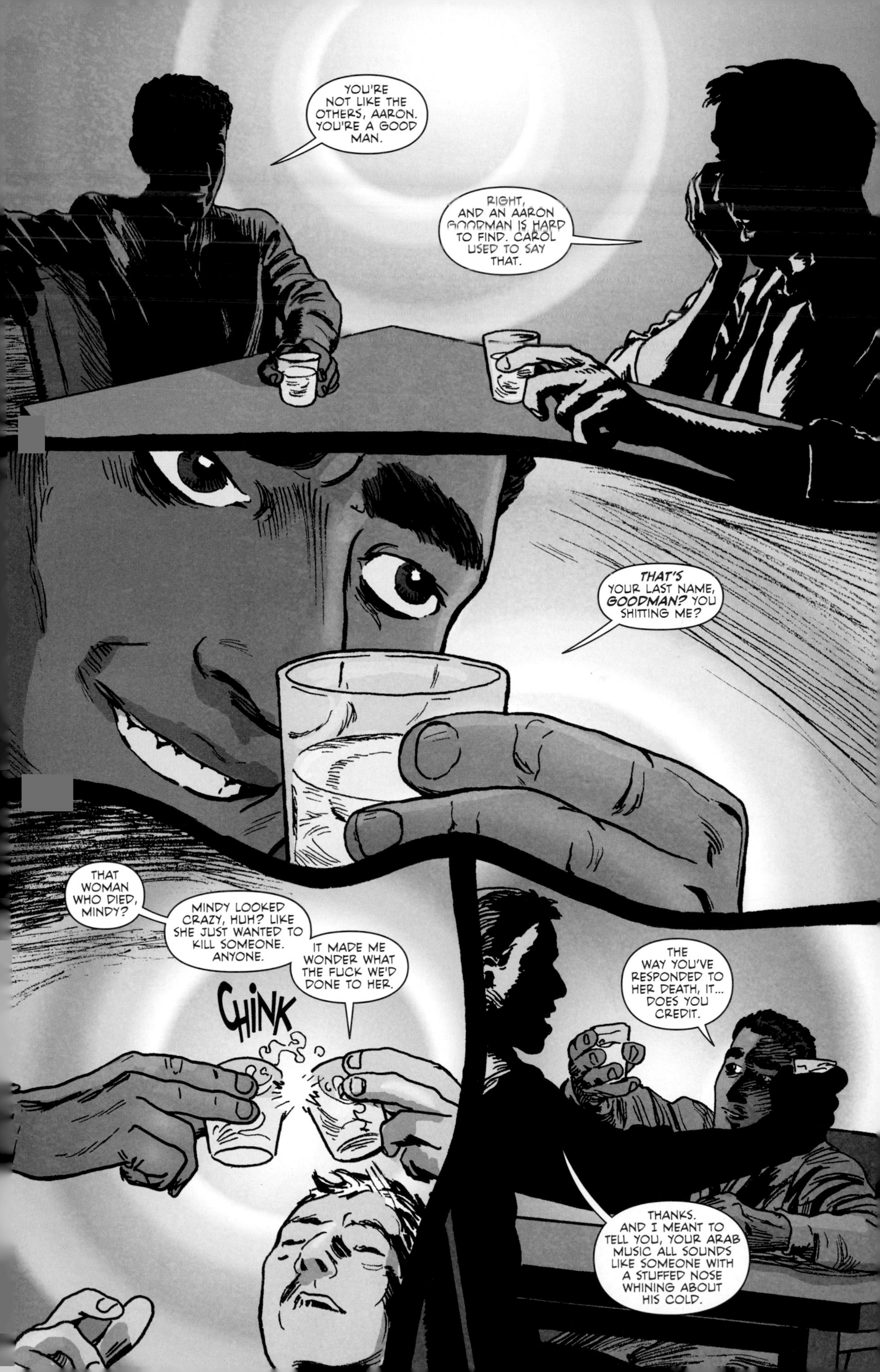
YOU'RE NOT LIKE THE OTHERS, AARON. YOU'RE A GOOD MAN.
RIGHT, AND AN AARON GOODMAN IS HARD TO FIND. CAROL USED TO SAY THAT.
THAT'S YOUR LAST NAME, GOODMAN? YOU SHITTING ME?
THAT WOMAN WHO DIED, MINDY?
MINDY LOOKED CRAZY, HUH? LIKE SHE JUST WANTED TO KILL SOMEONE. ANYONE.
IT MADE ME WONDER WHAT THE FUCK WE'D DONE TO HER.
CHINK
THE WAY YOU'VE RESPONDED TO HER DEATH, IT... DOES YOU CREDIT.
THANKS. AND I MEANT TO TELL YOU, YOUR ARAB MUSIC ALL SOUNDS LIKE SOMEONE WITH A STUFFED NOSE WHINING ABOUT HIS COLD.

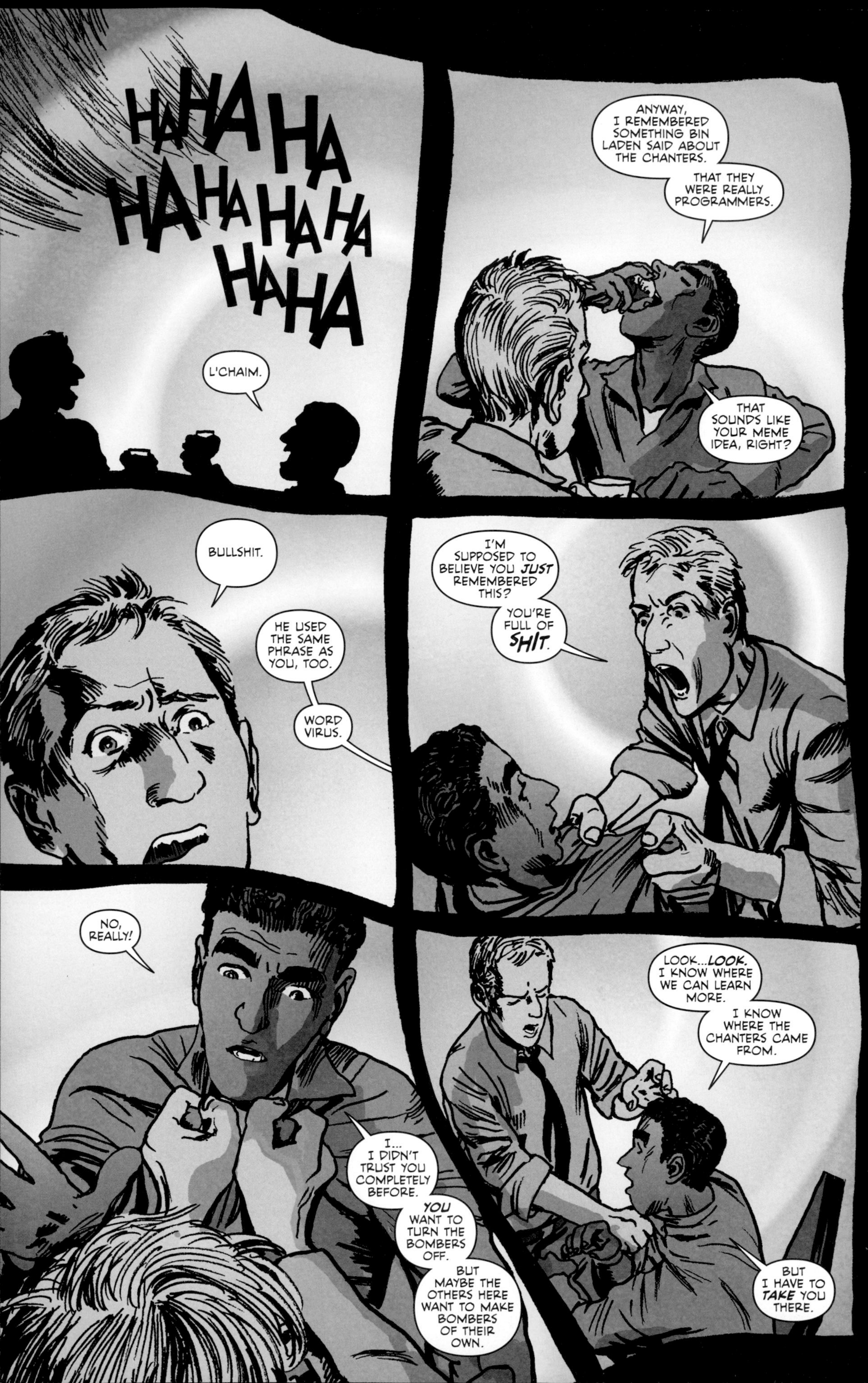
HA HA HA HA
HA HA HA HA HA
HA HA
L'CHAIM.
ANYWAY, I REMEMBERED SOMETHING BIN LADEN SAID ABOUT THE CHANTERS.
THAT THEY WERE REALLY PROGRAMMERS.
THAT SOUNDS LIKE YOUR MEME IDEA, RIGHT?
BULLSHIT.
HE USED THE SAME PHRASE AS YOU, TOO.
WORD VIRUS.
I'M SUPPOSED TO BELIEVE YOU *JUST* REMEMBERED THIS?
YOU'RE FULL OF *SHIT*.
NO, REALLY!
I... I DIDN'T TRUST YOU COMPLETELY BEFORE.
YOU WANT TO TURN THE BOMBERS OFF.
BUT MAYBE THE OTHERS HERE WANT TO MAKE BOMBERS OF THEIR OWN.
LOOK... *LOOK.* I KNOW WHERE WE CAN LEARN MORE.
I KNOW WHERE THE CHANTERS CAME FROM.
BUT I HAVE TO *TAKE* YOU THERE.

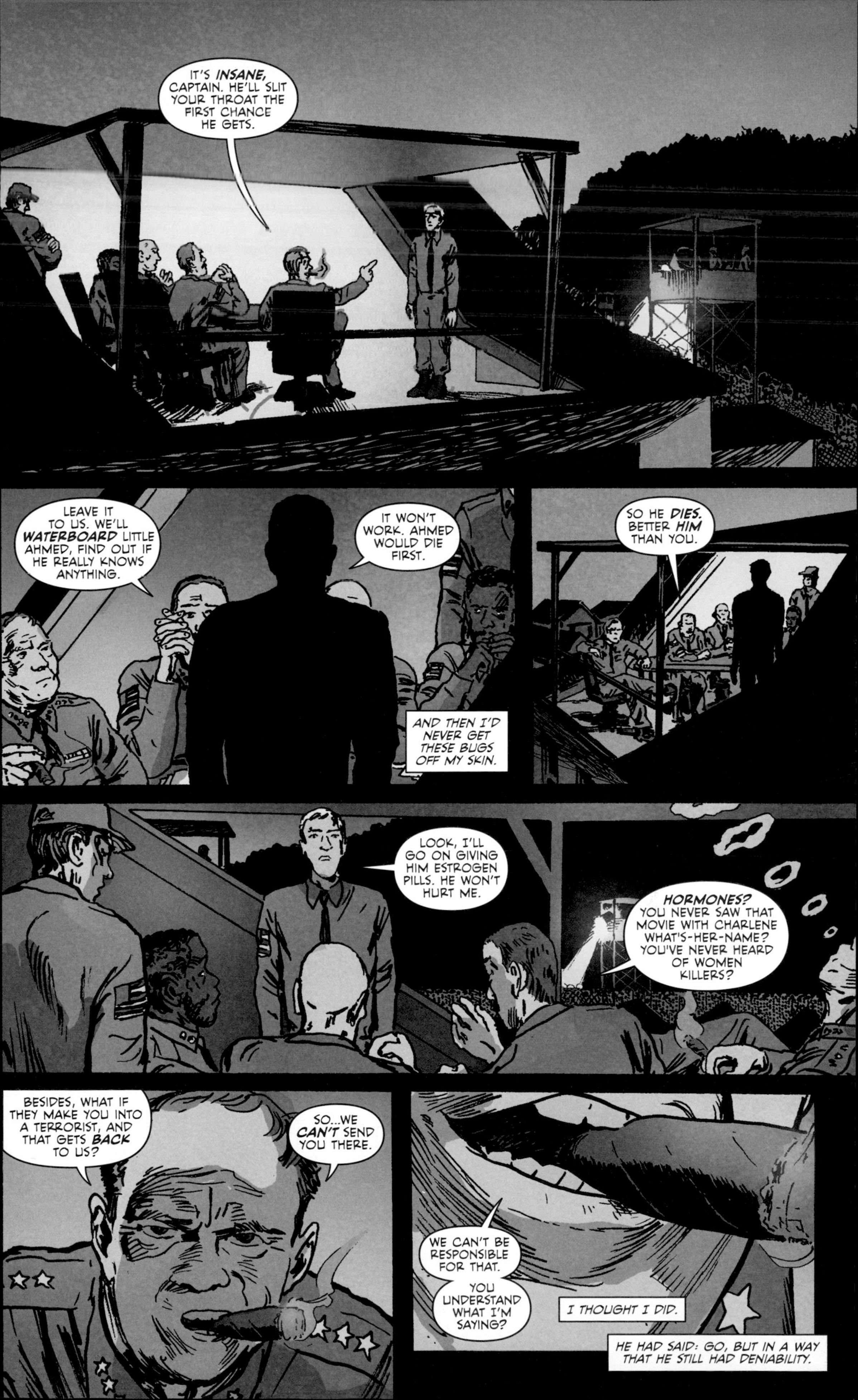
IT'S *INSANE,* CAPTAIN. HE'LL SLIT YOUR THROAT THE FIRST CHANCE HE GETS.
LEAVE IT TO US. WE'LL *WATERBOARD* LITTLE AHMED, FIND OUT IF HE REALLY KNOWS ANYTHING.
IT WON'T WORK. AHMED WOULD DIE FIRST.
AND THEN I'D NEVER GET THESE BUGS OFF MY SKIN.
SO HE *DIES.* BETTER *HIM* THAN YOU.
LOOK, I'LL GO ON GIVING HIM ESTROGEN PILLS. HE WON'T HURT ME.
HORMONES? YOU NEVER SAW THAT MOVIE WITH CHARLENE WHAT'S-HER-NAME? YOU'VE NEVER HEARD OF WOMEN KILLERS?
BESIDES, WHAT IF THEY MAKE YOU INTO A TERRORIST, AND THAT GETS *BACK* TO US?
SO...WE *CAN'T* SEND YOU THERE.
WE CAN'T BE RESPONSIBLE FOR THAT.
YOU UNDERSTAND WHAT I'M SAYING?
I THOUGHT I DID.
HE HAD SAID: GO, BUT IN A WAY THAT HE STILL HAD DENIABILITY.

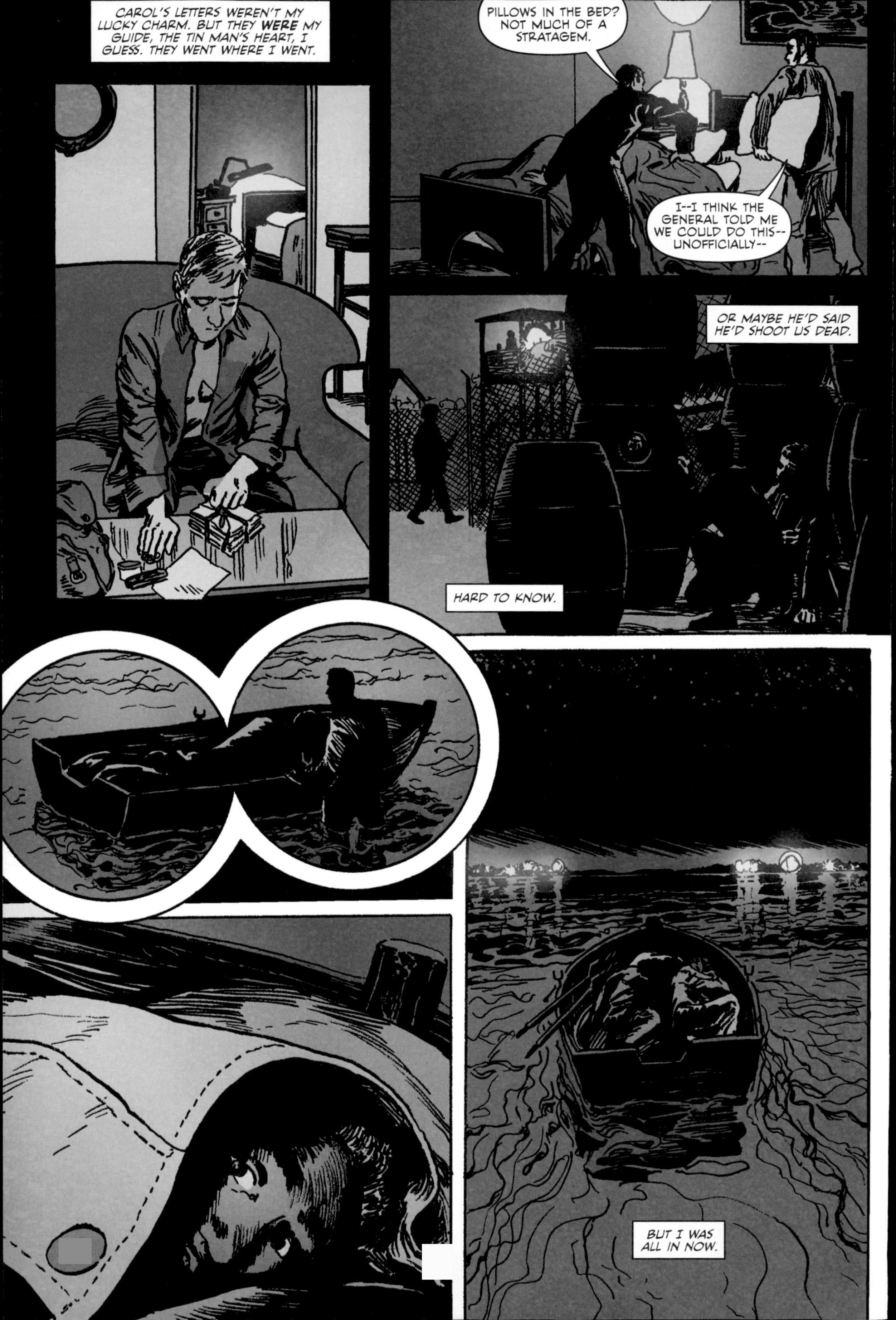
CAROL'S LETTERS WEREN'T MY LUCKY CHARM. BUT THEY WERE MY GUIDE, THE TIN MAN'S HEART, I GUESS. THEY WENT WHERE I WENT.
PILLOWS IN THE BED? NOT MUCH OF A STRATAGEM.
I--I THINK THE GENERAL TOLD ME WE COULD DO THIS--UNOFFICIALLY--
OR MAYBE HE'D SAID HE'D SHOOT US DEAD.
HARD TO KNOW.
BUT I WAS ALL IN NOW.

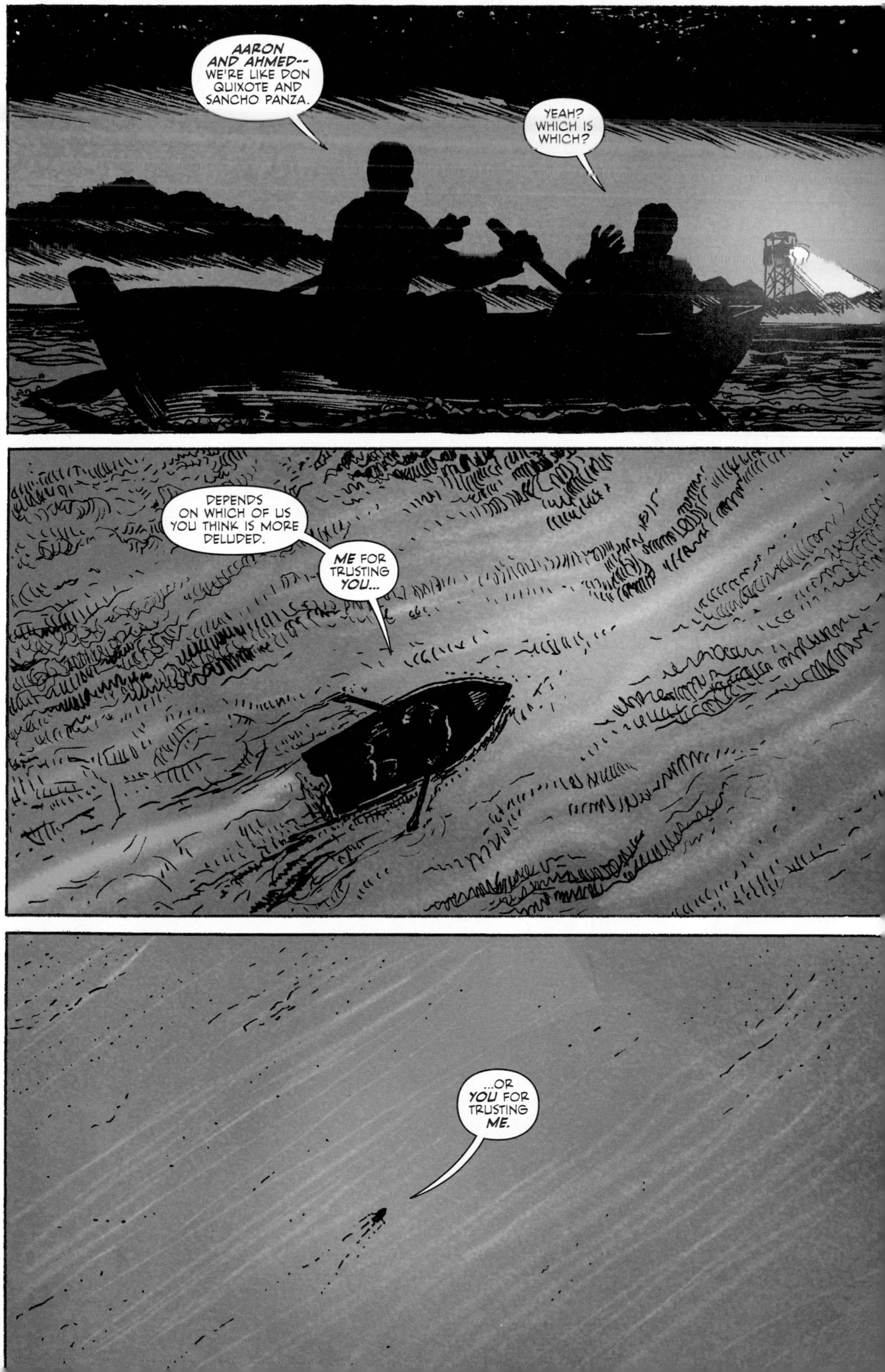
AARON AND AHMED-- WE'RE LIKE DON QUIXOTE AND SANCHO PANZA.
YEAH? WHICH IS WHICH?
DEPENDS ON WHICH OF US YOU THINK IS MORE DELUDED.
ME FOR TRUSTING YOU...
...OR YOU FOR TRUSTING ME.

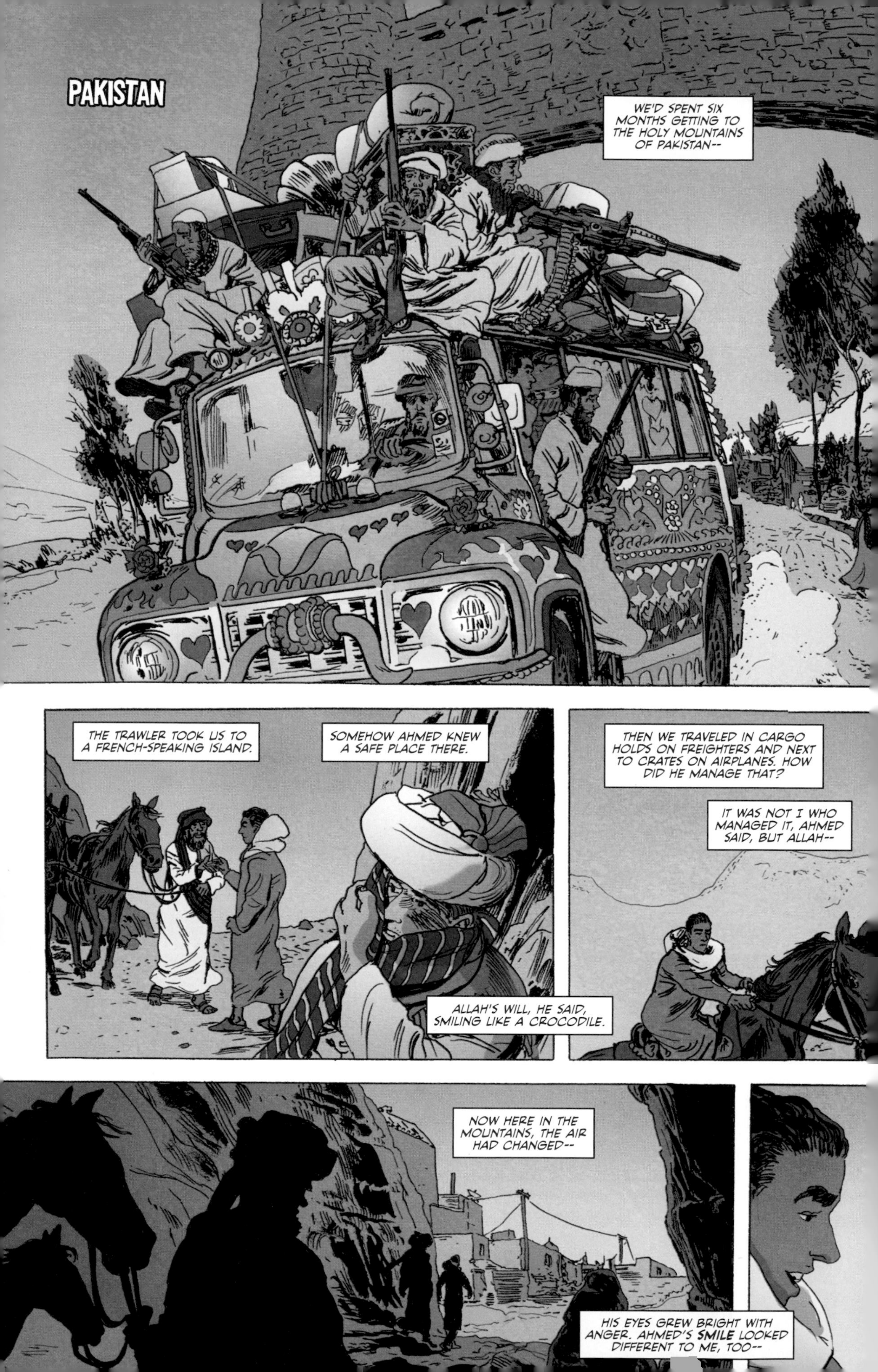
PAKISTAN
WE'D SPENT SIX MONTHS GETTING TO THE HOLY MOUNTAINS OF PAKISTAN--
THE TRAWLER TOOK US TO A FRENCH-SPEAKING ISLAND.
SOMEHOW AHMED KNEW A SAFE PLACE THERE.
ALLAH'S WILL, HE SAID, SMILING LIKE A CROCODILE.
THEN WE TRAVELED IN CARGO HOLDS ON FREIGHTERS AND NEXT TO CRATES ON AIRPLANES. HOW DID HE MANAGE THAT?
IT WAS NOT I WHO MANAGED IT, AHMED SAID, BUT ALLAH--
NOW HERE IN THE MOUNTAINS, THE AIR HAD CHANGED--
HIS EYES GREW BRIGHT WITH ANGER. AHMED'S SMILE LOOKED DIFFERENT TO ME, TOO--

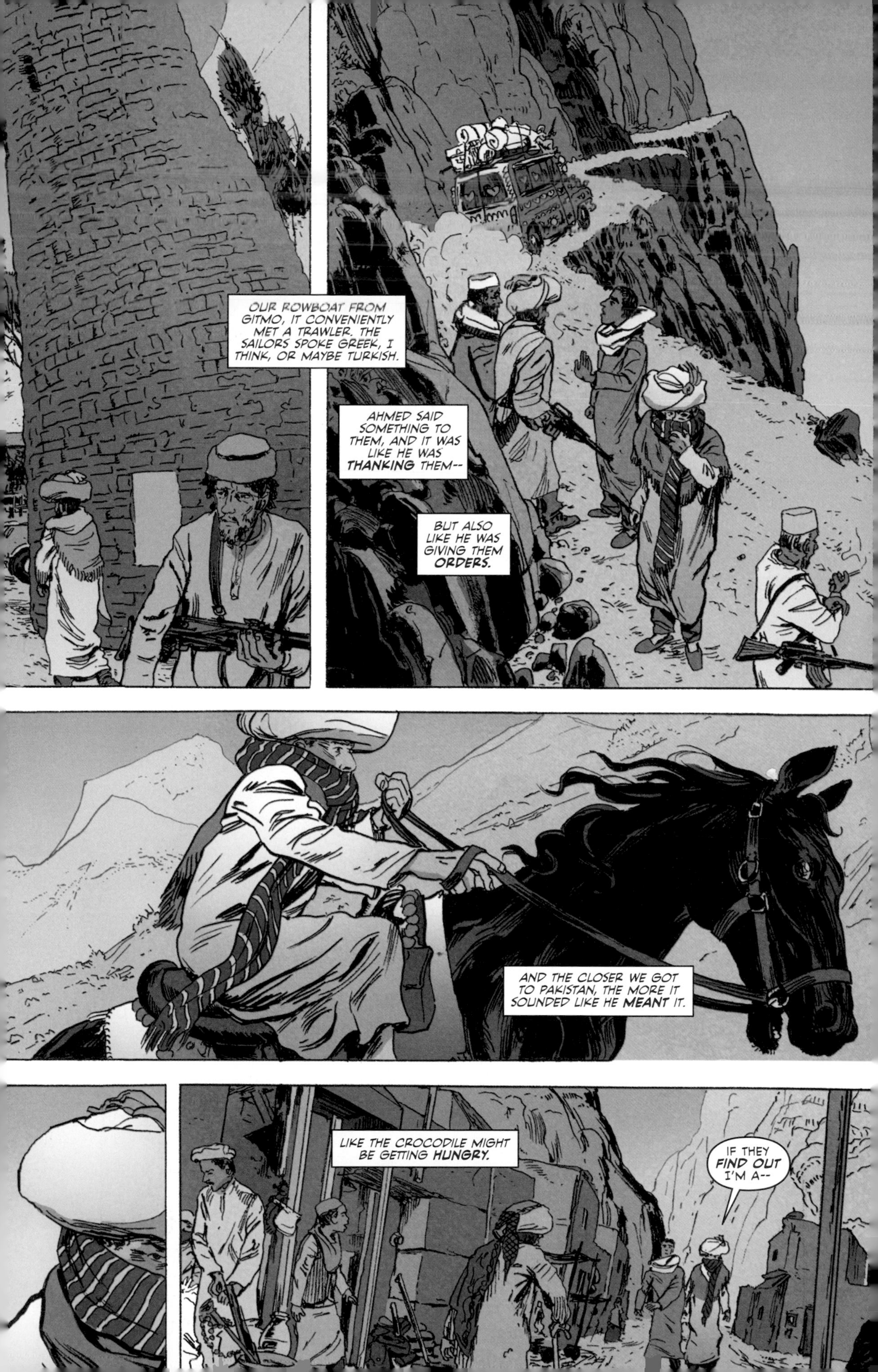

OUR ROWBOAT FROM GITMO, IT CONVENIENTLY MET A TRAWLER. THE SAILORS SPOKE GREEK, I THINK, OR MAYBE TURKISH.
AHMED SAID SOMETHING TO THEM, AND IT WAS LIKE HE WAS **THANKING** THEM--
BUT ALSO LIKE HE WAS GIVING THEM **ORDERS.**
AND THE CLOSER WE GOT TO PAKISTAN, THE MORE IT SOUNDED LIKE HE **MEANT** IT.
LIKE THE CROCODILE MIGHT BE GETTING **HUNGRY.**
IF THEY **FIND OUT** I'M A--

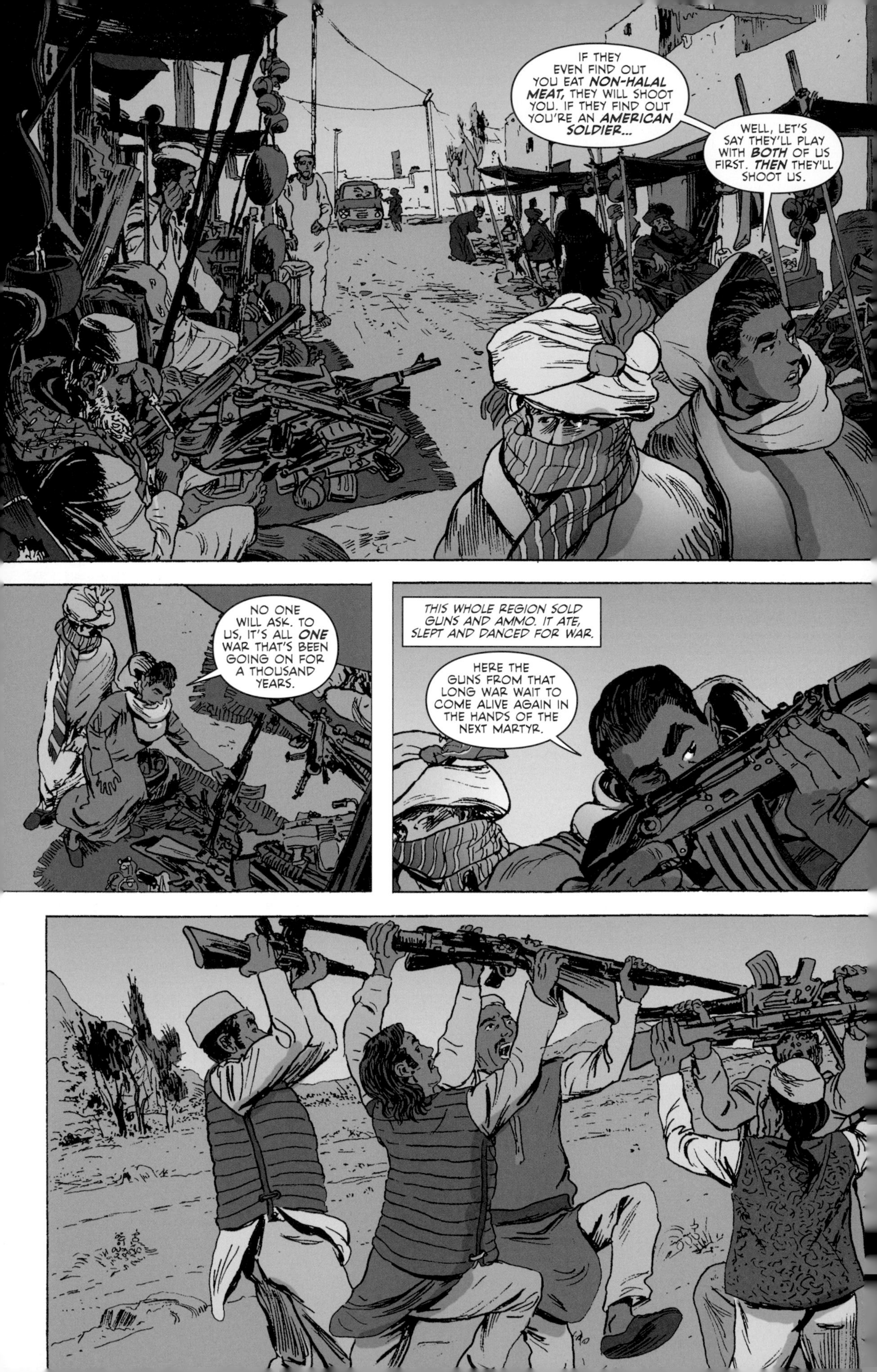
IF THEY EVEN FIND OUT YOU EAT **NON-HALAL MEAT,** THEY WILL SHOOT YOU. IF THEY FIND OUT YOU'RE AN **AMERICAN SOLDIER...**
WELL, LET'S SAY THEY'LL PLAY WITH **BOTH** OF US FIRST. ***THEN*** THEY'LL SHOOT US.
NO ONE WILL ASK. TO US, IT'S ALL *ONE* WAR THAT'S BEEN GOING ON FOR A THOUSAND YEARS.
THIS WHOLE REGION SOLD GUNS AND AMMO. IT ATE, SLEPT AND DANCED FOR WAR.
HERE THE GUNS FROM THAT LONG WAR WAIT TO COME ALIVE AGAIN IN THE HANDS OF THE NEXT MARTYR.

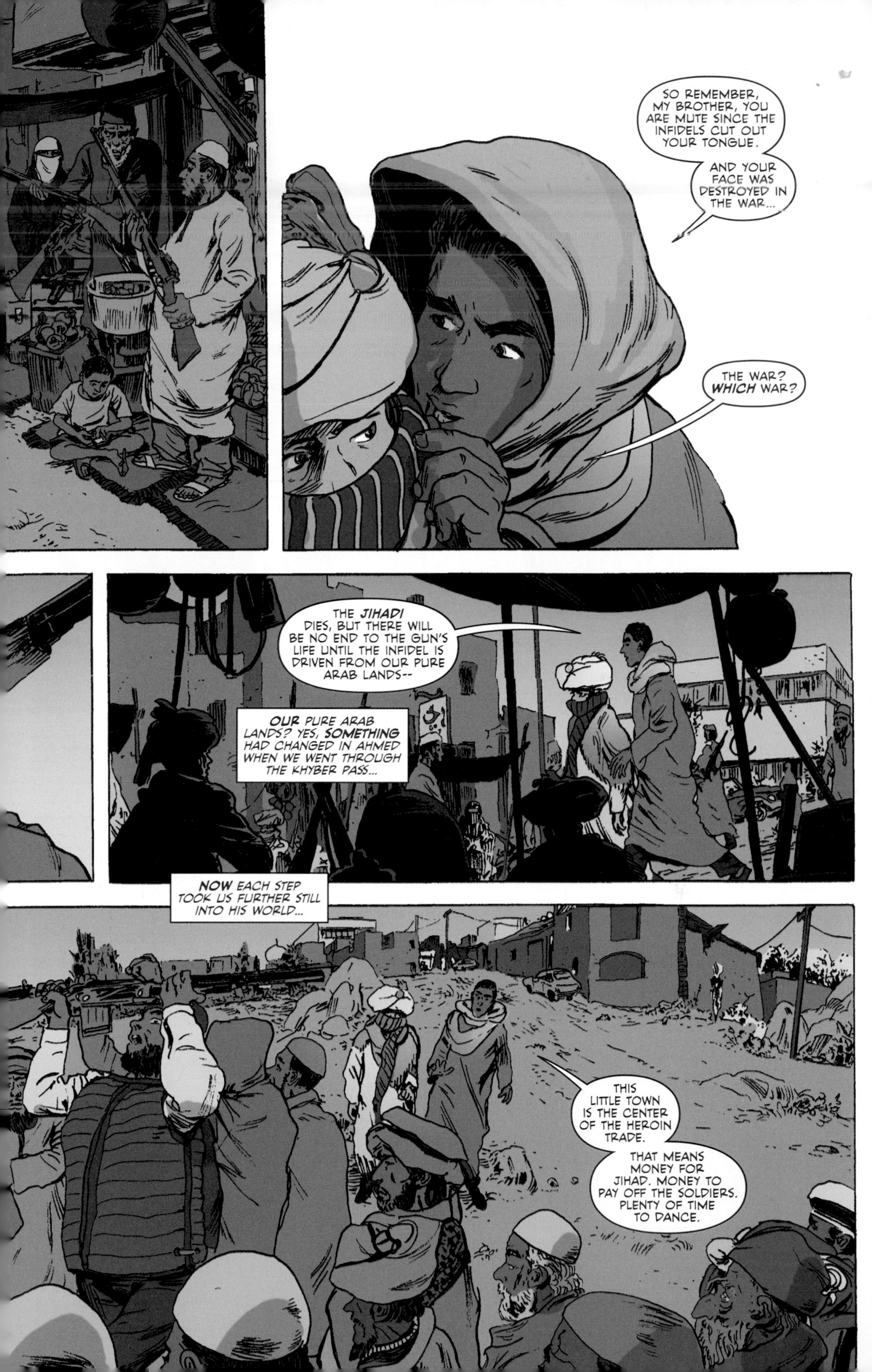
SO REMEMBER, MY BROTHER, YOU ARE MUTE SINCE THE INFIDELS CUT OUT YOUR TONGUE.
AND YOUR FACE WAS DESTROYED IN THE WAR...
THE WAR? WHICH WAR?
THE JIHADI DIES, BUT THERE WILL BE NO END TO THE GUN'S LIFE UNTIL THE INFIDEL IS DRIVEN FROM OUR PURE ARAB LANDS--
OUR PURE ARAB LANDS? YES, SOMETHING HAD CHANGED IN AHMED WHEN WE WENT THROUGH THE KHYBER PASS...
NOW EACH STEP TOOK US FURTHER STILL INTO HIS WORLD...
THIS LITTLE TOWN IS THE CENTER OF THE HEROIN TRADE.
THAT MEANS MONEY FOR JIHAD. MONEY TO PAY OFF THE SOLDIERS. PLENTY OF TIME TO DANCE.

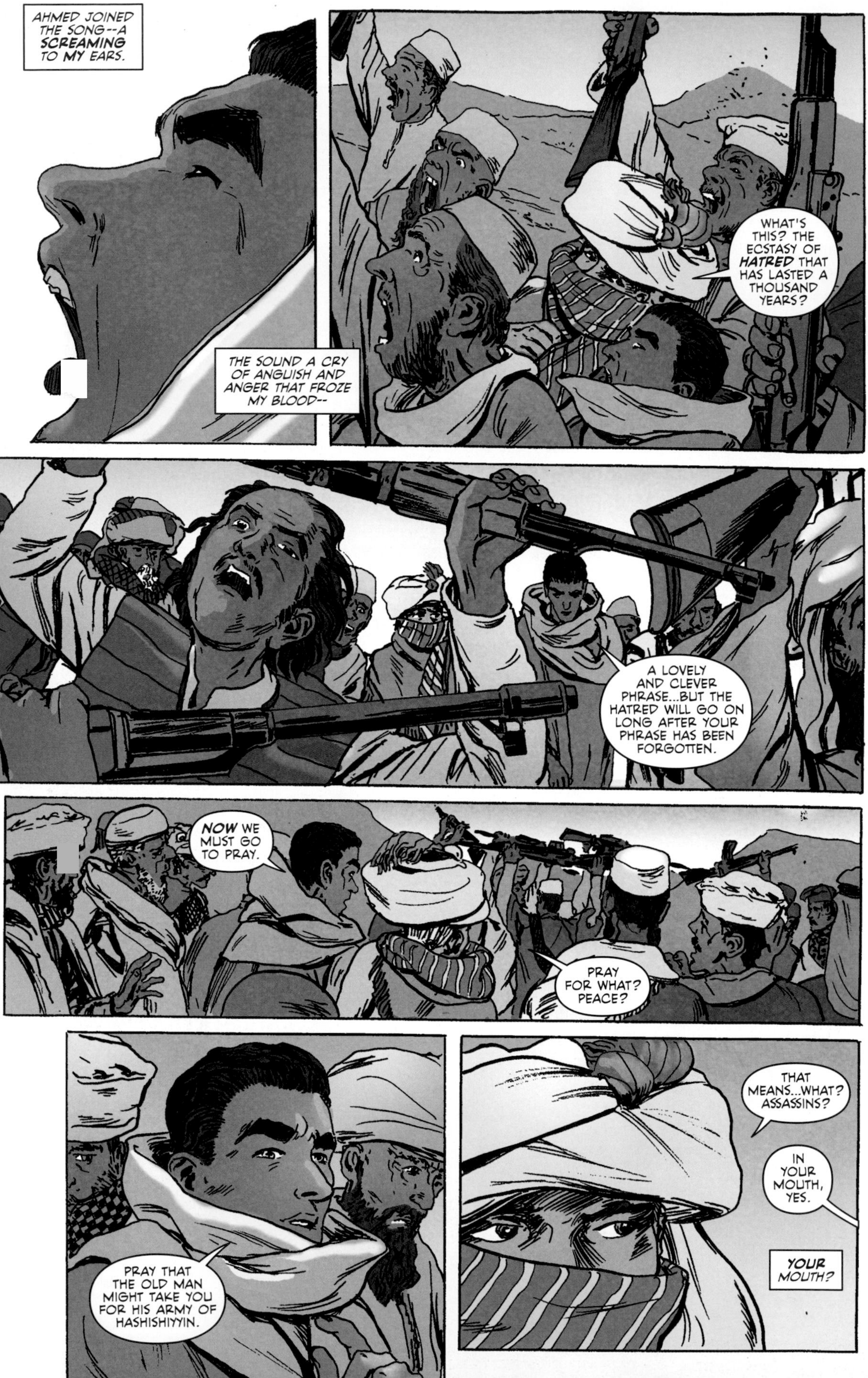
AHMED JOINED THE SONG--A SCREAMING TO MY EARS.
THE SOUND A CRY OF ANGUISH AND ANGER THAT FROZE MY BLOOD--
WHAT'S THIS? THE ECSTASY OF HATRED THAT HAS LASTED A THOUSAND YEARS?
A LOVELY AND CLEVER PHRASE...BUT THE HATRED WILL GO ON LONG AFTER YOUR PHRASE HAS BEEN FORGOTTEN.
NOW WE MUST GO TO PRAY.
PRAY FOR WHAT? PEACE?
PRAY THAT THE OLD MAN MIGHT TAKE YOU FOR HIS ARMY OF HASHISHIYYIN.
THAT MEANS...WHAT? ASSASSINS?
IN YOUR MOUTH, YES.
YOUR MOUTH?

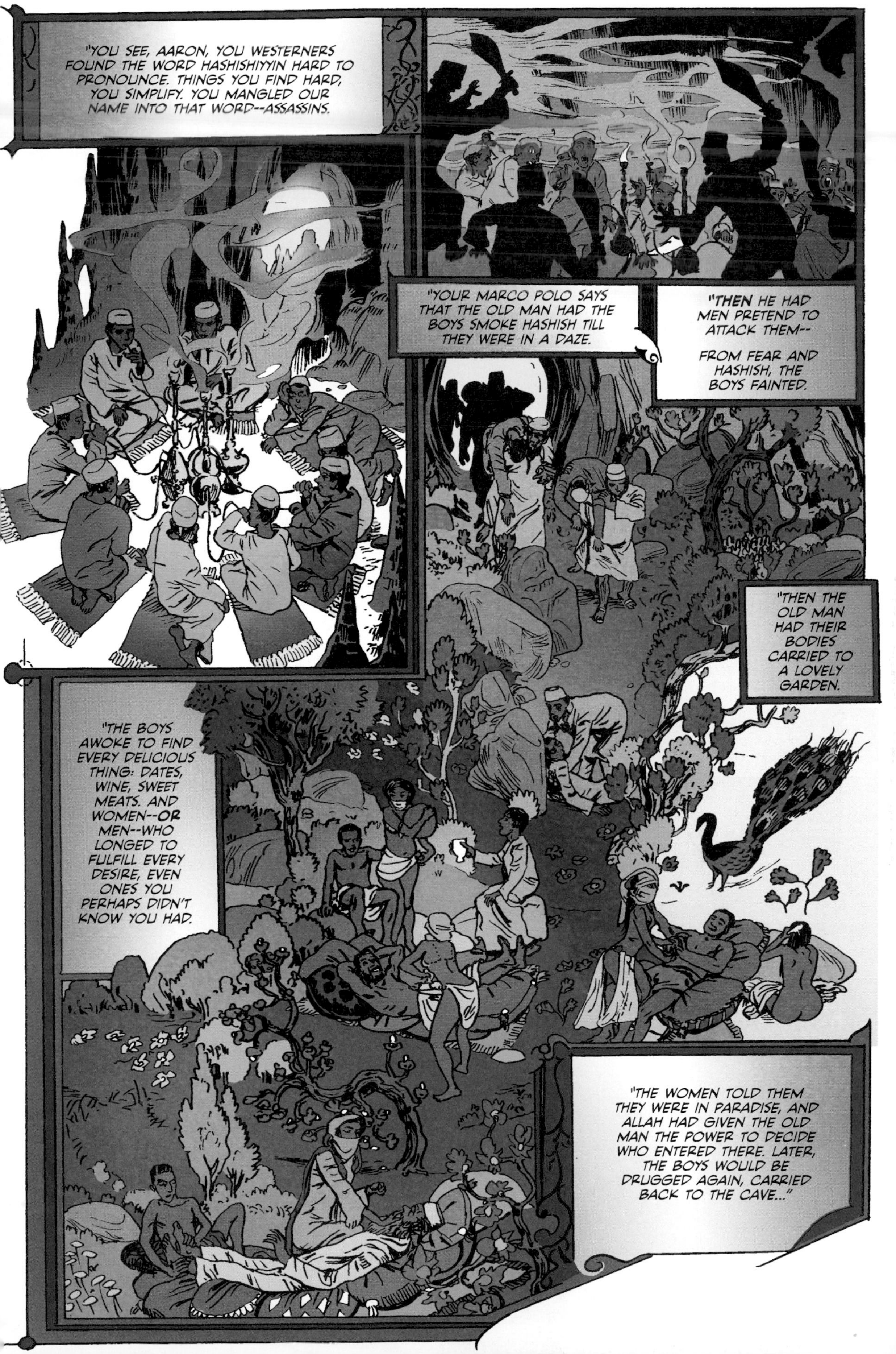
"YOU SEE, AARON, YOU WESTERNERS FOUND THE WORD HASHISHIYYIN HARD TO PRONOUNCE. THINGS YOU FIND HARD, YOU SIMPLIFY. YOU MANGLED OUR NAME INTO THAT WORD--ASSASSINS.
"YOUR MARCO POLO SAYS THAT THE OLD MAN HAD THE BOYS SMOKE HASHISH TILL THEY WERE IN A DAZE.
"THEN HE HAD MEN PRETEND TO ATTACK THEM--
FROM FEAR AND HASHISH, THE BOYS FAINTED.
"THEN THE OLD MAN HAD THEIR BODIES CARRIED TO A LOVELY GARDEN.
"THE BOYS AWOKE TO FIND EVERY DELICIOUS THING: DATES, WINE, SWEET MEATS. AND WOMEN--OR MEN--WHO LONGED TO FULFILL EVERY DESIRE, EVEN ONES YOU PERHAPS DIDN'T KNOW YOU HAD.
"THE WOMEN TOLD THEM THEY WERE IN PARADISE, AND ALLAH HAD GIVEN THE OLD MAN THE POWER TO DECIDE WHO ENTERED THERE. LATER, THE BOYS WOULD BE DRUGGED AGAIN, CARRIED BACK TO THE CAVE..."

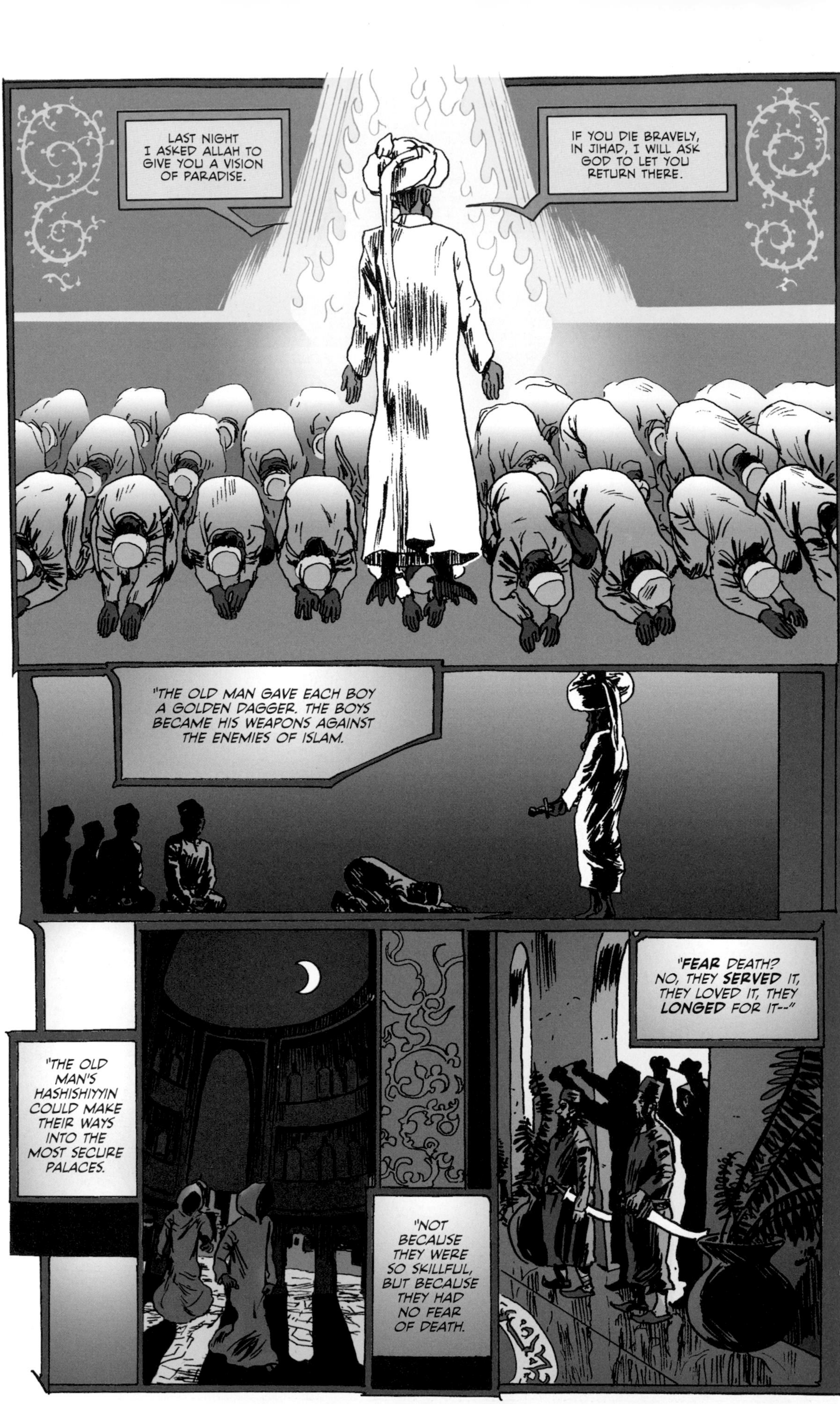

LAST NIGHT I ASKED ALLAH TO GIVE YOU A VISION OF PARADISE.
IF YOU DIE BRAVELY, IN JIHAD, I WILL ASK GOD TO LET YOU RETURN THERE.
"THE OLD MAN GAVE EACH BOY A GOLDEN DAGGER. THE BOYS BECAME HIS WEAPONS AGAINST THE ENEMIES OF ISLAM.
"THE OLD MAN'S HASHISHIYYIN COULD MAKE THEIR WAYS INTO THE MOST SECURE PALACES.
"NOT BECAUSE THEY WERE SO SKILLFUL, BUT BECAUSE THEY HAD NO FEAR OF DEATH.
"FEAR DEATH? NO, THEY SERVED IT, THEY LOVED IT, THEY LONGED FOR IT--"

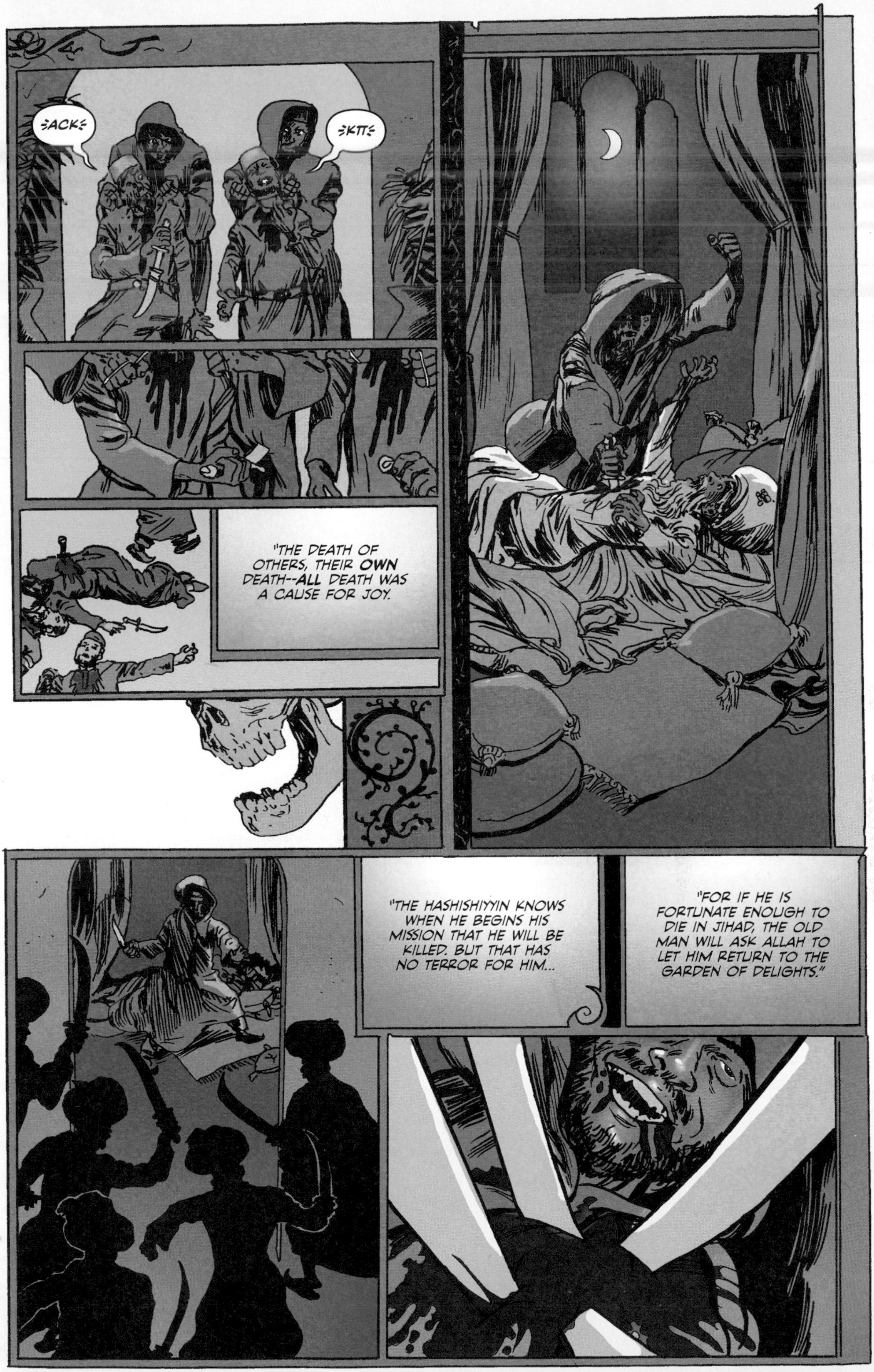

ACK
KTT
"THE DEATH OF OTHERS, THEIR OWN DEATH--ALL DEATH WAS A CAUSE FOR JOY.
"THE HASHISHIYYIN KNOWS WHEN HE BEGINS HIS MISSION THAT HE WILL BE KILLED. BUT THAT HAS NO TERROR FOR HIM...
"FOR IF HE IS FORTUNATE ENOUGH TO DIE IN JIHAD, THE OLD MAN WILL ASK ALLAH TO LET HIM RETURN TO THE GARDEN OF DELIGHTS."

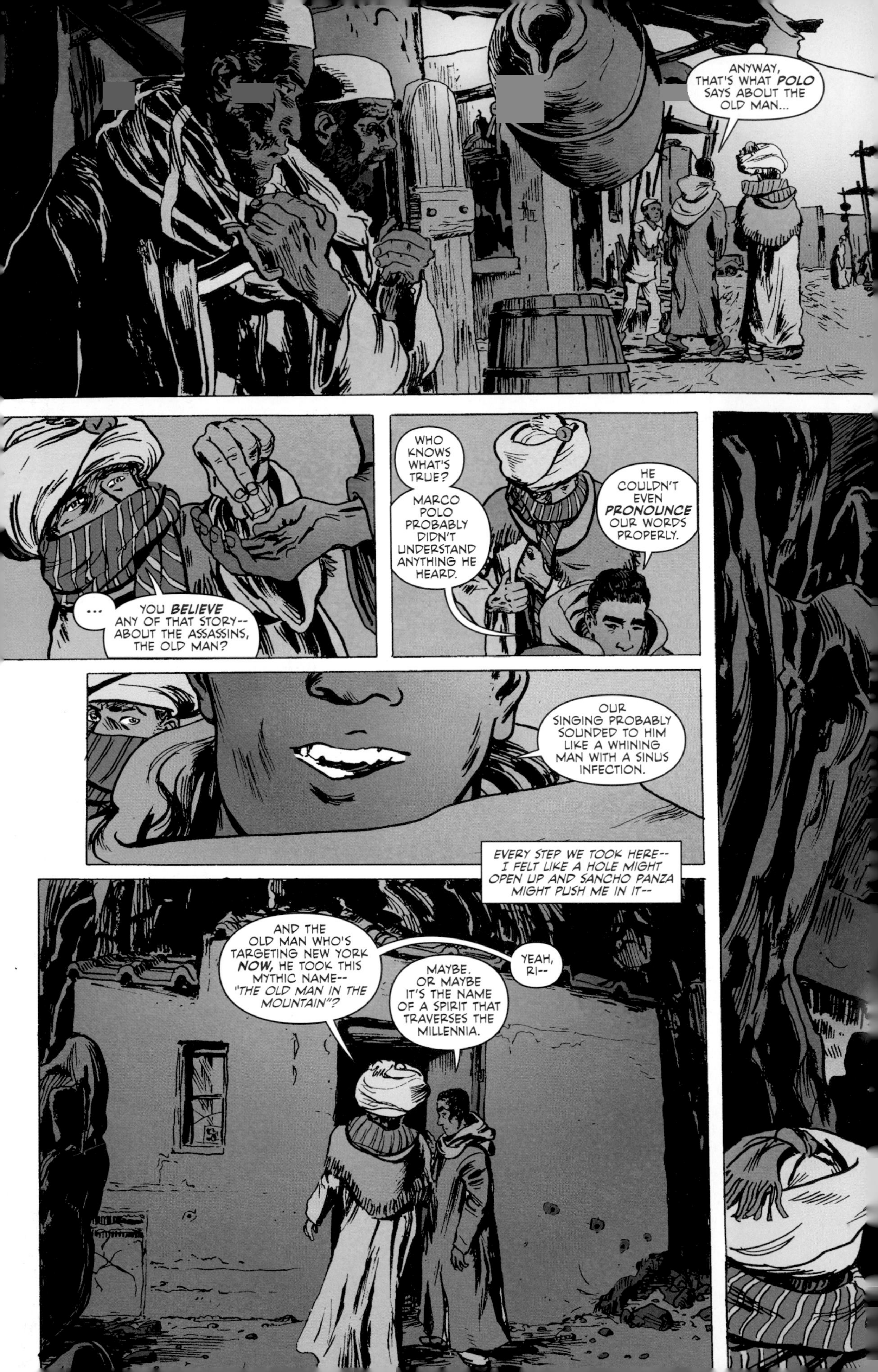

ANYWAY, THAT'S WHAT *POLO* SAYS ABOUT THE OLD MAN...
...
YOU *BELIEVE* ANY OF THAT STORY-- ABOUT THE ASSASSINS, THE OLD MAN?
WHO KNOWS WHAT'S TRUE?
MARCO POLO PROBABLY DIDN'T UNDERSTAND ANYTHING HE HEARD.
HE COULDN'T EVEN *PRONOUNCE* OUR WORDS PROPERLY.
OUR SINGING PROBABLY SOUNDED TO HIM LIKE A WHINING MAN WITH A SINUS INFECTION.
EVERY STEP WE TOOK HERE-- I FELT LIKE A HOLE MIGHT OPEN UP AND SANCHO PANZA MIGHT PUSH ME IN IT--
AND THE OLD MAN WHO'S TARGETING NEW YORK *NOW,* HE TOOK THIS MYTHIC NAME-- *"THE OLD MAN IN THE MOUNTAIN"?*
MAYBE. OR MAYBE IT'S THE NAME OF A SPIRIT THAT TRAVERSES THE MILLENNIA.
YEAH, RI--

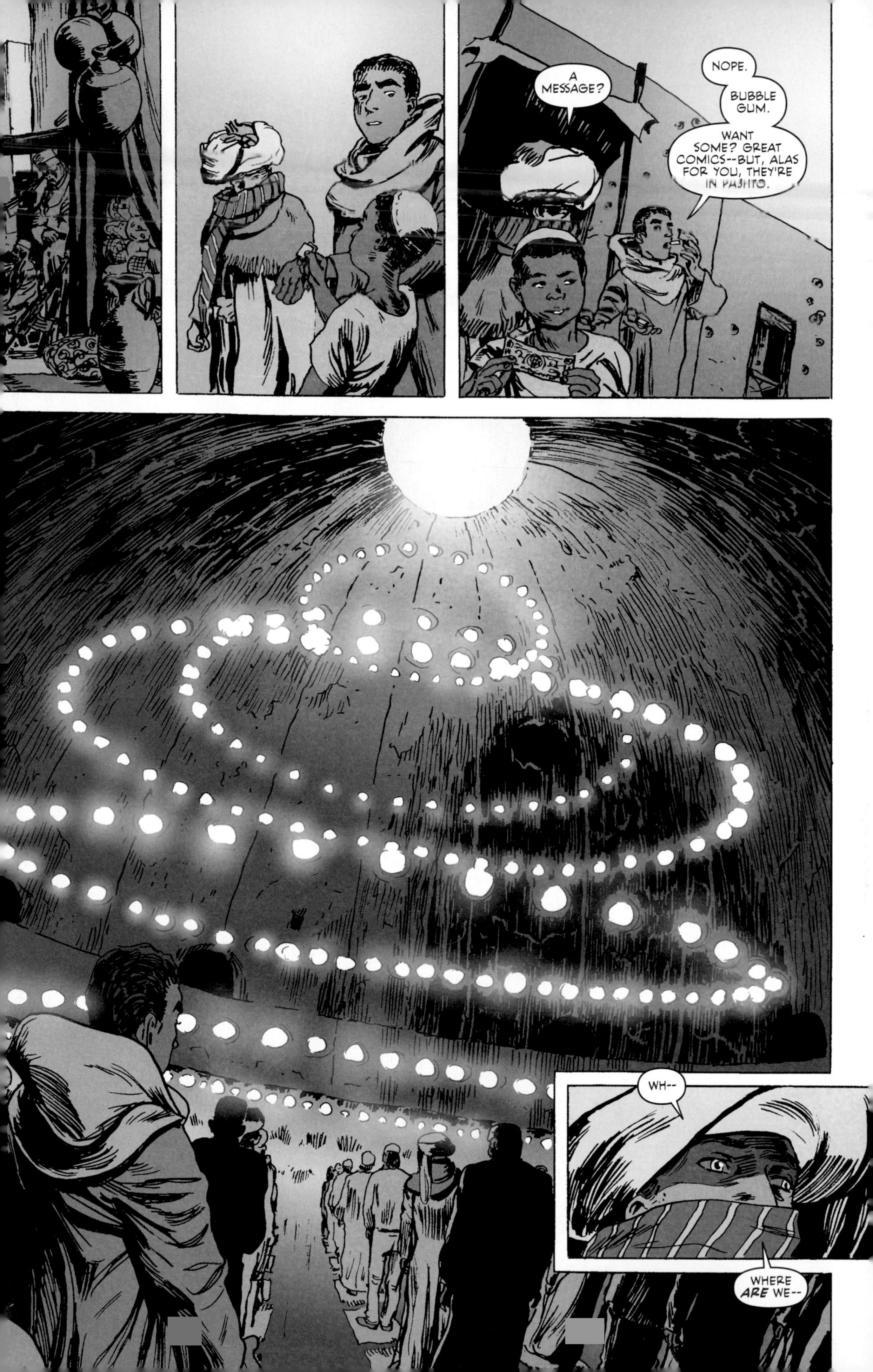
A MESSAGE?
NOPE.
BUBBLE GUM.
WANT SOME? GREAT COMICS--BUT, ALAS FOR YOU, THEY'RE IN PASHTO.
WH--
WHERE ARE WE--

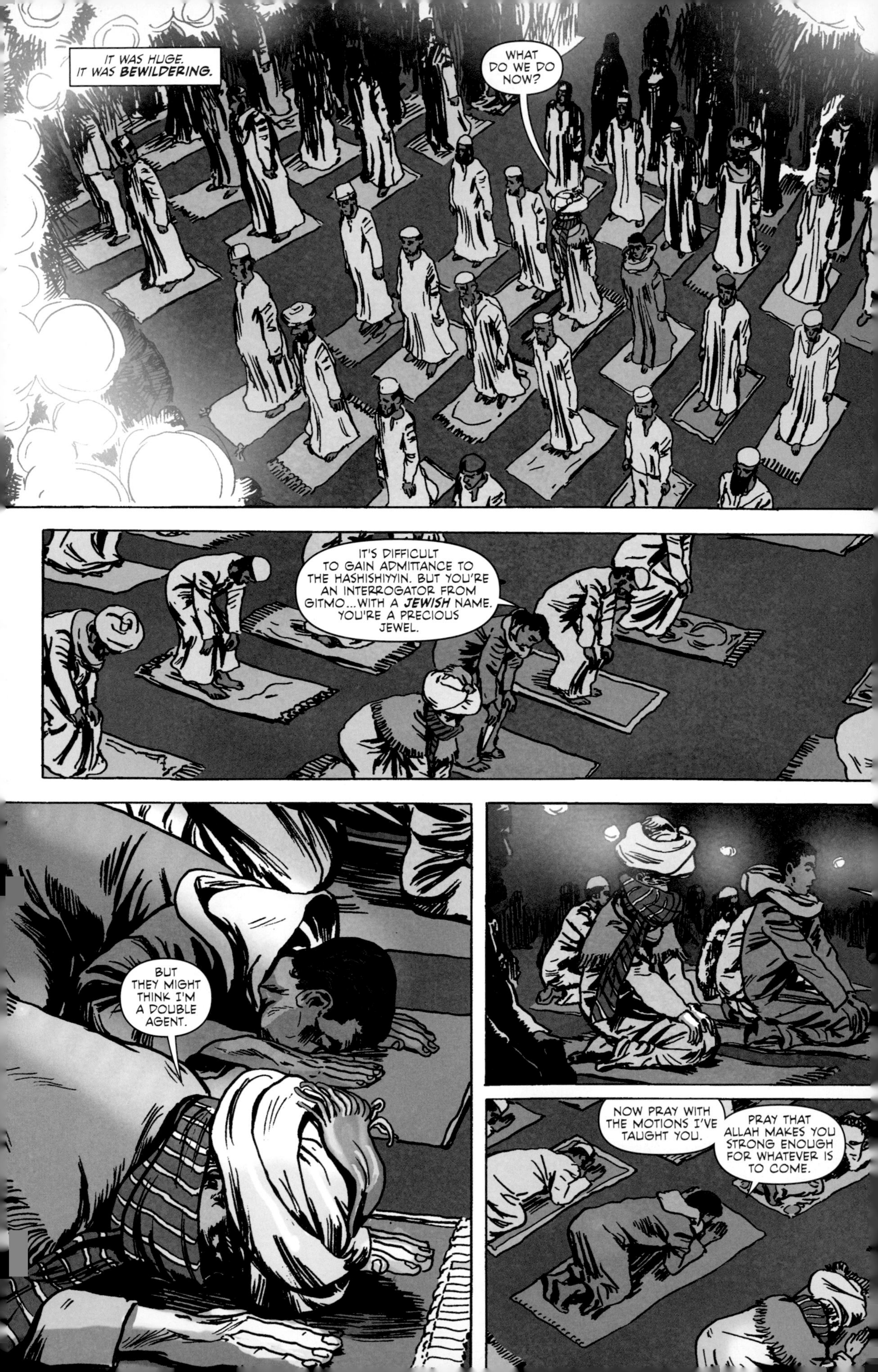
IT WAS HUGE.
IT WAS BEWILDERING.
WHAT DO WE DO NOW?
IT'S DIFFICULT TO GAIN ADMITTANCE TO THE HASHISHIYYIN. BUT YOU'RE AN INTERROGATOR FROM GITMO...WITH A JEWISH NAME. YOU'RE A PRECIOUS JEWEL.
BUT THEY MIGHT THINK I'M A DOUBLE AGENT.
NOW PRAY WITH THE MOTIONS I'VE TAUGHT YOU.
PRAY THAT ALLAH MAKES YOU STRONG ENOUGH FOR WHATEVER IS TO COME.

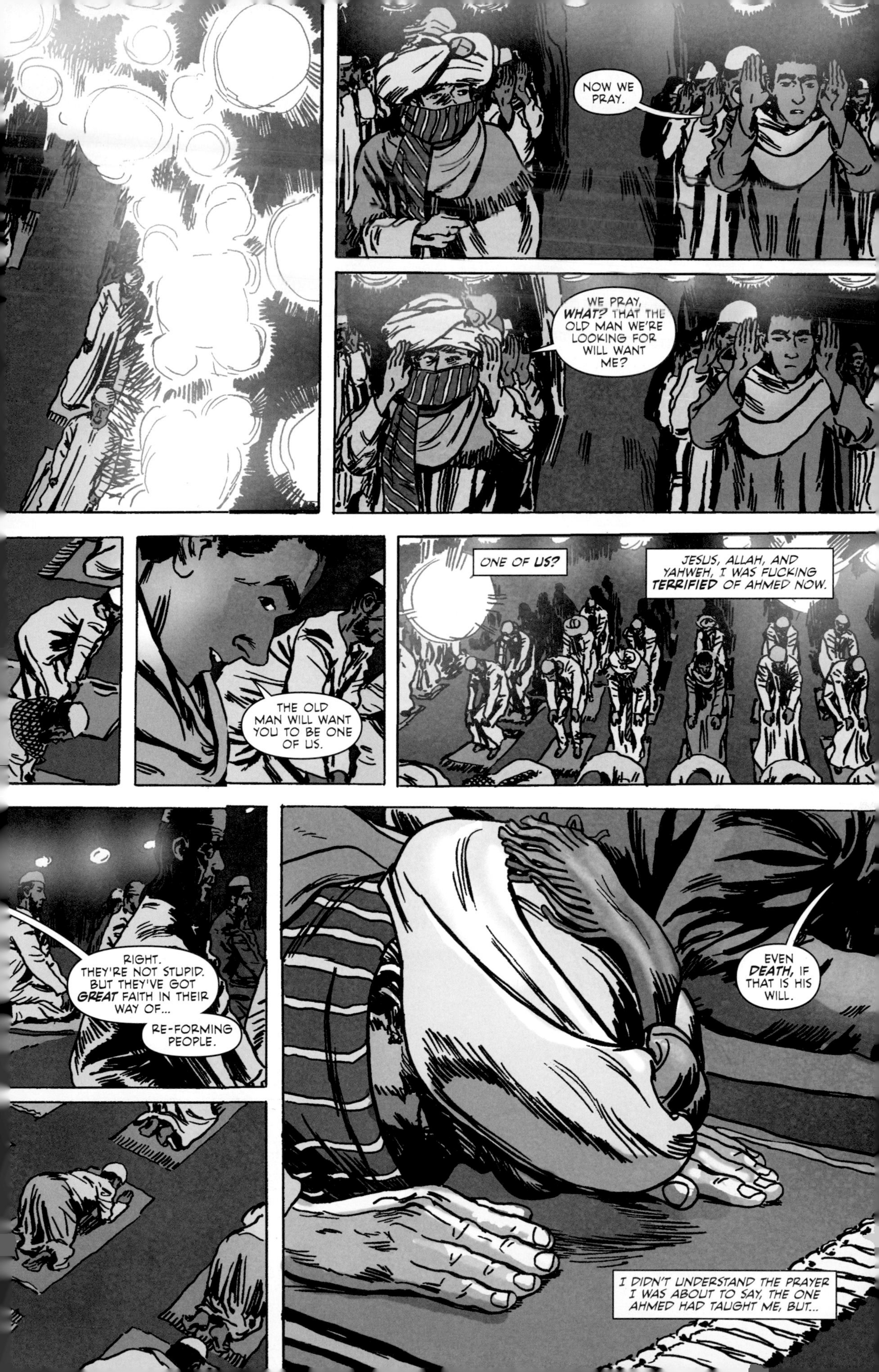
NOW WE PRAY.
WE PRAY, WHAT? THAT THE OLD MAN WE'RE LOOKING FOR WILL WANT ME?
THE OLD MAN WILL WANT YOU TO BE ONE OF US.
ONE OF US?
JESUS, ALLAH, AND YAHWEH, I WAS FUCKING TERRIFIED OF AHMED NOW.
RIGHT. THEY'RE NOT STUPID. BUT THEY'VE GOT GREAT FAITH IN THEIR WAY OF...
RE-FORMING PEOPLE.
EVEN DEATH, IF THAT IS HIS WILL.
I DIDN'T UNDERSTAND THE PRAYER I WAS ABOUT TO SAY, THE ONE AHMED HAD TAUGHT ME, BUT...

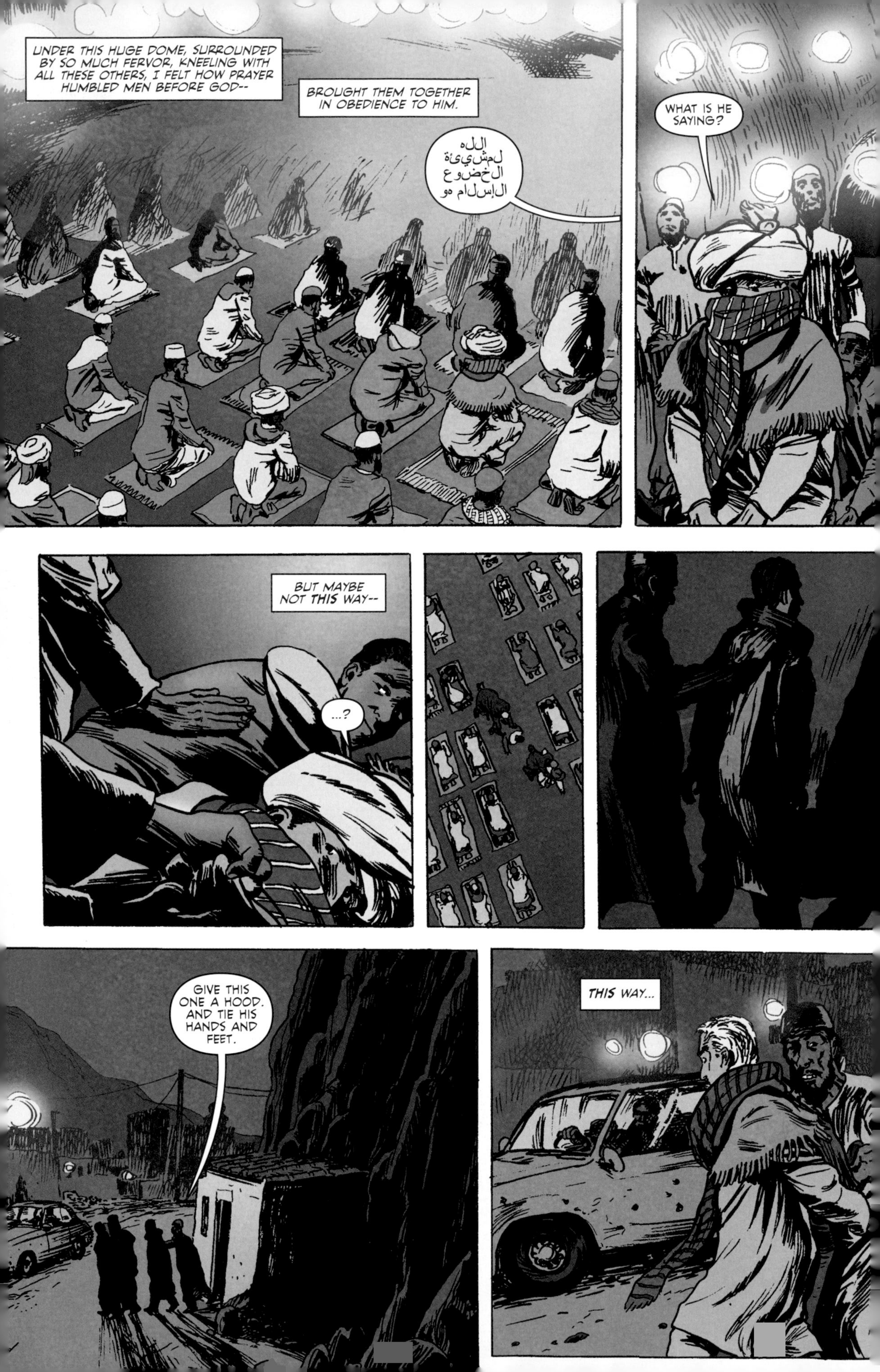
UNDER THIS HUGE DOME, SURROUNDED BY SO MUCH FERVOR, KNEELING WITH ALL THESE OTHERS, I FELT HOW PRAYER HUMBLED MEN BEFORE GOD--
BROUGHT THEM TOGETHER IN OBEDIENCE TO HIM.
الله
لمشيئة
الخضوع
الإسلام هو
WHAT IS HE SAYING?
BUT MAYBE NOT THIS WAY--
...?
GIVE THIS ONE A HOOD. AND TIE HIS HANDS AND FEET.
THIS WAY...

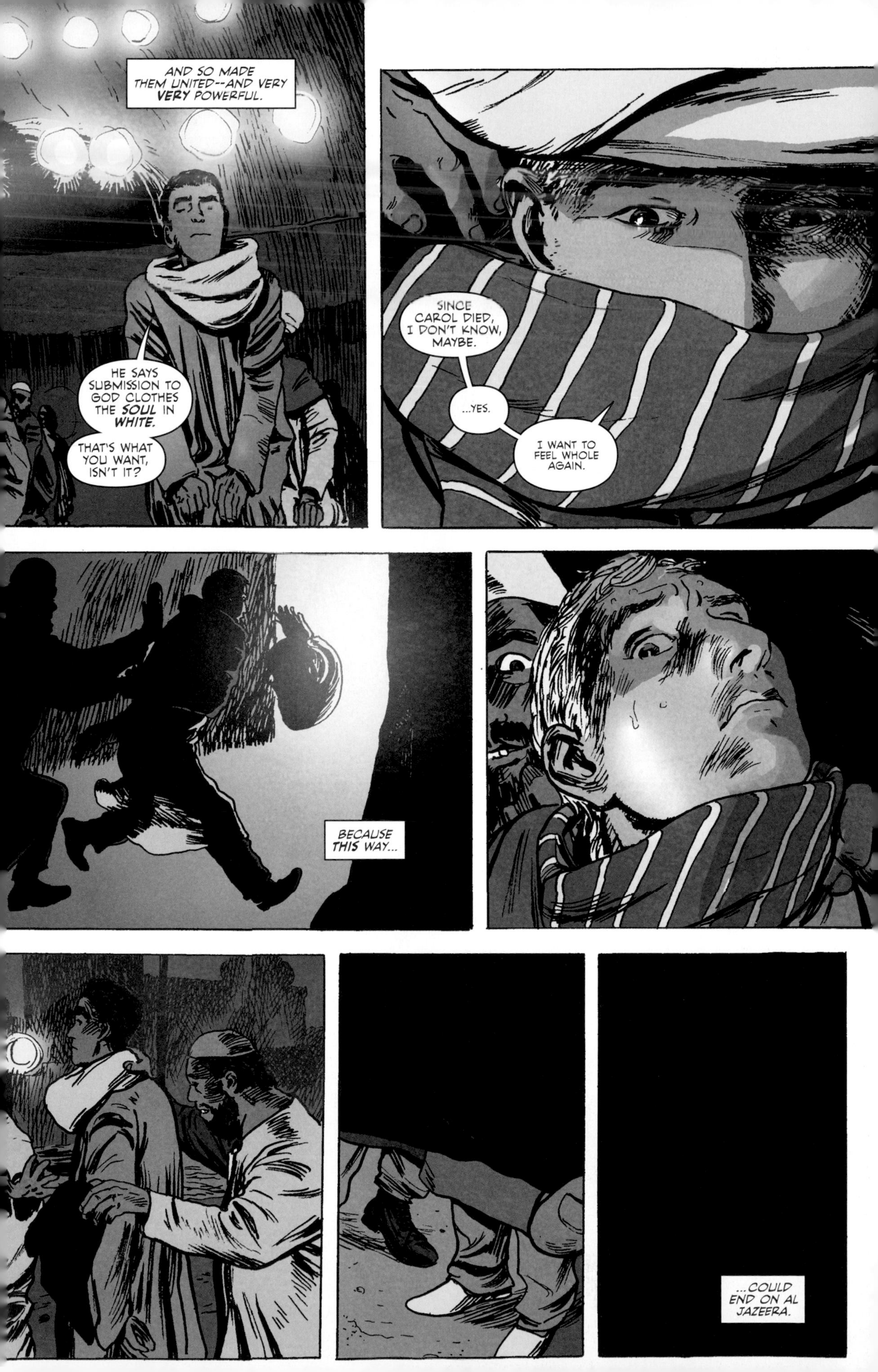

AND SO MADE THEM UNITED--AND VERY VERY POWERFUL.
HE SAYS SUBMISSION TO GOD CLOTHES THE SOUL IN WHITE.
THAT'S WHAT YOU WANT, ISN'T IT?
SINCE CAROL DIED, I DON'T KNOW, MAYBE.
...YES.
I WANT TO FEEL WHOLE AGAIN.
BECAUSE THIS WAY...
...COULD END ON AL JAZEERA.

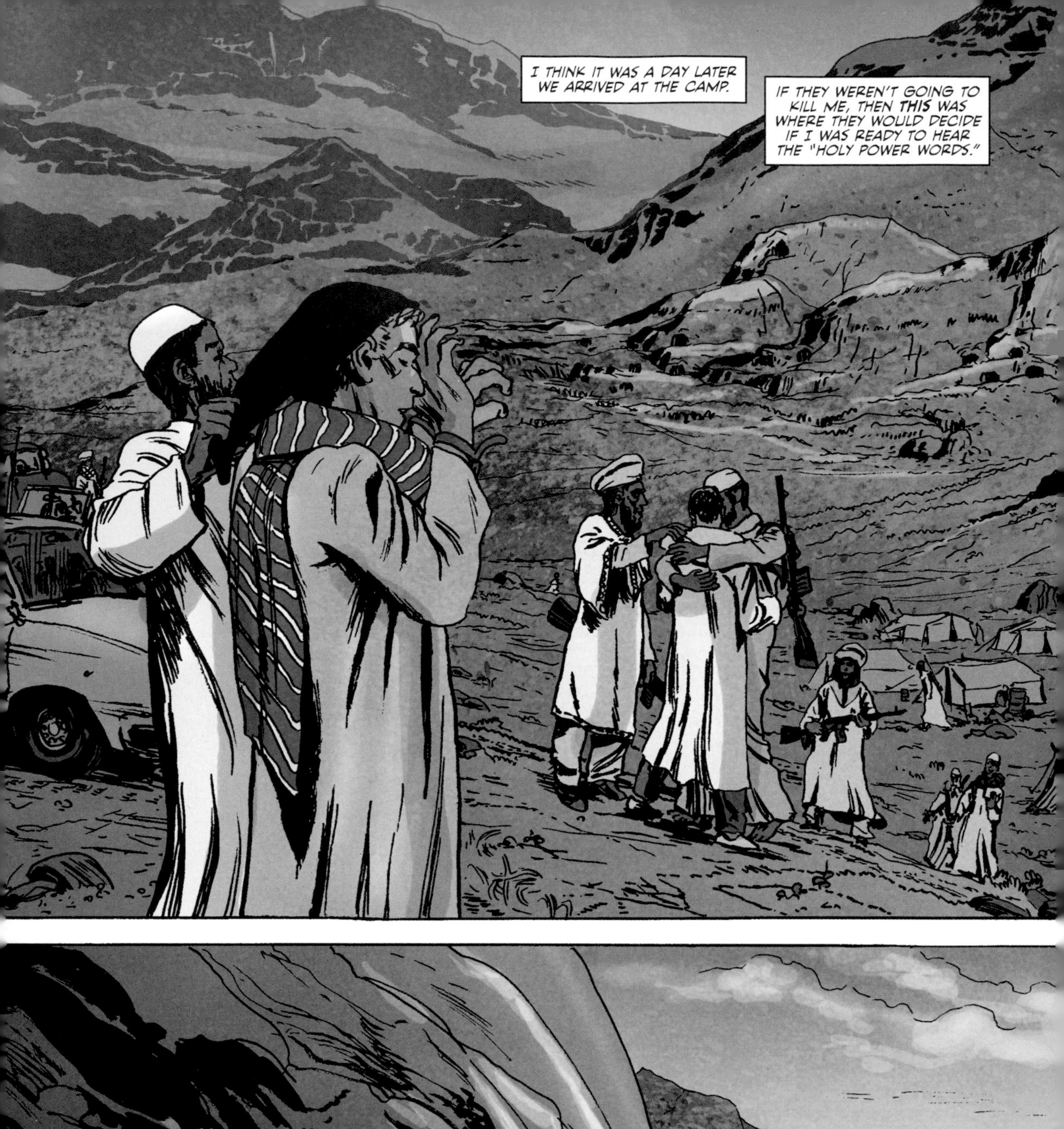
I THINK IT WAS A DAY LATER WE ARRIVED AT THE CAMP.
IF THEY WEREN'T GOING TO KILL ME, THEN THIS WAS WHERE THEY WOULD DECIDE IF I WAS READY TO HEAR THE "HOLY POWER WORDS."

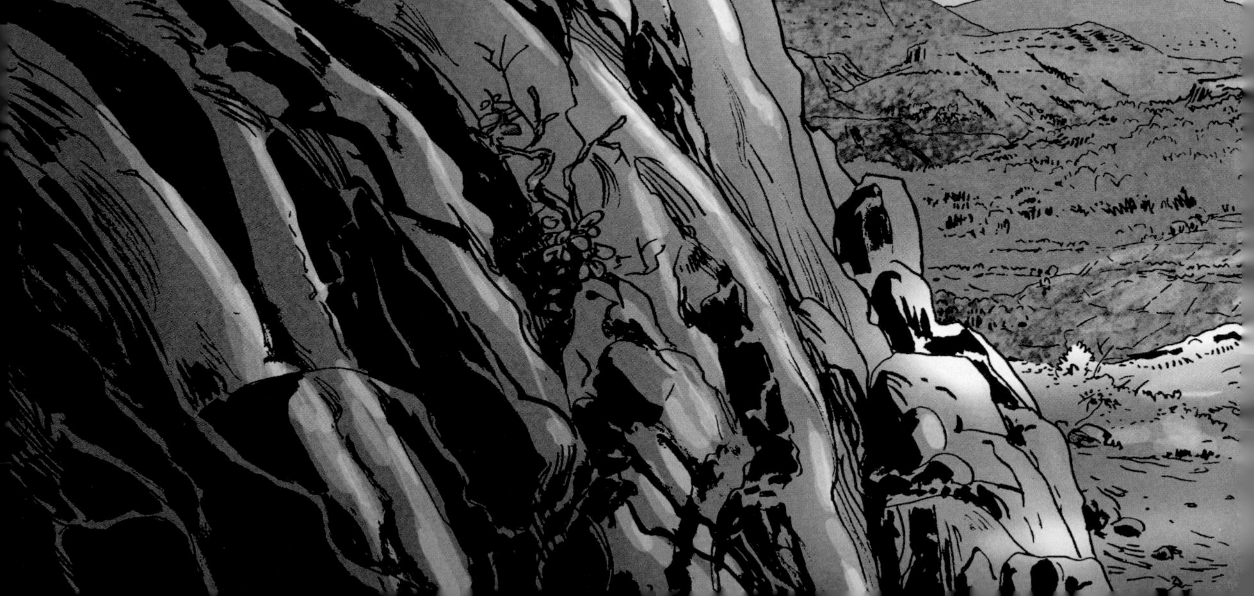

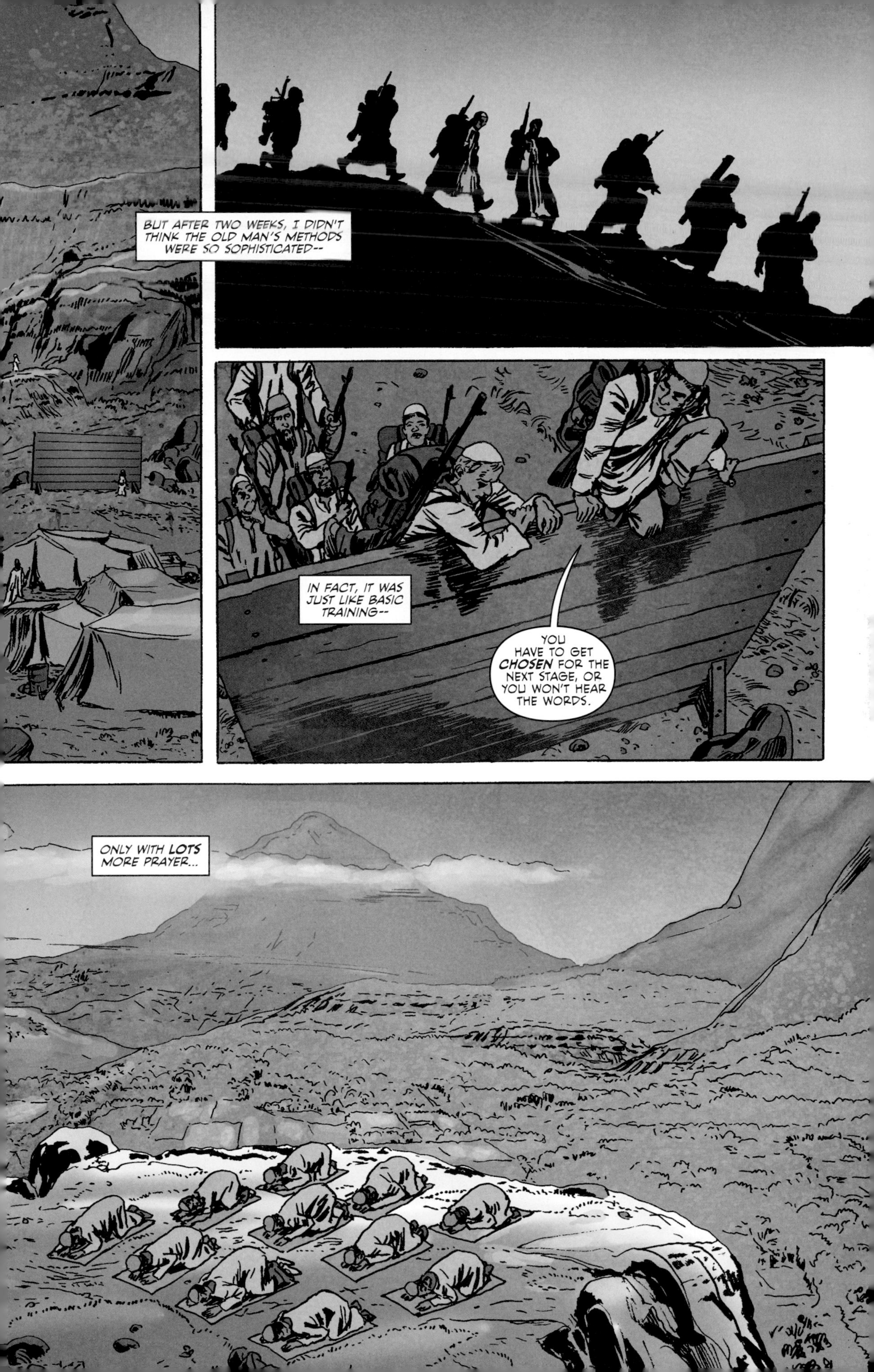

BUT AFTER TWO WEEKS, I DIDN'T THINK THE OLD MAN'S METHODS WERE SO SOPHISTICATED--
IN FACT, IT WAS JUST LIKE BASIC TRAINING--
YOU HAVE TO GET CHOSEN FOR THE NEXT STAGE, OR YOU WON'T HEAR THE WORDS.
ONLY WITH LOTS MORE PRAYER...

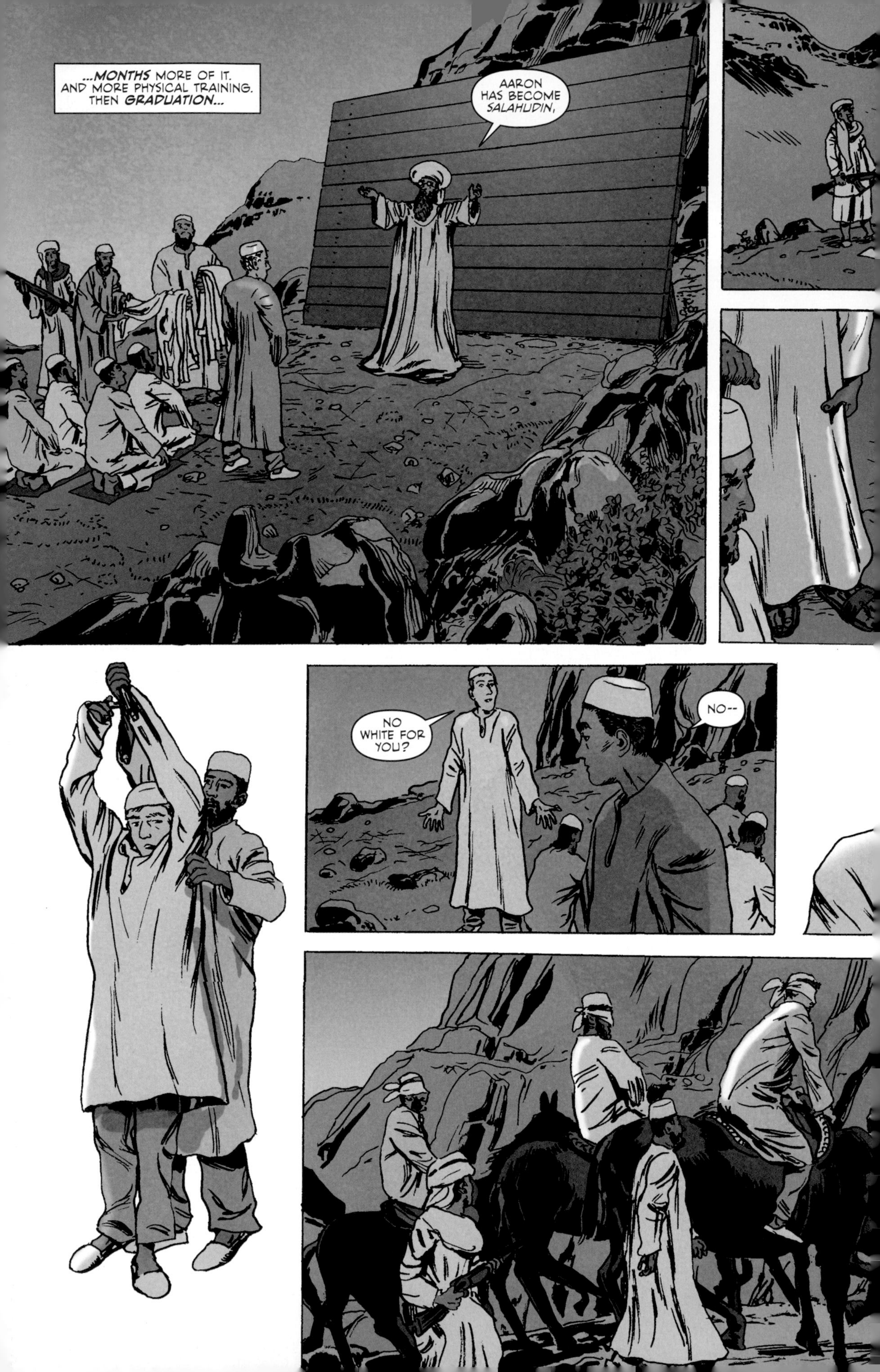
...MONTHS MORE OF IT. AND MORE PHYSICAL TRAINING. THEN GRADUATION...
AARON HAS BECOME SALAHUDIN,
NO WHITE FOR YOU?
NO--

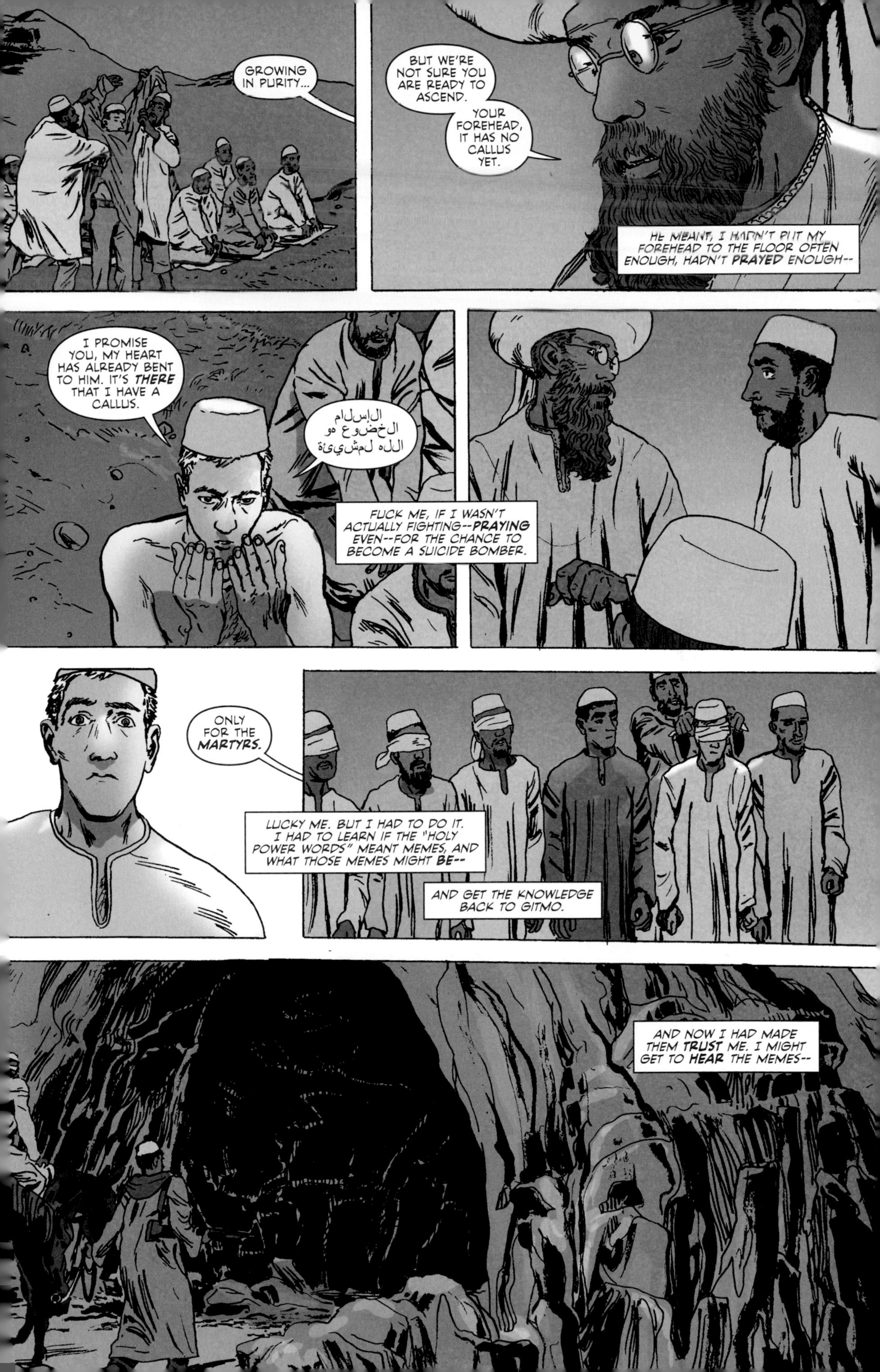
GROWING IN PURITY...
BUT WE'RE NOT SURE YOU ARE READY TO ASCEND.
YOUR FOREHEAD, IT HAS NO CALLUS YET.
HE MEANT, I HADN'T PUT MY FOREHEAD TO THE FLOOR OFTEN ENOUGH, HADN'T **PRAYED** ENOUGH--
I PROMISE YOU, MY HEART HAS ALREADY BENT TO HIM. IT'S ***THERE*** THAT I HAVE A CALLUS.
الإسلام
الخضوع هو
الله لمشيئة
*FUCK ME, IF I WASN'T ACTUALLY FIGHTING--**PRAYING** EVEN--FOR THE CHANCE TO BECOME A SUICIDE BOMBER.*
ONLY FOR THE ***MARTYRS.***
*LUCKY ME. BUT I HAD TO DO IT. I HAD TO LEARN IF THE "HOLY POWER WORDS" MEANT MEMES, AND WHAT THOSE MEMES MIGHT **BE--***
AND GET THE KNOWLEDGE BACK TO GITMO.
*AND NOW I HAD MADE THEM **TRUST** ME. I MIGHT GET TO **HEAR** THE MEMES--*

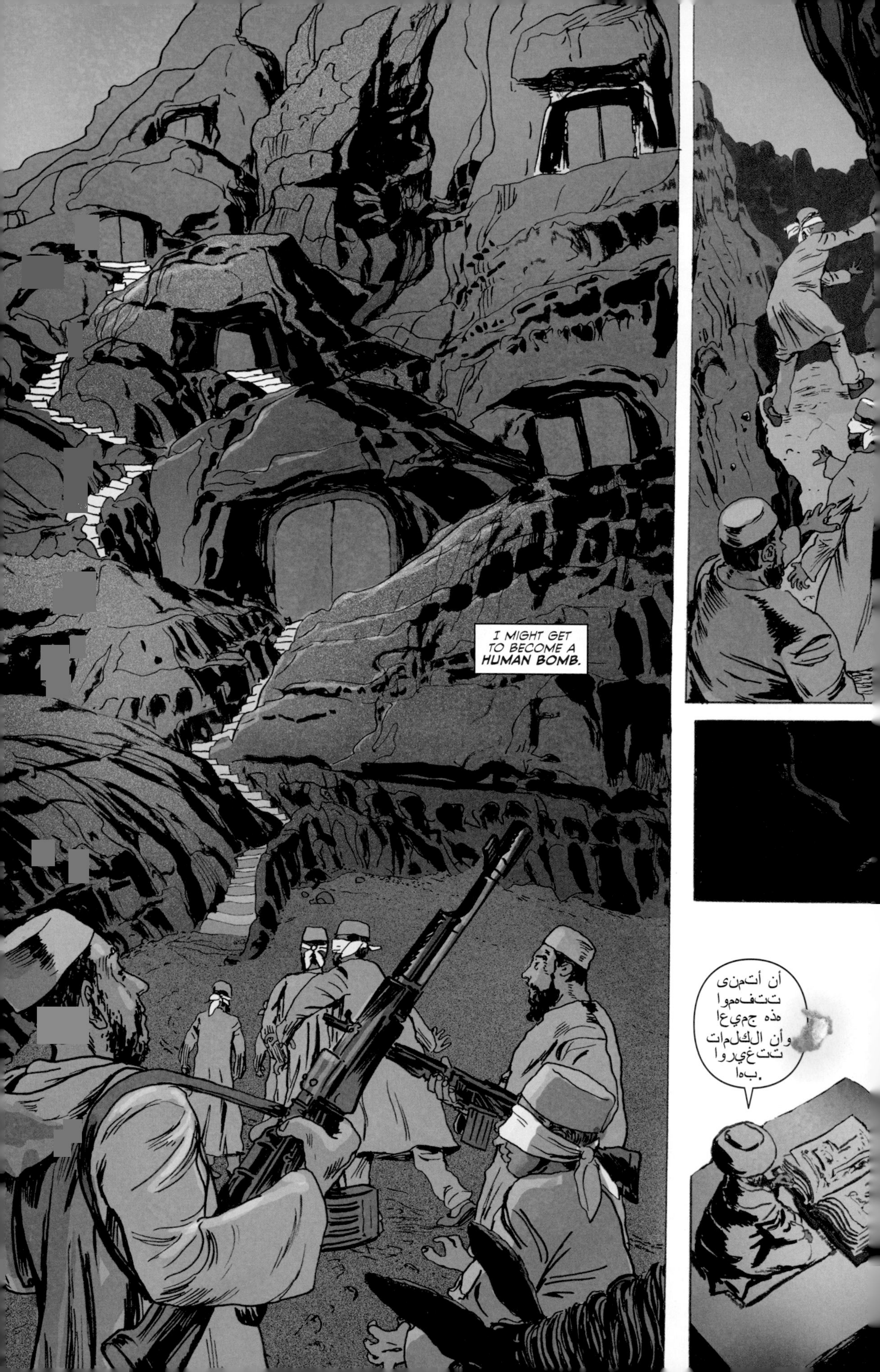
I MIGHT GET TO BECOME A HUMAN BOMB.
أن أتمنى تتفهموا هذه جميعا وأن الكلمات تتغيروا بها.

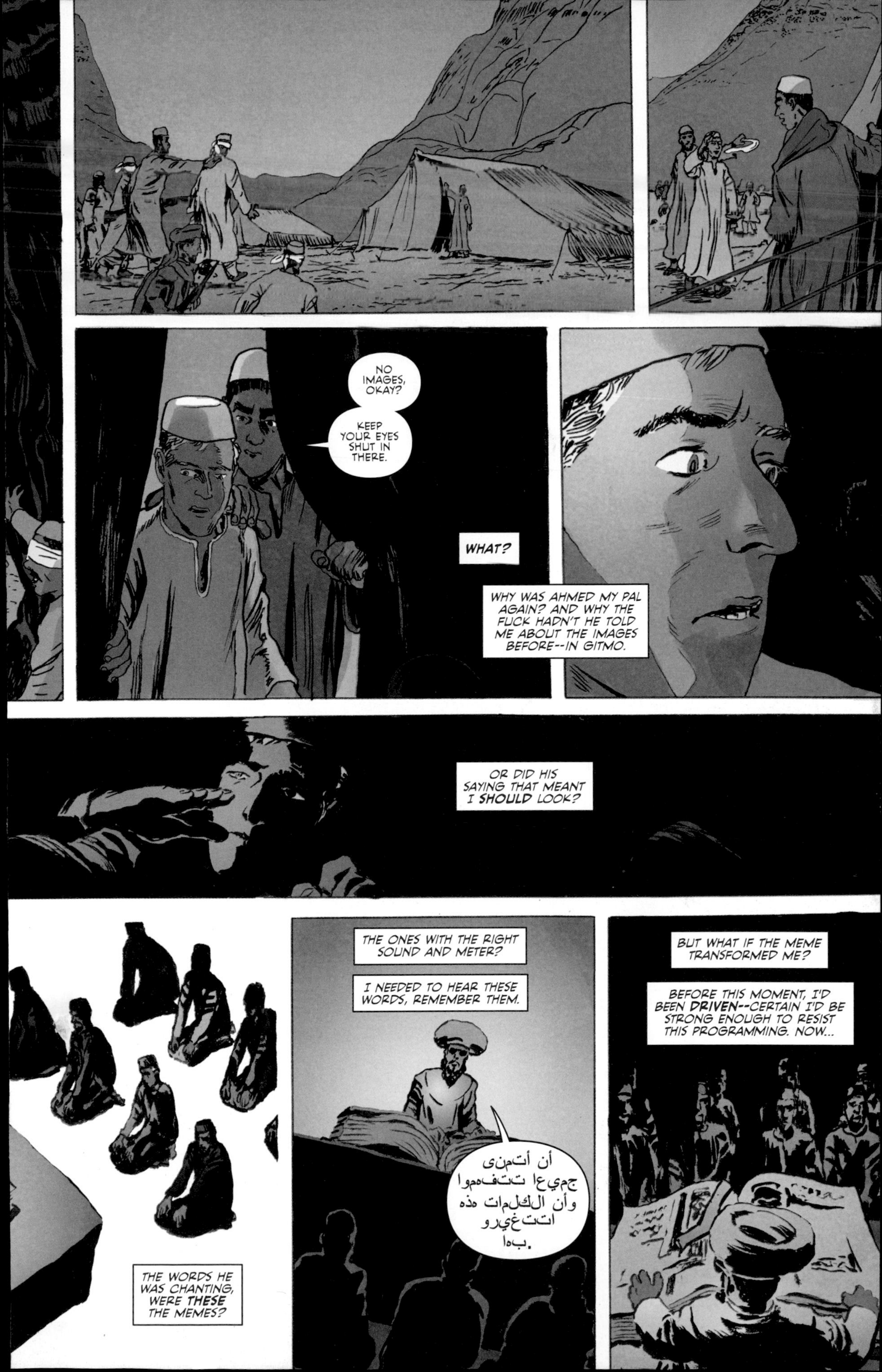
NO IMAGES, OKAY?
KEEP YOUR EYES SHUT IN THERE.
WHAT?
WHY WAS AHMED MY PAL AGAIN? AND WHY THE FUCK HADN'T HE TOLD ME ABOUT THE IMAGES BEFORE--IN GITMO.
OR DID HIS SAYING THAT MEANT I SHOULD LOOK?
THE WORDS HE WAS CHANTING, WERE THESE THE MEMES?
THE ONES WITH THE RIGHT SOUND AND METER?
I NEEDED TO HEAR THESE WORDS, REMEMBER THEM.
أن أتمنى جميعا تتفهموا وأن الكلمات هذه اتتغيرو بها.
BUT WHAT IF THE MEME TRANSFORMED ME?
BEFORE THIS MOMENT, I'D BEEN DRIVEN--CERTAIN I'D BE STRONG ENOUGH TO RESIST THIS PROGRAMMING. NOW...

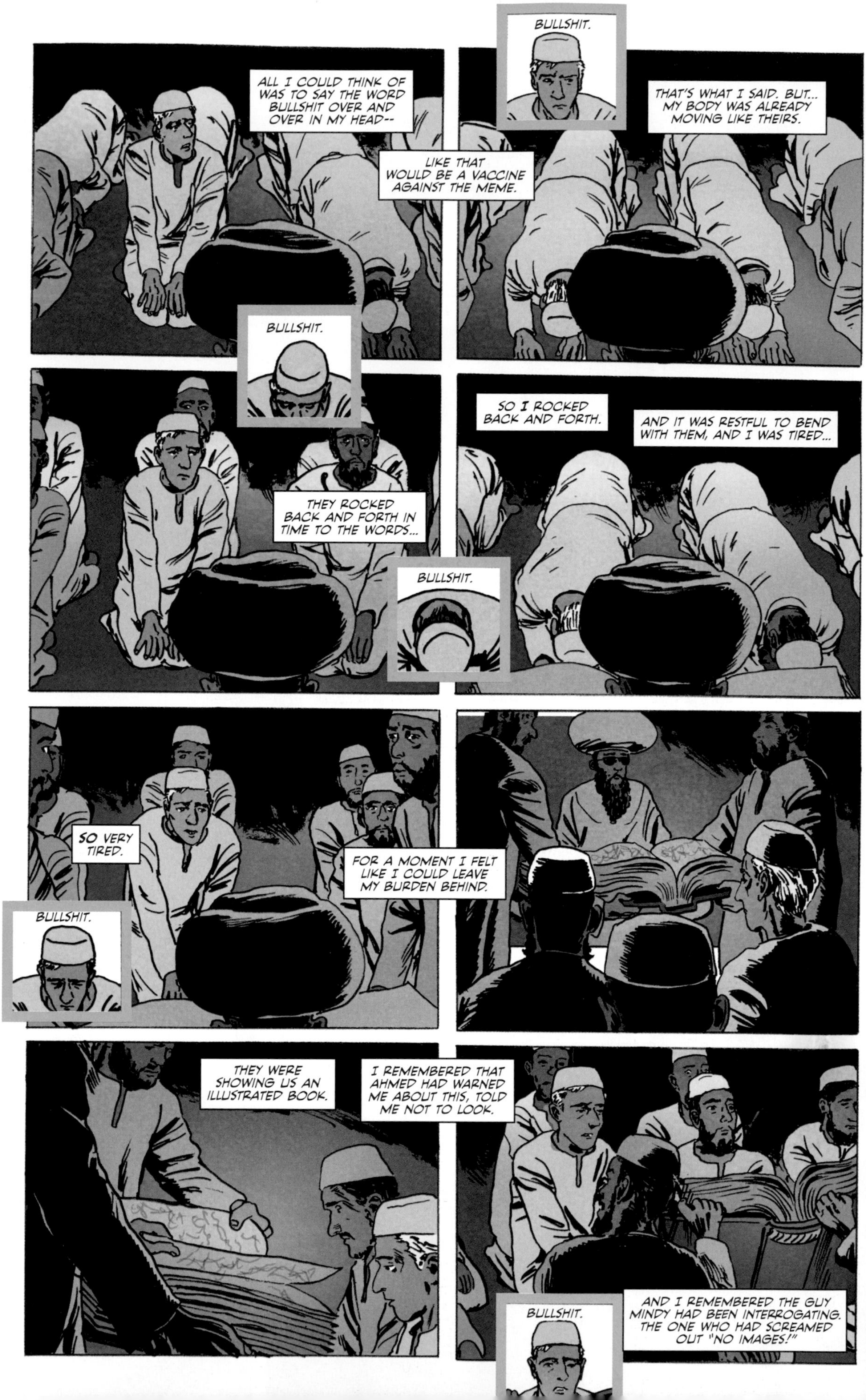
ALL I COULD THINK OF WAS TO SAY THE WORD BULLSHIT OVER AND OVER IN MY HEAD--
LIKE THAT WOULD BE A VACCINE AGAINST THE MEME.
BULLSHIT.
BULLSHIT.
THAT'S WHAT I SAID. BUT... MY BODY WAS ALREADY MOVING LIKE THEIRS.
THEY ROCKED BACK AND FORTH IN TIME TO THE WORDS...
BULLSHIT.
SO I ROCKED BACK AND FORTH.
AND IT WAS RESTFUL TO BEND WITH THEM, AND I WAS TIRED...
SO VERY TIRED.
BULLSHIT.
FOR A MOMENT I FELT LIKE I COULD LEAVE MY BURDEN BEHIND.
THEY WERE SHOWING US AN ILLUSTRATED BOOK.
I REMEMBERED THAT AHMED HAD WARNED ME ABOUT THIS, TOLD ME NOT TO LOOK.
AND I REMEMBERED THE GUY MINDY HAD BEEN INTERROGATING. THE ONE WHO HAD SCREAMED OUT "NO IMAGES!"
BULLSHIT.

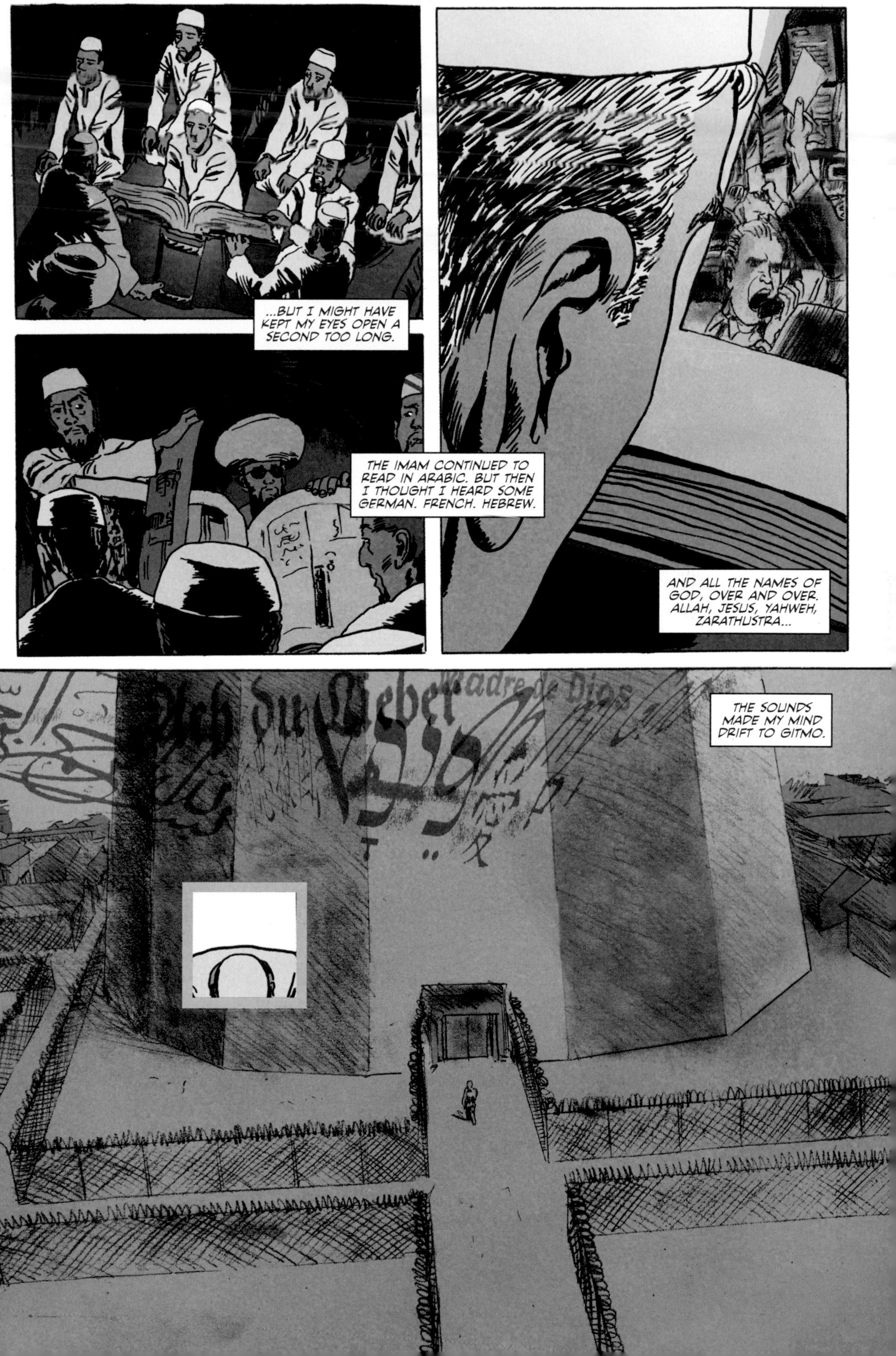
...BUT I MIGHT HAVE KEPT MY EYES OPEN A SECOND TOO LONG.
THE IMAM CONTINUED TO READ IN ARABIC. BUT THEN I THOUGHT I HEARD SOME GERMAN. FRENCH. HEBREW.
AND ALL THE NAMES OF GOD, OVER AND OVER. ALLAH, JESUS, YAHWEH, ZARATHUSTRA...
Madre de Dios
THE SOUNDS MADE MY MIND DRIFT TO GITMO.

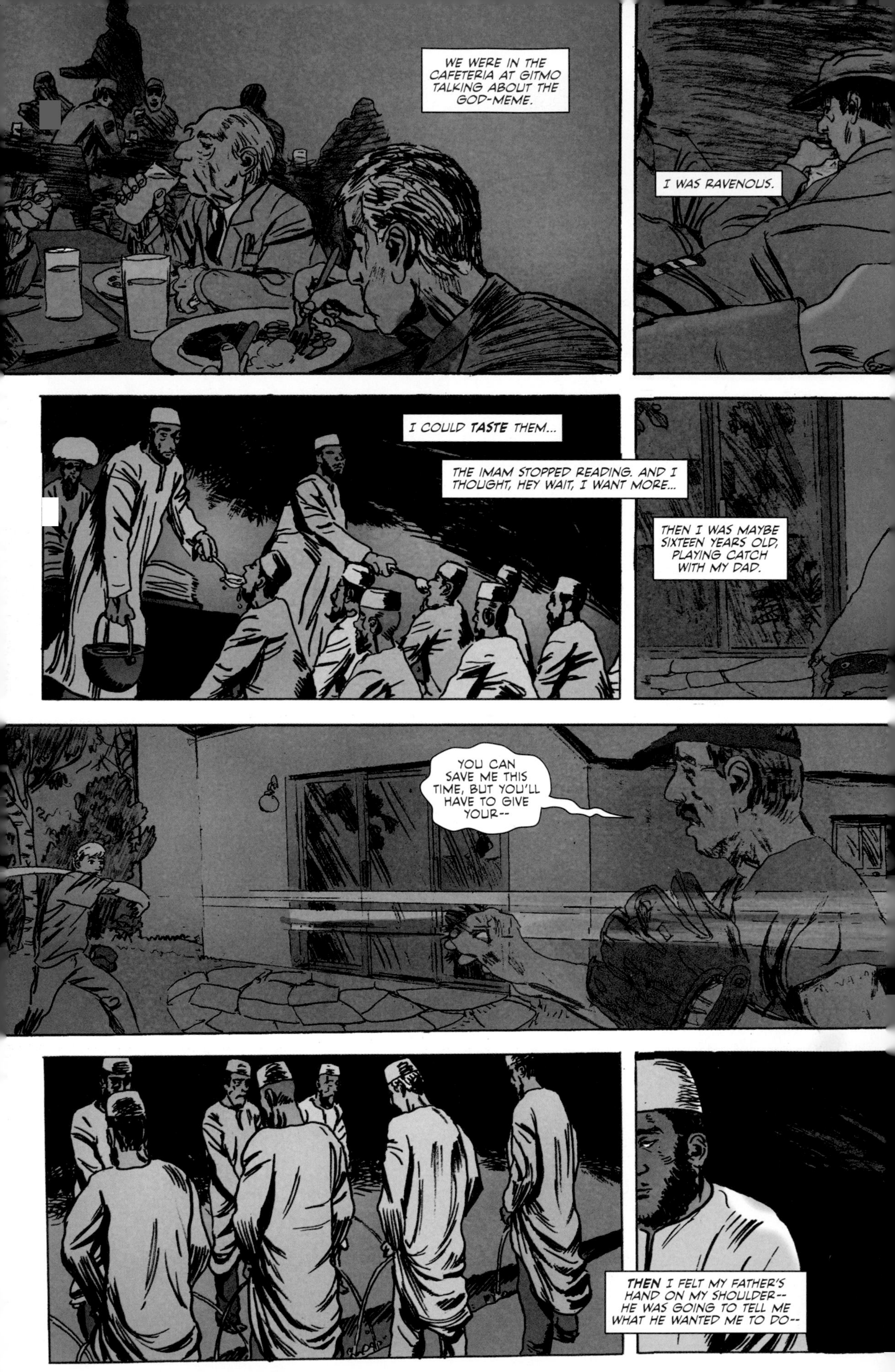
WE WERE IN THE CAFETERIA AT GITMO TALKING ABOUT THE GOD-MEME.
I WAS RAVENOUS.
I COULD **TASTE** THEM...
THE IMAM STOPPED READING. AND I THOUGHT, HEY WAIT, I WANT MORE...
THEN I WAS MAYBE SIXTEEN YEARS OLD, PLAYING CATCH WITH MY DAD.
YOU CAN SAVE ME THIS TIME, BUT YOU'LL HAVE TO GIVE YOUR--
THEN I FELT MY FATHER'S HAND ON MY SHOULDER-- HE WAS GOING TO TELL ME WHAT HE WANTED ME TO DO--

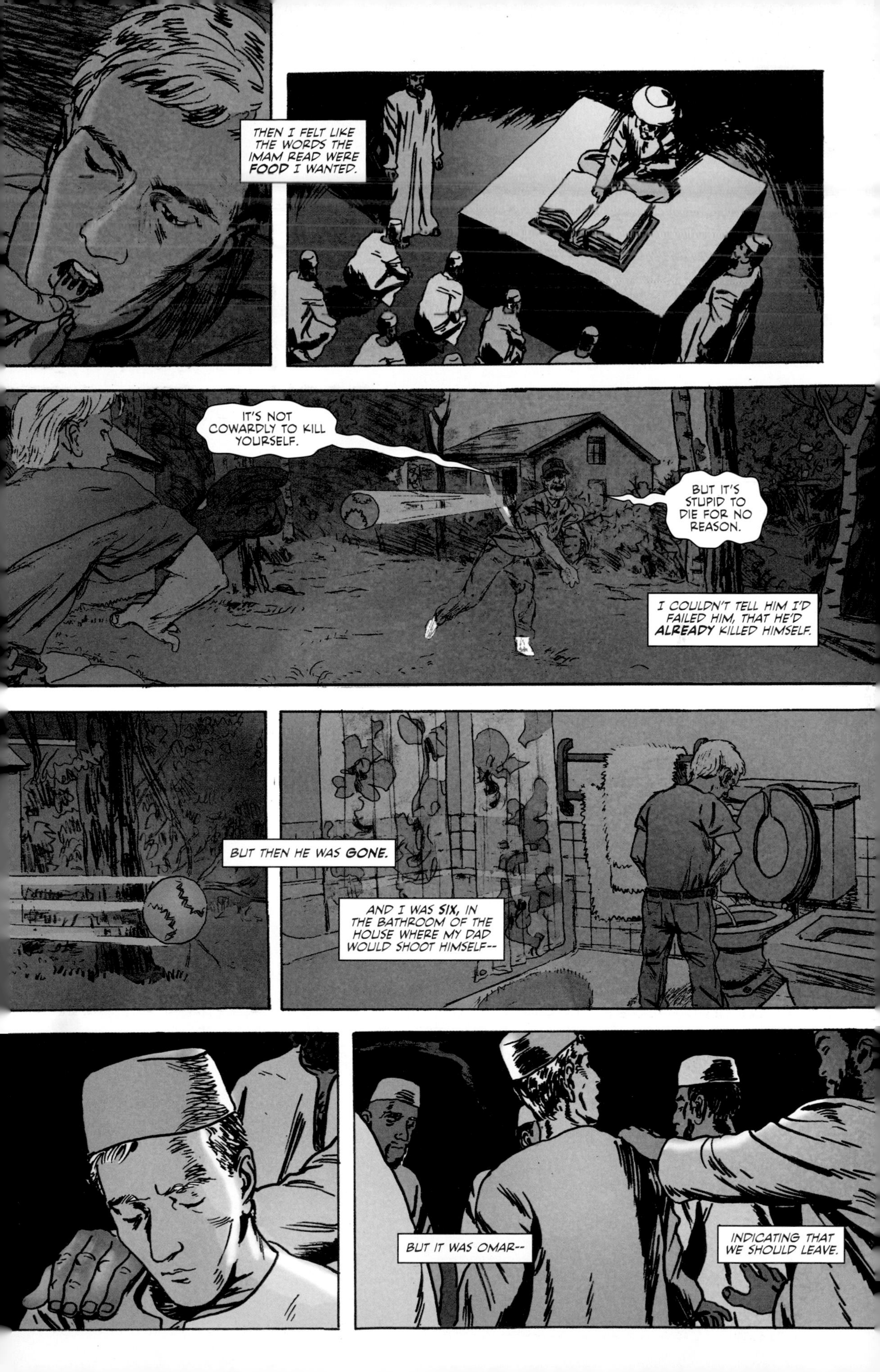

THEN I FELT LIKE THE WORDS THE IMAM READ WERE **FOOD** I WANTED.
IT'S NOT COWARDLY TO KILL YOURSELF.
BUT IT'S STUPID TO DIE FOR NO REASON.
I COULDN'T TELL HIM I'D FAILED HIM, THAT HE'D **ALREADY** KILLED HIMSELF.
BUT THEN HE WAS **GONE.**
AND I WAS **SIX,** IN THE BATHROOM OF THE HOUSE WHERE MY DAD WOULD SHOOT HIMSELF--
BUT IT WAS OMAR--
INDICATING THAT WE SHOULD LEAVE.

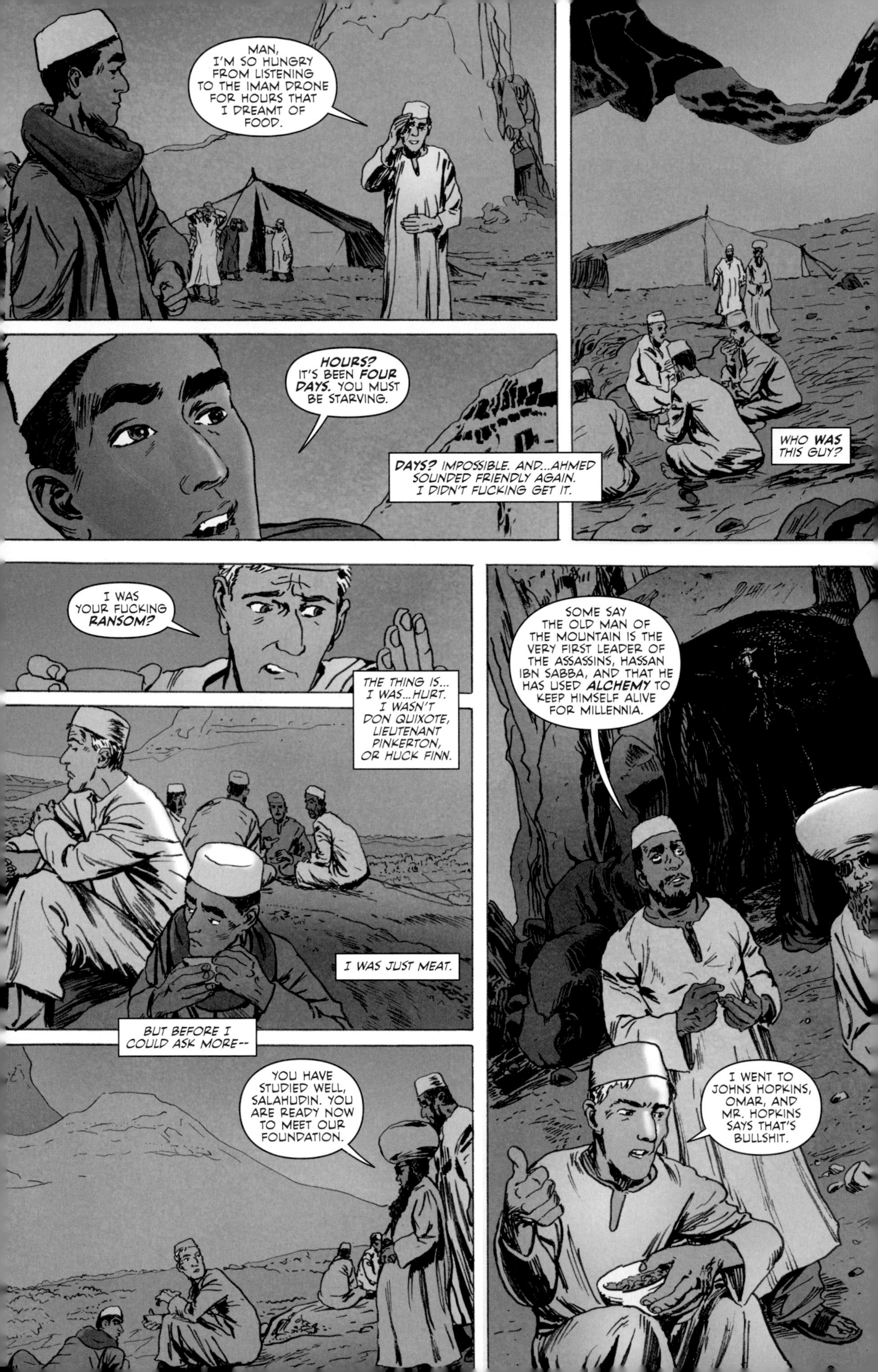
MAN, I'M SO HUNGRY FROM LISTENING TO THE IMAM DRONE FOR HOURS THAT I DREAMT OF FOOD.
HOURS? IT'S BEEN FOUR DAYS. YOU MUST BE STARVING.
DAYS? IMPOSSIBLE. AND...AHMED SOUNDED FRIENDLY AGAIN. I DIDN'T FUCKING GET IT.
WHO WAS THIS GUY?
I WAS YOUR FUCKING RANSOM?
THE THING IS... I WAS...HURT. I WASN'T DON QUIXOTE, LIEUTENANT PINKERTON, OR HUCK FINN.
I WAS JUST MEAT.
BUT BEFORE I COULD ASK MORE--
YOU HAVE STUDIED WELL, SALAHUDIN. YOU ARE READY NOW TO MEET OUR FOUNDATION.
SOME SAY THE OLD MAN OF THE MOUNTAIN IS THE VERY FIRST LEADER OF THE ASSASSINS, HASSAN IBN SABBA, AND THAT HE HAS USED ALCHEMY TO KEEP HIMSELF ALIVE FOR MILLENNIA.
I WENT TO JOHNS HOPKINS, OMAR, AND MR. HOPKINS SAYS THAT'S BULLSHIT.

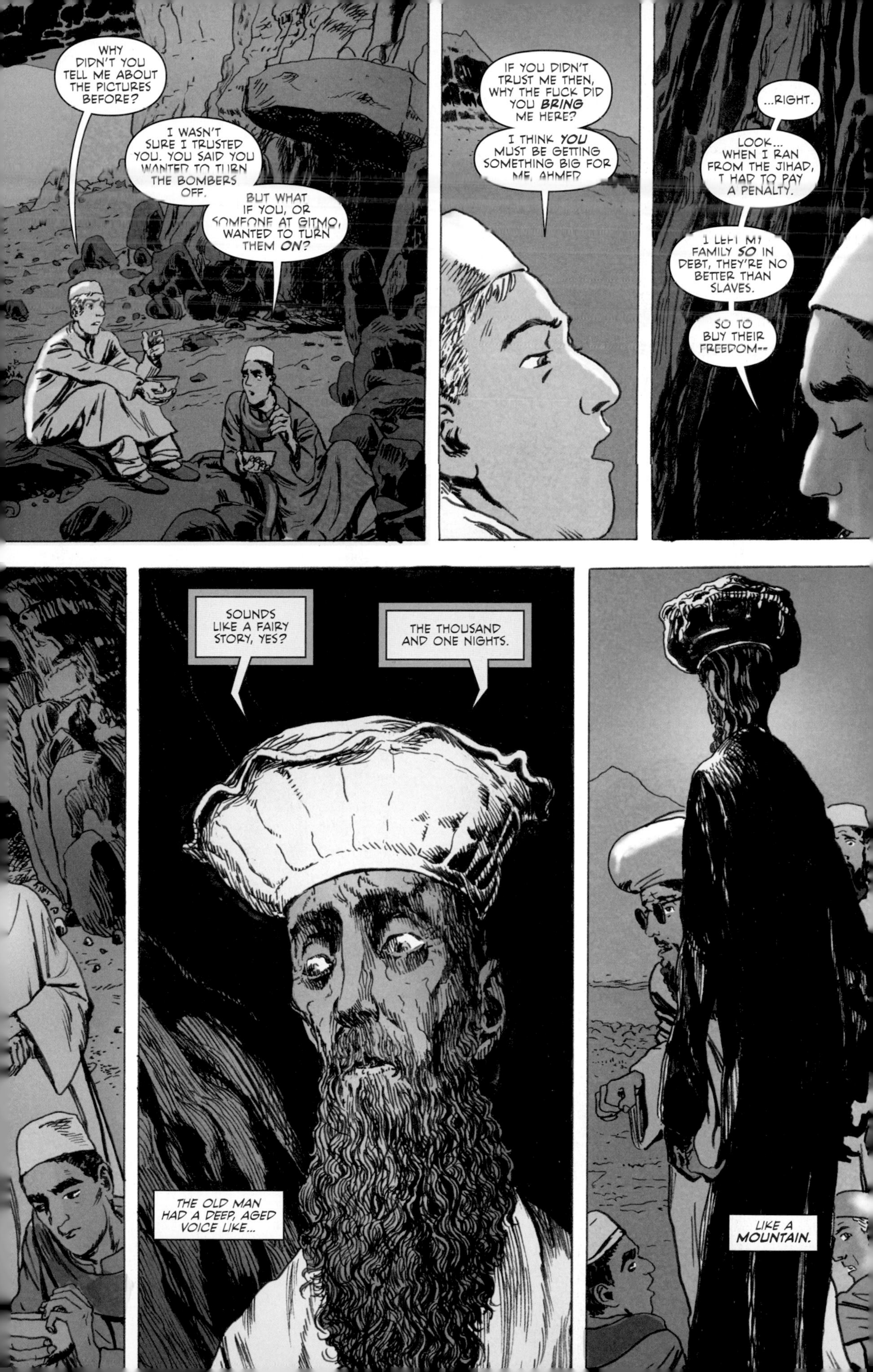
WHY DIDN'T YOU TELL ME ABOUT THE PICTURES BEFORE?
I WASN'T SURE I TRUSTED YOU. YOU SAID YOU WANTED TO TURN THE BOMBERS OFF.
BUT WHAT IF YOU, OR SOMEONE AT GITMO, WANTED TO TURN THEM ON?
IF YOU DIDN'T TRUST ME THEN, WHY THE FUCK DID YOU BRING ME HERE?
I THINK YOU MUST BE GETTING SOMETHING BIG FOR ME, AHMED?
...RIGHT.
LOOK... WHEN I RAN FROM THE JIHAD, I HAD TO PAY A PENALTY.
I LEFT MY FAMILY SO IN DEBT, THEY'RE NO BETTER THAN SLAVES.
SO TO BUY THEIR FREEDOM--
SOUNDS LIKE A FAIRY STORY, YES?
THE THOUSAND AND ONE NIGHTS.
THE OLD MAN HAD A DEEP, AGED VOICE LIKE...
LIKE A MOUNTAIN.

THIS *HAD* TO BE THE HIDDEN IMAM, THE FOUNDATION. THE OLD MAN IN THE MOUNTAIN. *THE LEADER OF THE ASSASSINS...*

THE BELIEF HAS ITS USES, NO?

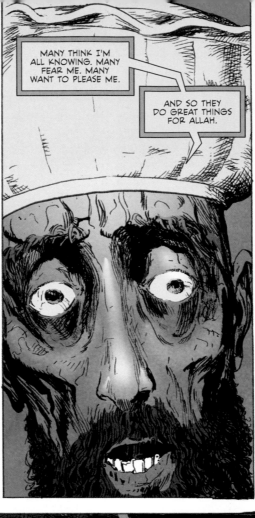

MANY THINK I'M ALL KNOWING. MANY FEAR ME. MANY WANT TO PLEASE ME.

AND SO THEY DO GREAT THINGS FOR ALLAH.

PERHAPS DEAR AHMED WON YOU TO OUR CAUSE--

HE *DID*, SIR. HE IS VERY PERSUASIVE--

"FORCING YOUR BODY TO DO *HIS* BIDDING."

NOW YOU ARE READY FOR OUR SACRAMENT, FOR HASHISH. THE WAY OF THE ONES YOU CALL--

--THE ASSASSINS. AHMED TOLD ME THAT.

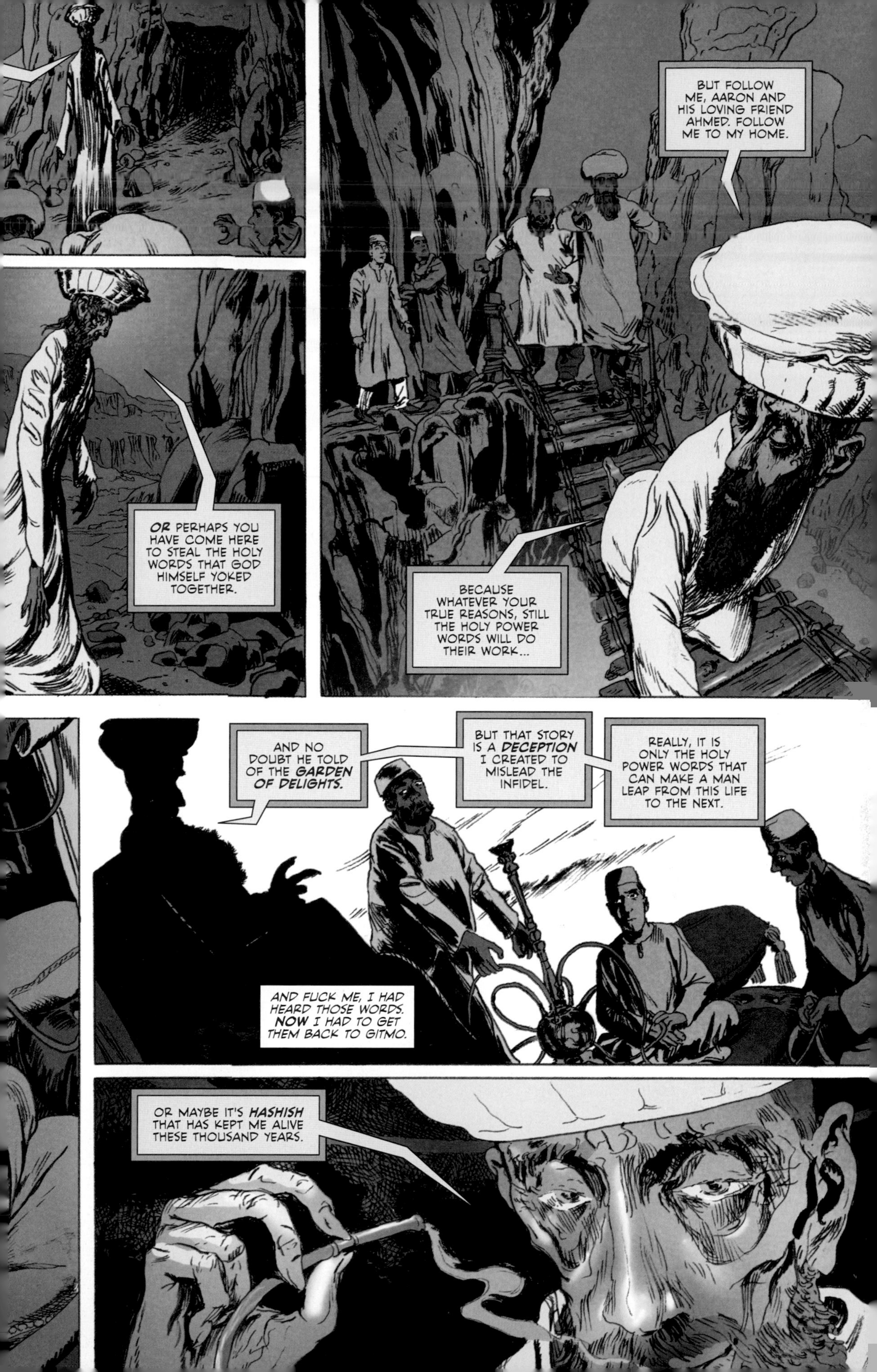
BUT FOLLOW ME, AARON AND HIS LOVING FRIEND AHMED. FOLLOW ME TO MY HOME.
OR PERHAPS YOU HAVE COME HERE TO STEAL THE HOLY WORDS THAT GOD HIMSELF YOKED TOGETHER.
BECAUSE WHATEVER YOUR TRUE REASONS, STILL THE HOLY POWER WORDS WILL DO THEIR WORK...
AND NO DOUBT HE TOLD OF THE GARDEN OF DELIGHTS.
BUT THAT STORY IS A DECEPTION I CREATED TO MISLEAD THE INFIDEL.
REALLY, IT IS ONLY THE HOLY POWER WORDS THAT CAN MAKE A MAN LEAP FROM THIS LIFE TO THE NEXT.
AND FUCK ME, I HAD HEARD THOSE WORDS. NOW I HAD TO GET THEM BACK TO GITMO.
OR MAYBE IT'S HASHISH THAT HAS KEPT ME ALIVE THESE THOUSAND YEARS.

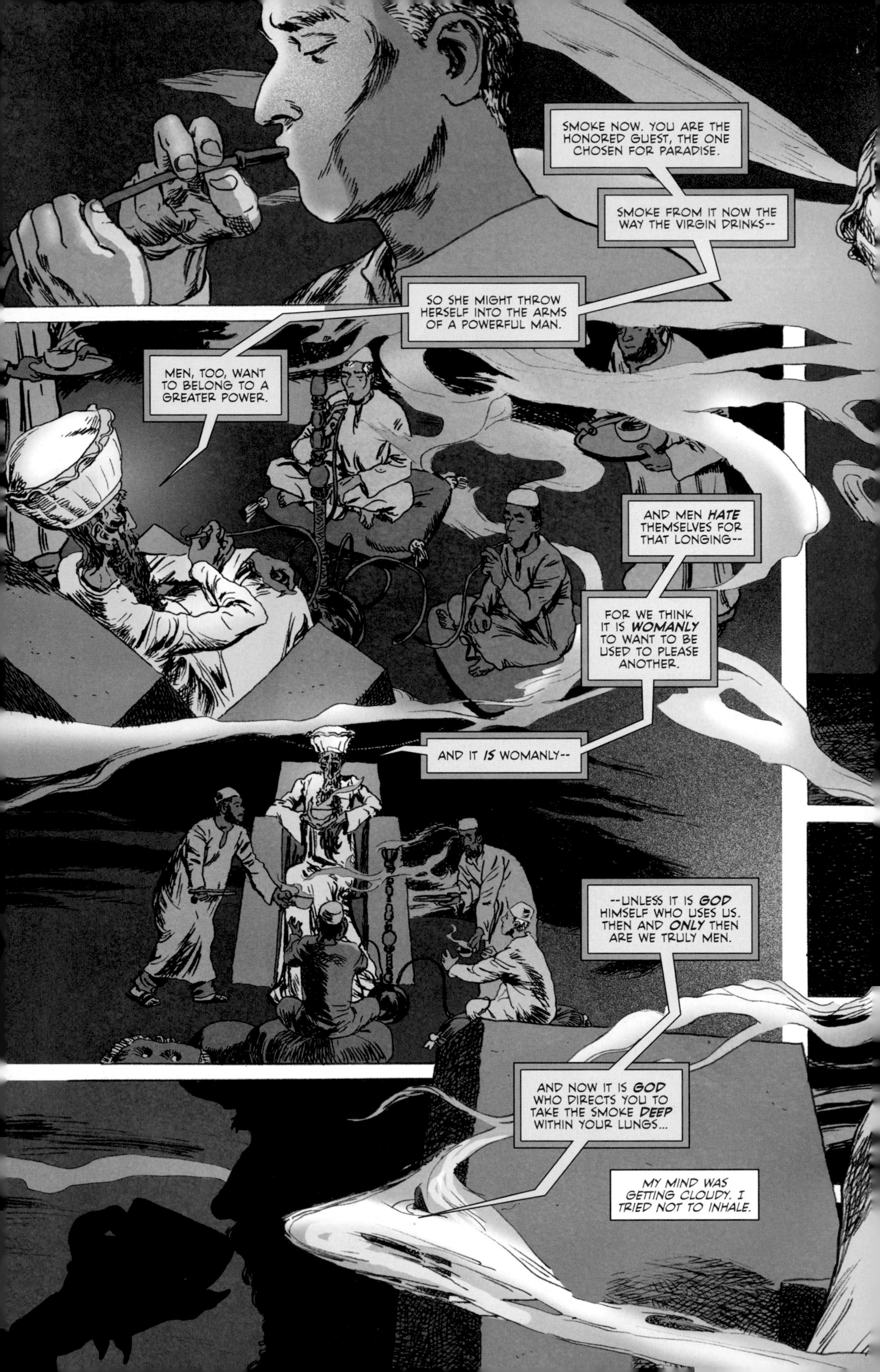
SMOKE NOW. YOU ARE THE HONORED GUEST, THE ONE CHOSEN FOR PARADISE.
SMOKE FROM IT NOW THE WAY THE VIRGIN DRINKS--
SO SHE MIGHT THROW HERSELF INTO THE ARMS OF A POWERFUL MAN.
MEN, TOO, WANT TO BELONG TO A GREATER POWER.
AND MEN *HATE* THEMSELVES FOR THAT LONGING--
FOR WE THINK IT IS *WOMANLY* TO WANT TO BE USED TO PLEASE ANOTHER.
AND IT *IS* WOMANLY--
--UNLESS IT IS *GOD* HIMSELF WHO USES US. THEN AND *ONLY* THEN ARE WE TRULY MEN.
AND NOW IT IS *GOD* WHO DIRECTS YOU TO TAKE THE SMOKE *DEEP* WITHIN YOUR LUNGS...
MY MIND WAS GETTING CLOUDY. I TRIED NOT TO INHALE.

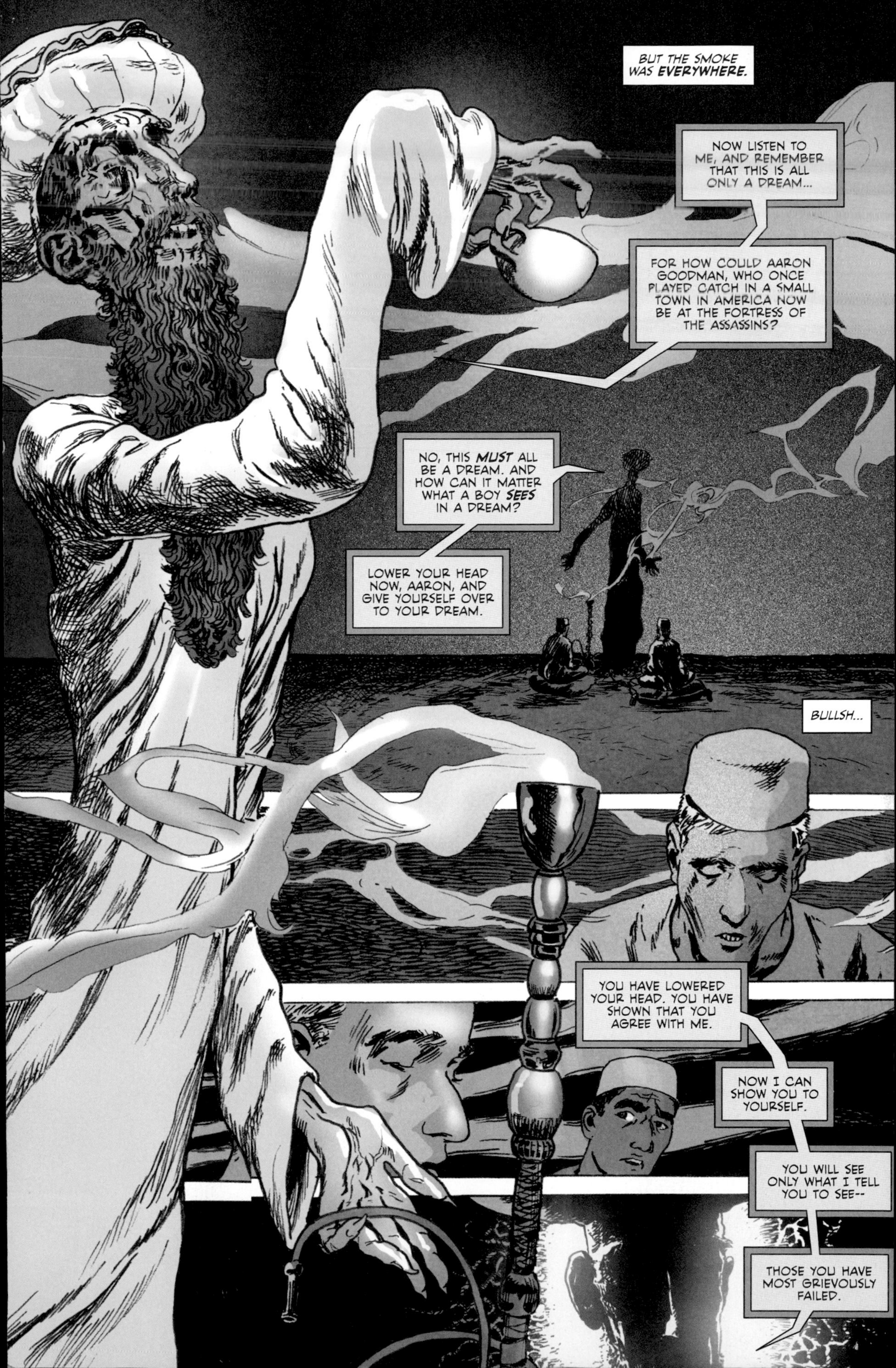
BUT THE SMOKE WAS EVERYWHERE.
NOW LISTEN TO ME, AND REMEMBER THAT THIS IS ALL ONLY A DREAM...
FOR HOW COULD AARON GOODMAN, WHO ONCE PLAYED CATCH IN A SMALL TOWN IN AMERICA NOW BE AT THE FORTRESS OF THE ASSASSINS?
NO, THIS MUST ALL BE A DREAM. AND HOW CAN IT MATTER WHAT A BOY SEES IN A DREAM?
LOWER YOUR HEAD NOW, AARON, AND GIVE YOURSELF OVER TO YOUR DREAM.
BULLSH...
YOU HAVE LOWERED YOUR HEAD. YOU HAVE SHOWN THAT YOU AGREE WITH ME.
NOW I CAN SHOW YOU TO YOURSELF.
YOU WILL SEE ONLY WHAT I TELL YOU TO SEE--
THOSE YOU HAVE MOST GRIEVOUSLY FAILED.

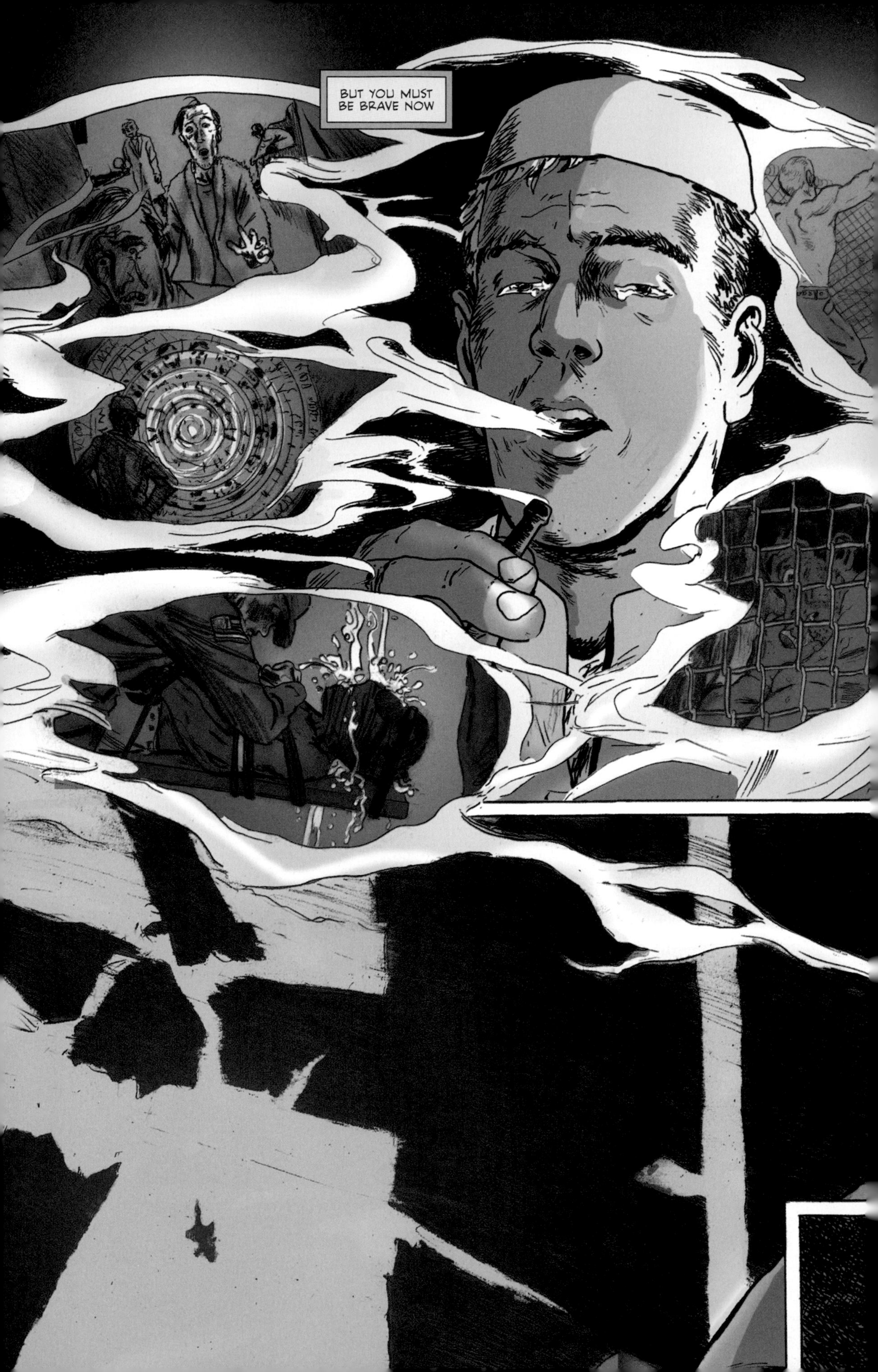
BUT YOU MUST
BE BRAVE NOW

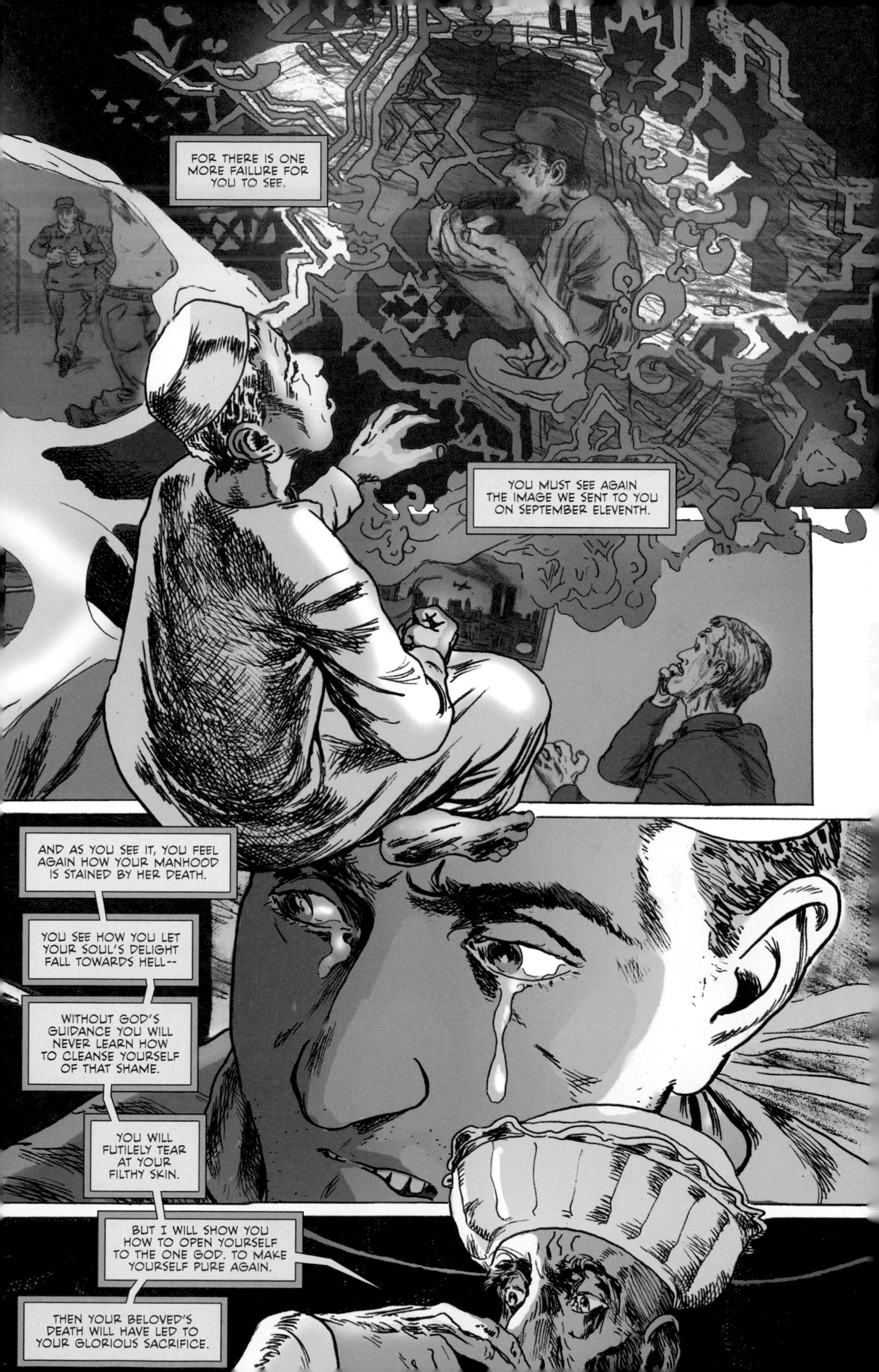
FOR THERE IS ONE MORE FAILURE FOR YOU TO SEE.
YOU MUST SEE AGAIN THE IMAGE WE SENT TO YOU ON SEPTEMBER ELEVENTH.
AND AS YOU SEE IT, YOU FEEL AGAIN HOW YOUR MANHOOD IS STAINED BY HER DEATH.
YOU SEE HOW YOU LET YOUR SOUL'S DELIGHT FALL TOWARDS HELL--
WITHOUT GOD'S GUIDANCE YOU WILL NEVER LEARN HOW TO CLEANSE YOURSELF OF THAT SHAME.
YOU WILL FUTILELY TEAR AT YOUR FILTHY SKIN.
BUT I WILL SHOW YOU HOW TO OPEN YOURSELF TO THE ONE GOD. TO MAKE YOURSELF PURE AGAIN.
THEN YOUR BELOVED'S DEATH WILL HAVE LED TO YOUR GLORIOUS SACRIFICE.

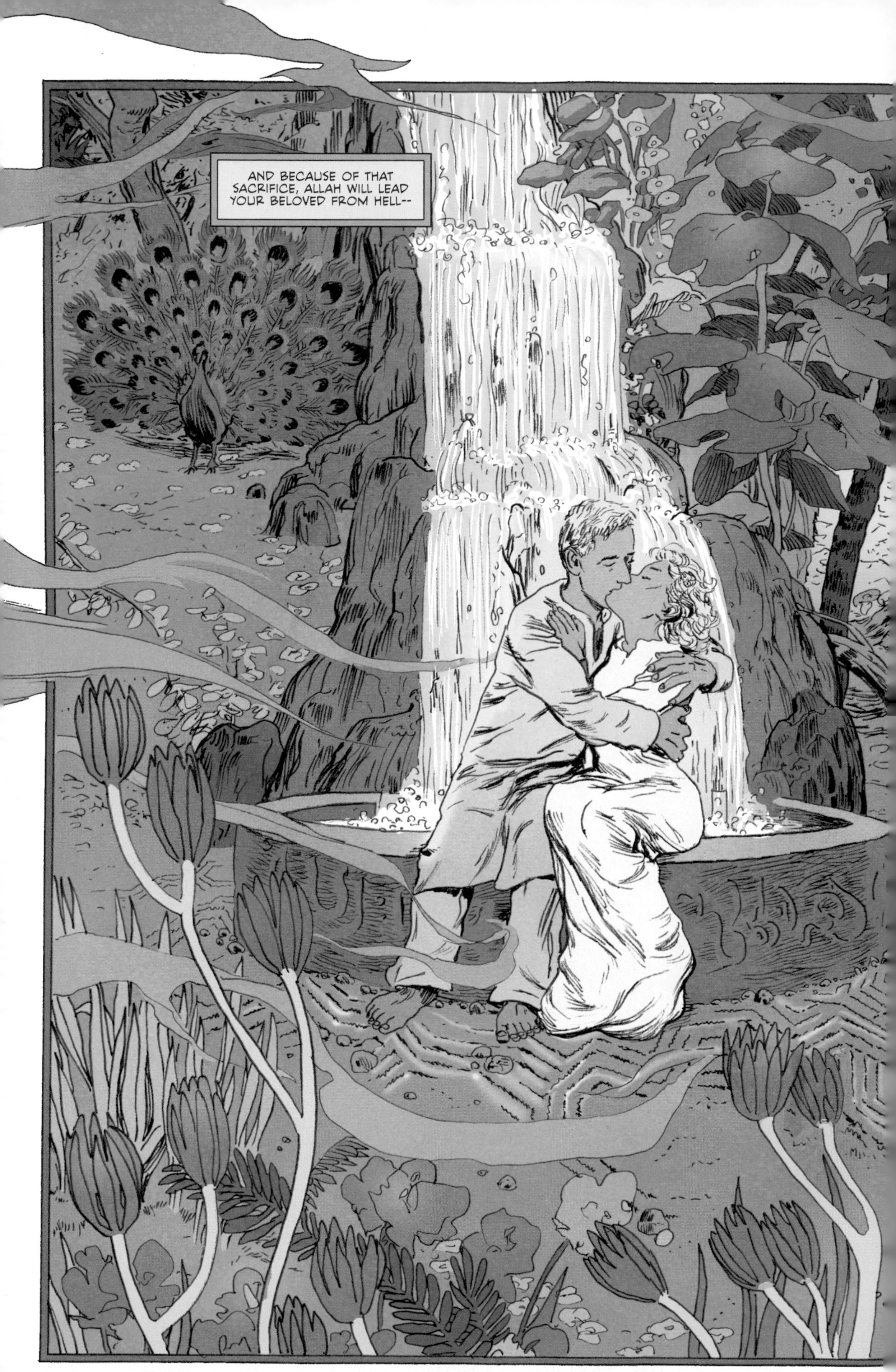
AND BECAUSE OF THAT SACRIFICE, ALLAH WILL LEAD YOUR BELOVED FROM HELL--

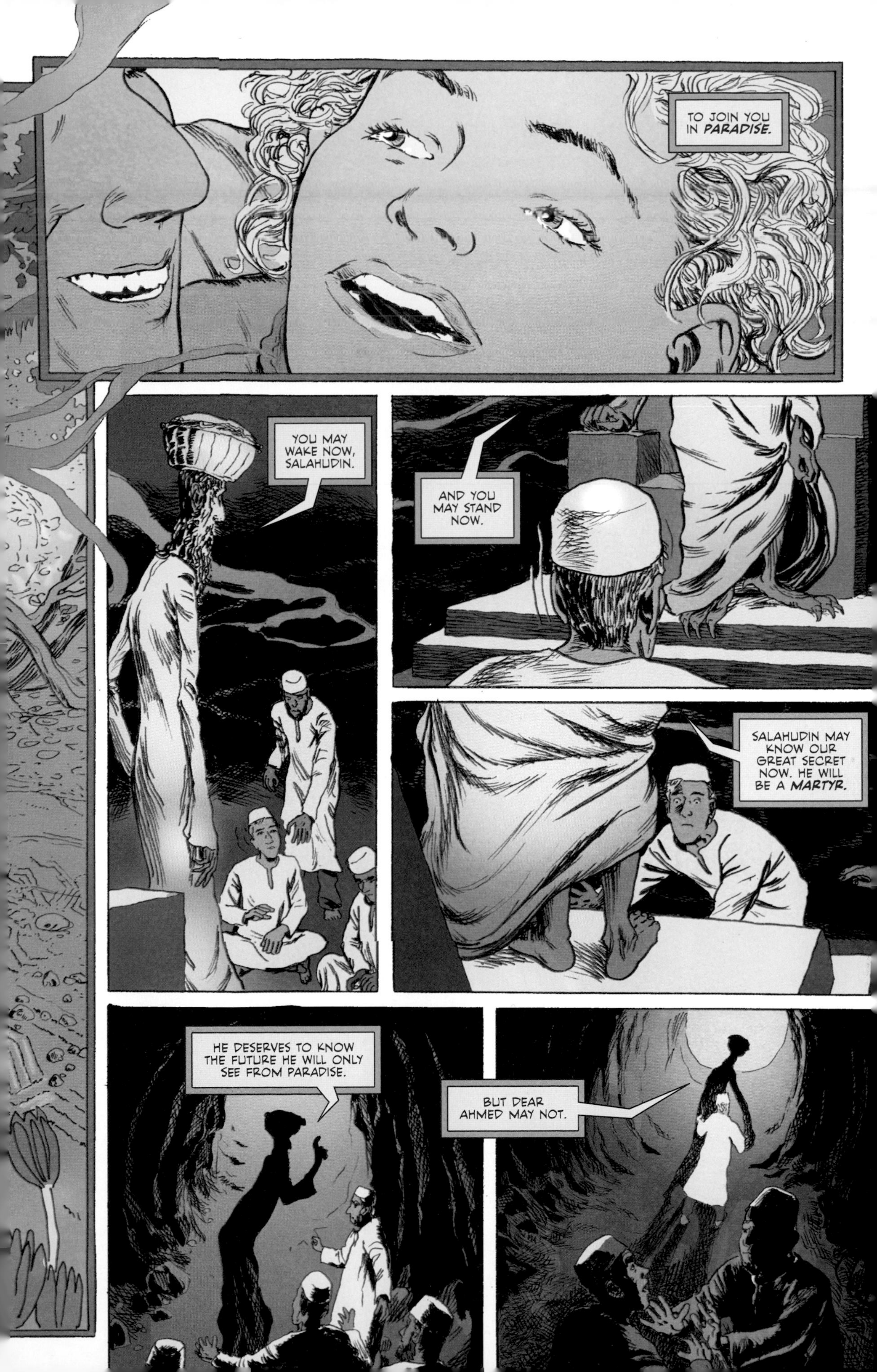
TO JOIN YOU IN *PARADISE.*
YOU MAY WAKE NOW, SALAHUDIN.
AND YOU MAY STAND NOW.
SALAHUDIN MAY KNOW OUR GREAT SECRET NOW. HE WILL BE A *MARTYR.*
HE DESERVES TO KNOW THE FUTURE HE WILL ONLY SEE FROM PARADISE.
BUT DEAR AHMED MAY NOT.

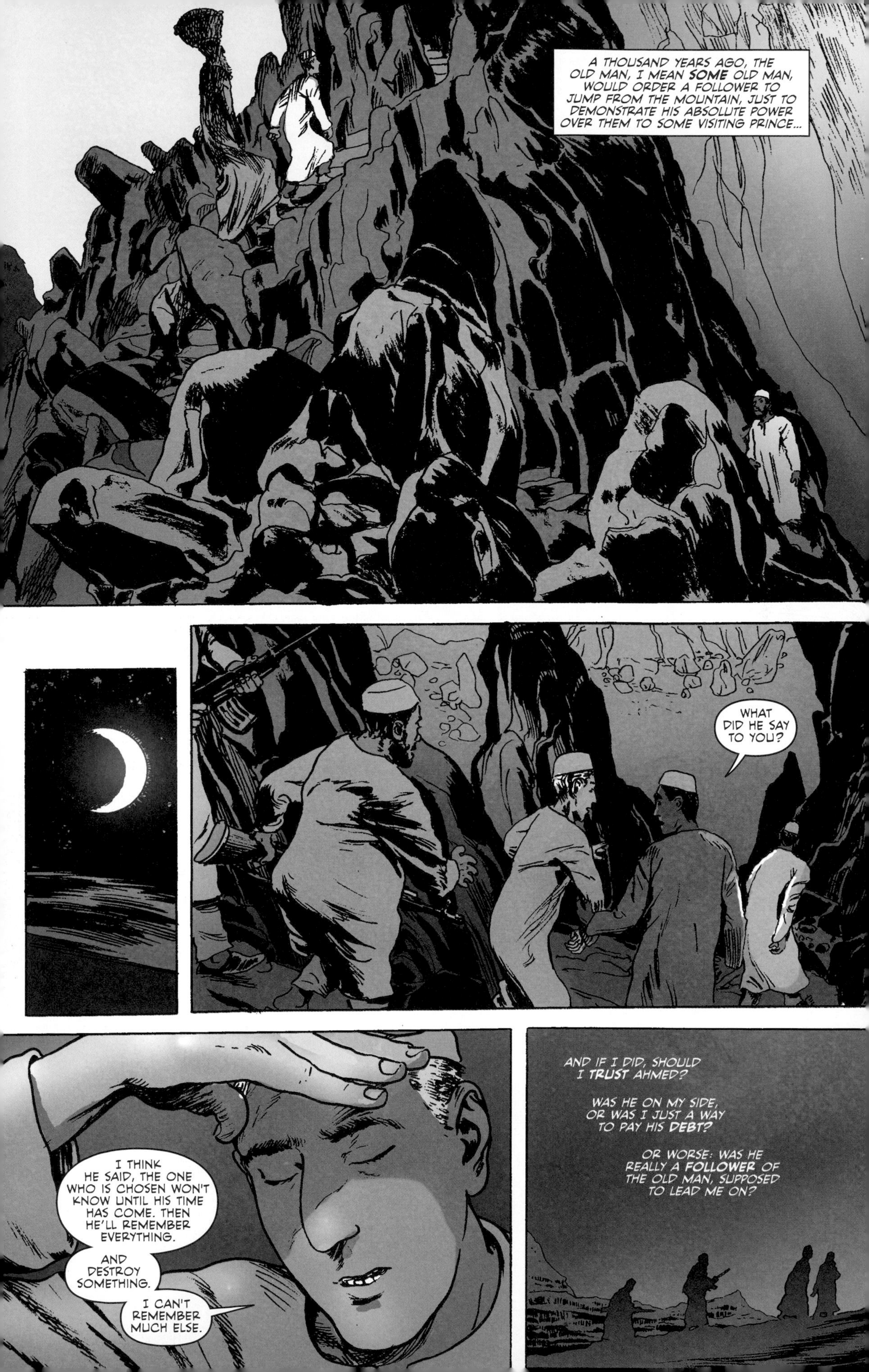
A THOUSAND YEARS AGO, THE OLD MAN, I MEAN SOME OLD MAN, WOULD ORDER A FOLLOWER TO JUMP FROM THE MOUNTAIN, JUST TO DEMONSTRATE HIS ABSOLUTE POWER OVER THEM TO SOME VISITING PRINCE...
WHAT DID HE SAY TO YOU?
I THINK HE SAID, THE ONE WHO IS CHOSEN WON'T KNOW UNTIL HIS TIME HAS COME. THEN HE'LL REMEMBER EVERYTHING.
AND DESTROY SOMETHING.
I CAN'T REMEMBER MUCH ELSE.
AND IF I DID, SHOULD I TRUST AHMED?
WAS HE ON MY SIDE, OR WAS I JUST A WAY TO PAY HIS DEBT?
OR WORSE: WAS HE REALLY A FOLLOWER OF THE OLD MAN, SUPPOSED TO LEAD ME ON?

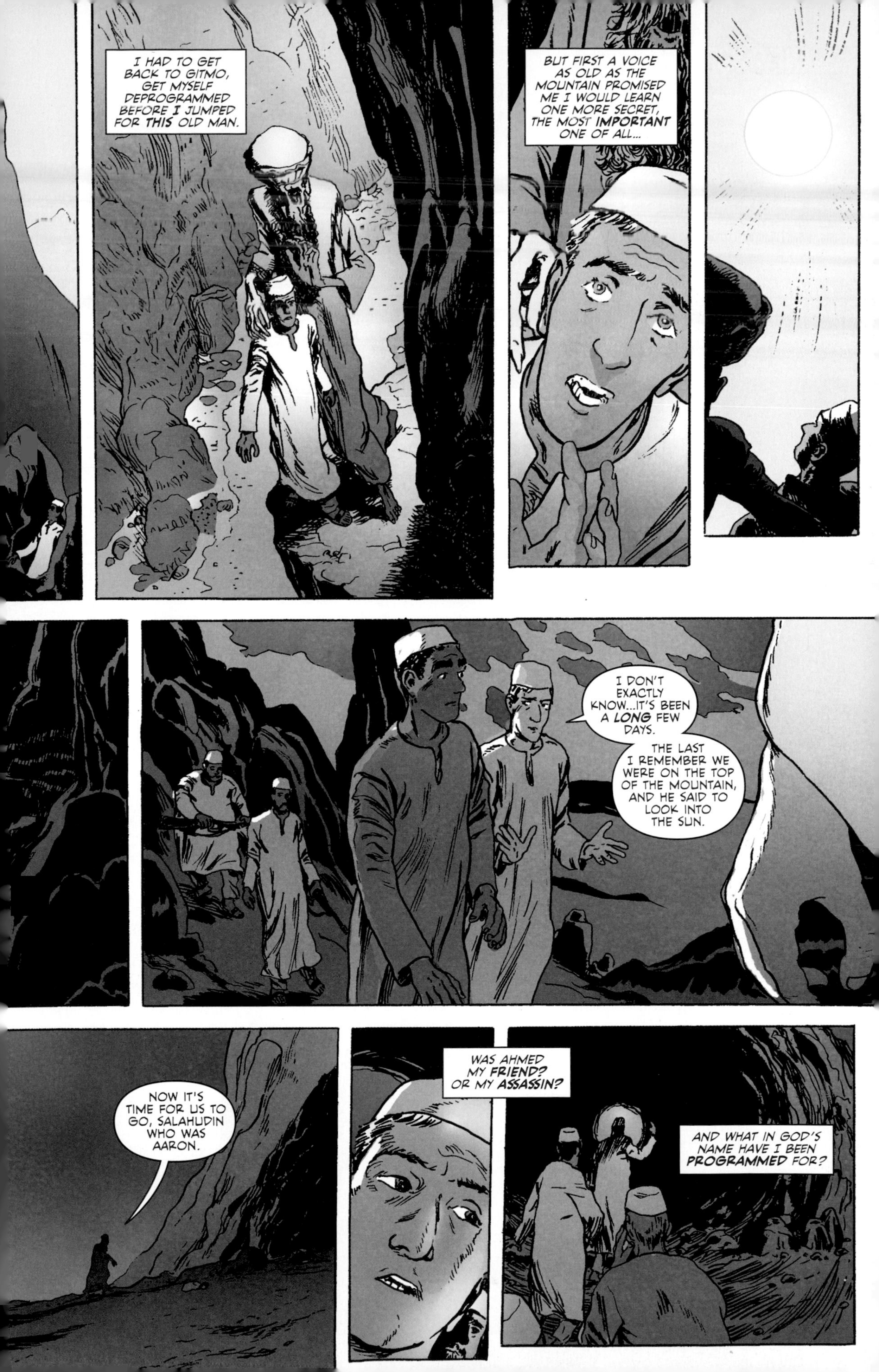
I HAD TO GET BACK TO GITMO, GET MYSELF DEPROGRAMMED BEFORE I JUMPED FOR THIS OLD MAN.
BUT FIRST A VOICE AS OLD AS THE MOUNTAIN PROMISED ME I WOULD LEARN ONE MORE SECRET, THE MOST IMPORTANT ONE OF ALL...
I DON'T EXACTLY KNOW...IT'S BEEN A LONG FEW DAYS.
THE LAST I REMEMBER WE WERE ON THE TOP OF THE MOUNTAIN, AND HE SAID TO LOOK INTO THE SUN.
NOW IT'S TIME FOR US TO GO, SALAHUDIN WHO WAS AARON.
WAS AHMED MY FRIEND? OR MY ASSASSIN?
AND WHAT IN GOD'S NAME HAVE I BEEN PROGRAMMED FOR?

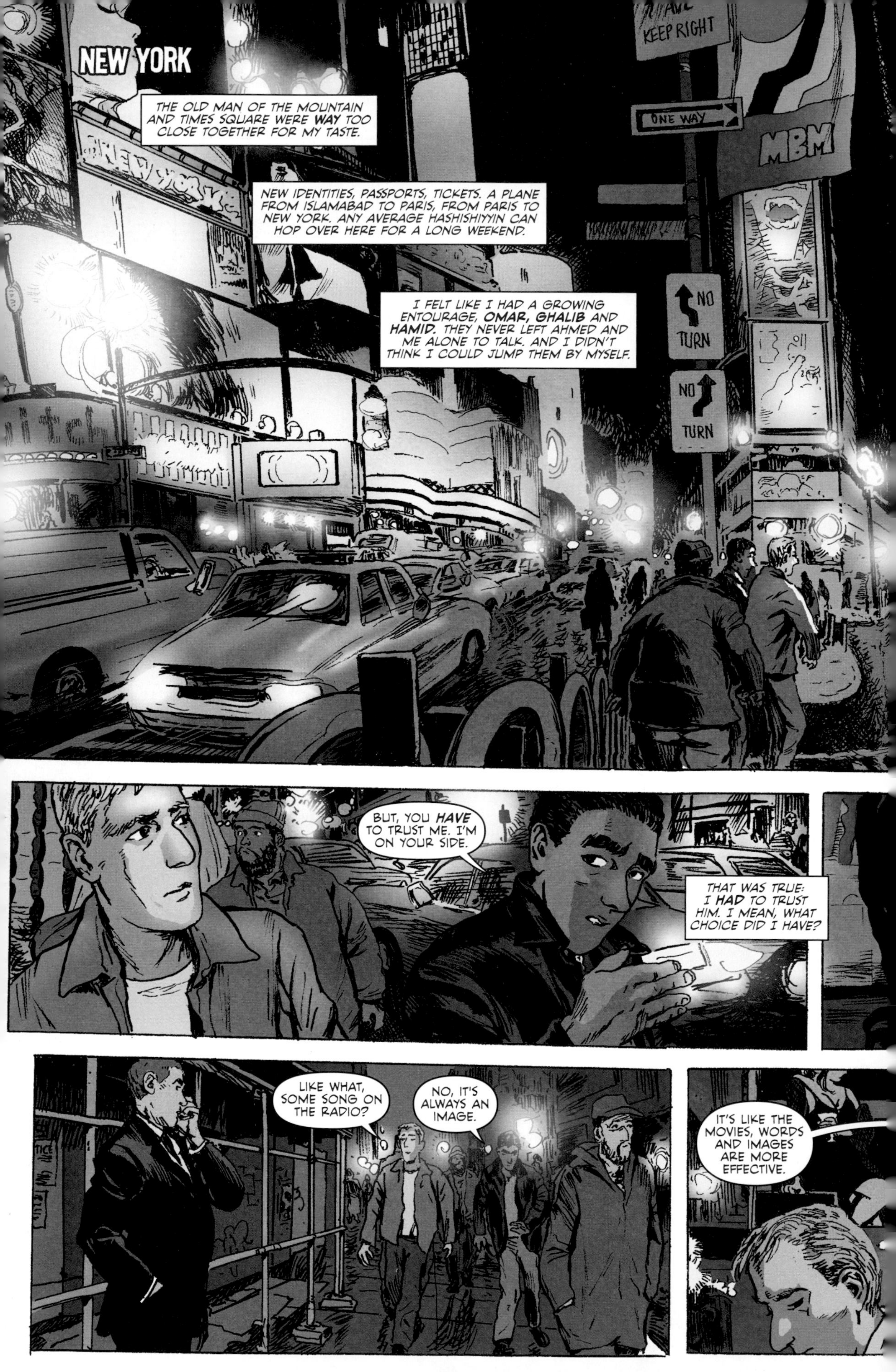
NEW YORK
THE OLD MAN OF THE MOUNTAIN AND TIMES SQUARE WERE WAY TOO CLOSE TOGETHER FOR MY TASTE.
NEW IDENTITIES, PASSPORTS, TICKETS. A PLANE FROM ISLAMABAD TO PARIS, FROM PARIS TO NEW YORK. ANY AVERAGE HASHISHIYYIN CAN HOP OVER HERE FOR A LONG WEEKEND.
I FELT LIKE I HAD A GROWING ENTOURAGE, OMAR, GHALIB AND HAMID. THEY NEVER LEFT AHMED AND ME ALONE TO TALK. AND I DIDN'T THINK I COULD JUMP THEM BY MYSELF.
KEEP RIGHT
ONE WAY
MBM
NO TURN
NO TURN
BUT, YOU HAVE TO TRUST ME. I'M ON YOUR SIDE.
THAT WAS TRUE: I HAD TO TRUST HIM. I MEAN, WHAT CHOICE DID I HAVE?
LIKE WHAT, SOME SONG ON THE RADIO?
NO, IT'S ALWAYS AN IMAGE.
IT'S LIKE THE MOVIES, WORDS AND IMAGES ARE MORE EFFECTIVE.

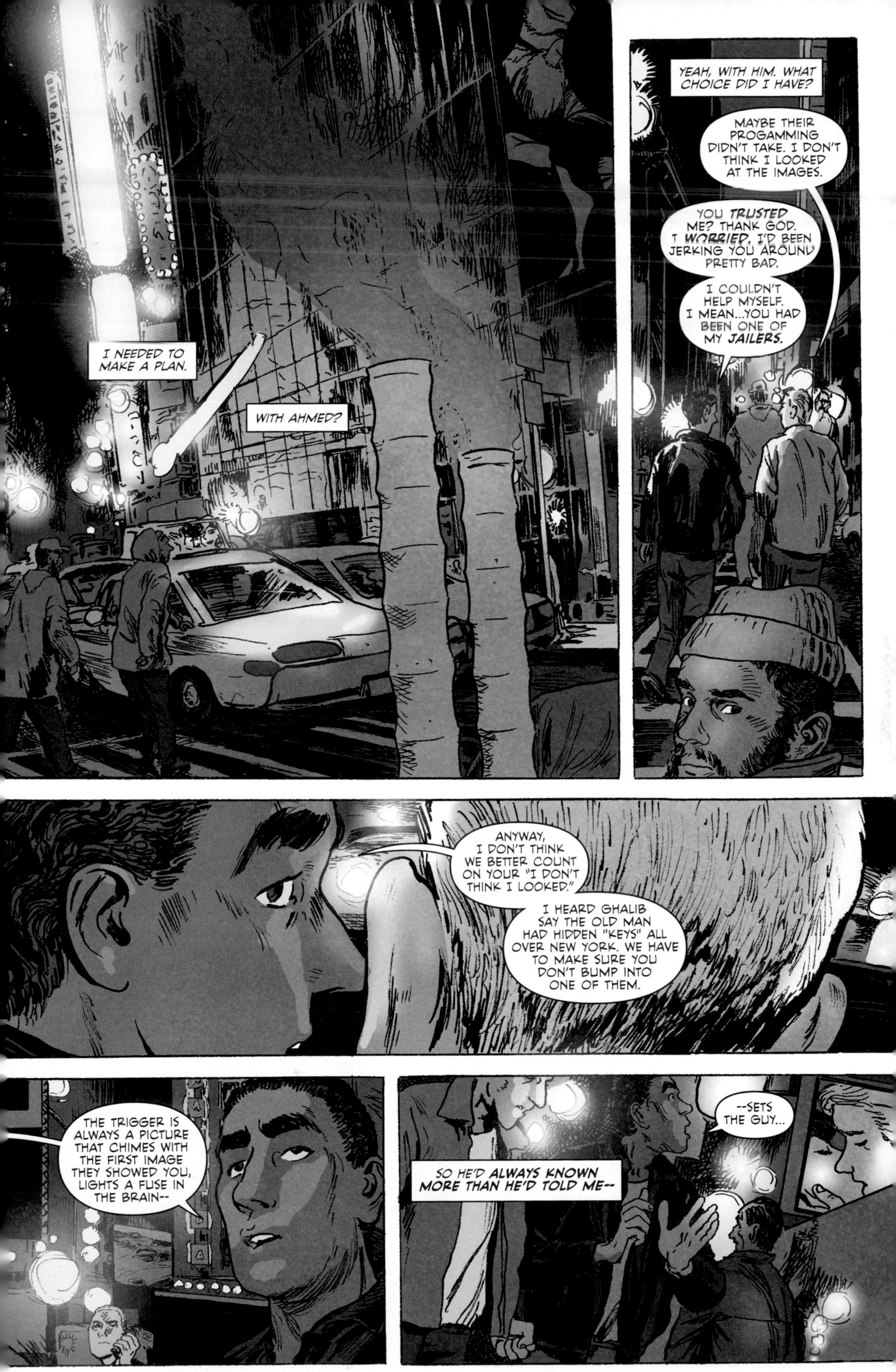
I NEEDED TO MAKE A PLAN.
WITH AHMED?
YEAH, WITH HIM. WHAT CHOICE DID I HAVE?
MAYBE THEIR PROGAMMING DIDN'T TAKE. I DON'T THINK I LOOKED AT THE IMAGES.
YOU TRUSTED ME? THANK GOD. I WORRIED. I'D BEEN JERKING YOU AROUND PRETTY BAD.
I COULDN'T HELP MYSELF. I MEAN...YOU HAD BEEN ONE OF MY JAILERS.
ANYWAY, I DON'T THINK WE BETTER COUNT ON YOUR "I DON'T THINK I LOOKED."
I HEARD GHALIB SAY THE OLD MAN HAD HIDDEN "KEYS" ALL OVER NEW YORK. WE HAVE TO MAKE SURE YOU DON'T BUMP INTO ONE OF THEM.
THE TRIGGER IS ALWAYS A PICTURE THAT CHIMES WITH THE FIRST IMAGE THEY SHOWED YOU, LIGHTS A FUSE IN THE BRAIN--
--SETS THE GUY...
SO HE'D ALWAYS KNOWN MORE THAN HE'D TOLD ME--

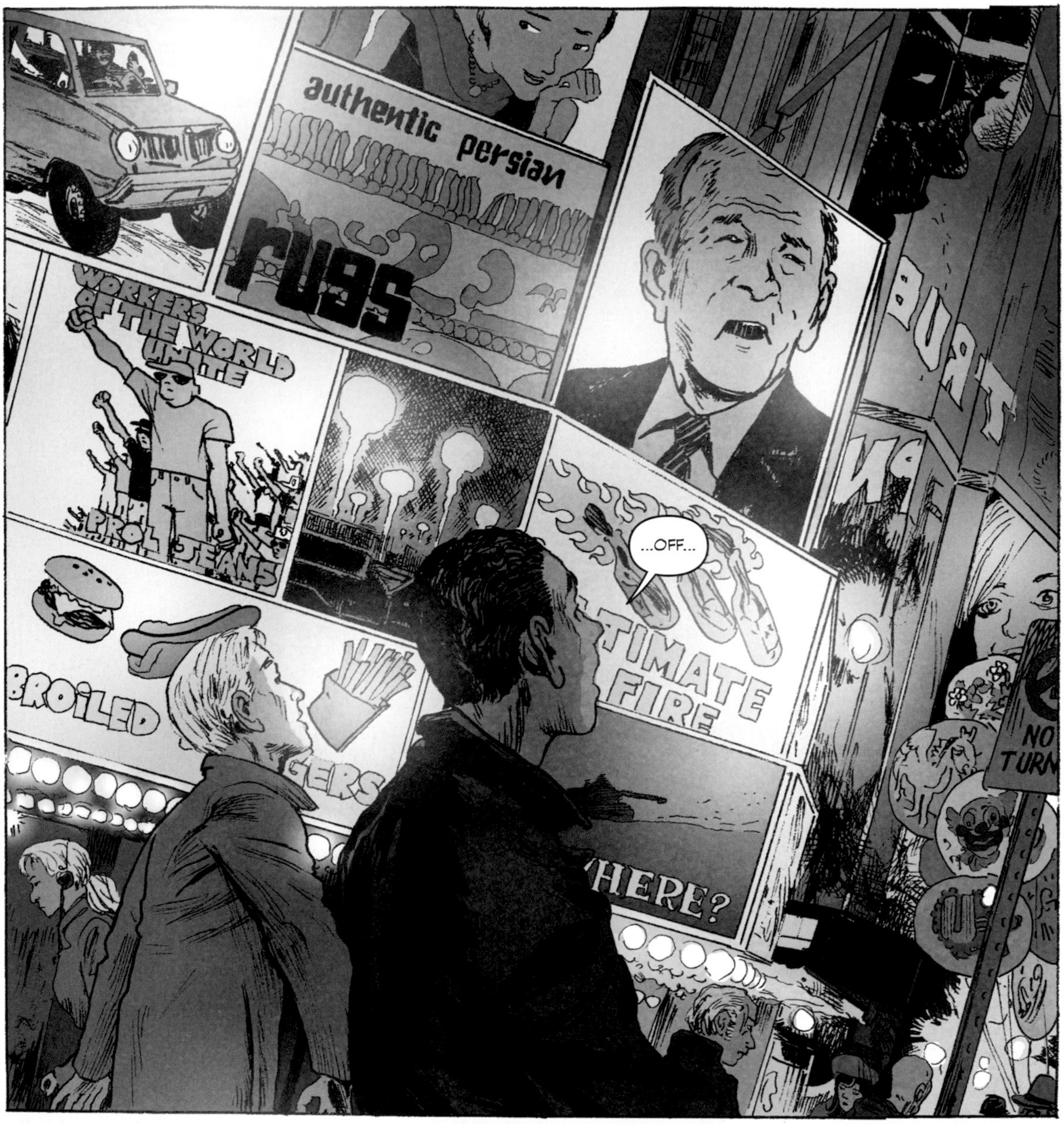
authentic persian
rugs
WORKERS OF THE WORLD UNITE
PROL JEANS
BROILED
...OFF...
NO TURN

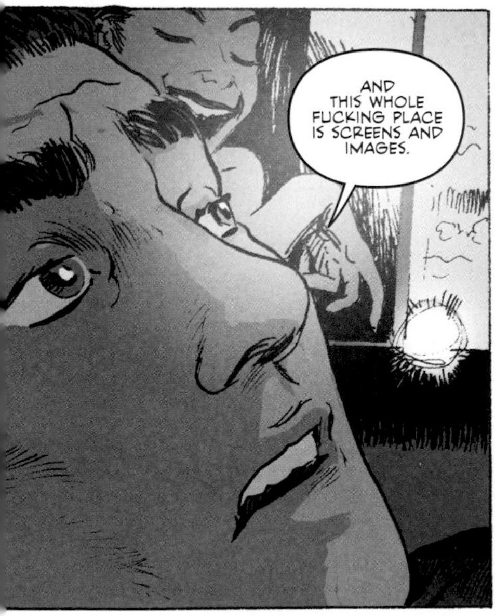
AND THIS WHOLE FUCKING PLACE IS SCREENS AND IMAGES.

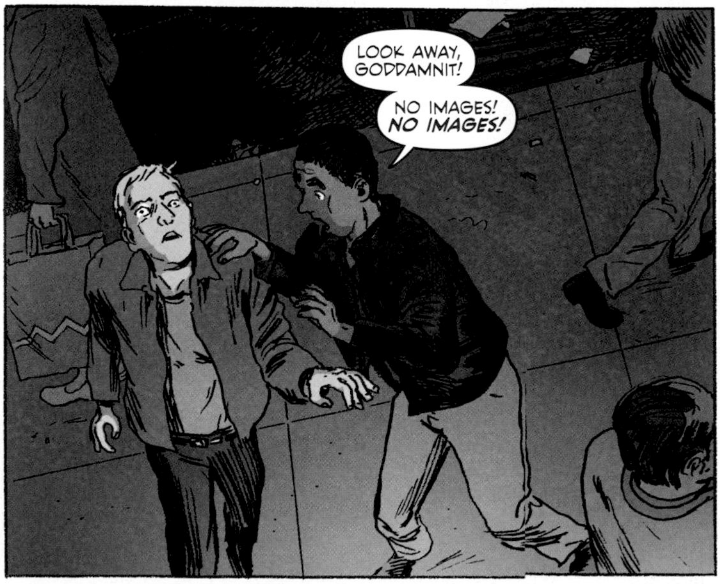
LOOK AWAY, GODDAMNIT!
NO IMAGES! *NO IMAGES!*

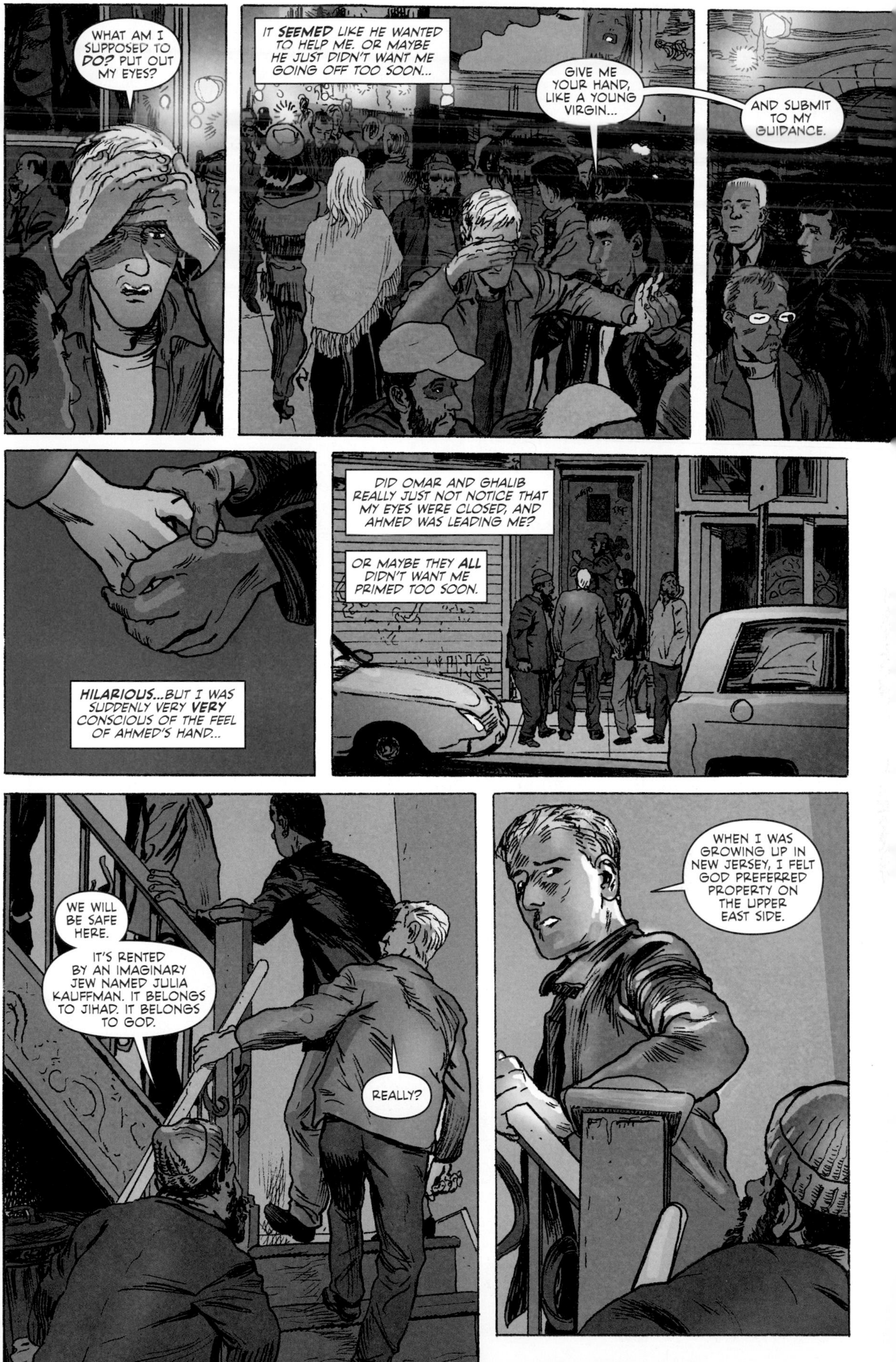
WHAT AM I SUPPOSED TO DO? PUT OUT MY EYES?
IT SEEMED LIKE HE WANTED TO HELP ME. OR MAYBE HE JUST DIDN'T WANT ME GOING OFF TOO SOON...
GIVE ME YOUR HAND, LIKE A YOUNG VIRGIN...
AND SUBMIT TO MY GUIDANCE.
HILARIOUS...BUT I WAS SUDDENLY VERY VERY CONSCIOUS OF THE FEEL OF AHMED'S HAND...
DID OMAR AND GHALIB REALLY JUST NOT NOTICE THAT MY EYES WERE CLOSED, AND AHMED WAS LEADING ME?
OR MAYBE THEY ALL DIDN'T WANT ME PRIMED TOO SOON.
WE WILL BE SAFE HERE.
IT'S RENTED BY AN IMAGINARY JEW NAMED JULIA KAUFFMAN. IT BELONGS TO JIHAD. IT BELONGS TO GOD.
REALLY?
WHEN I WAS GROWING UP IN NEW JERSEY, I FELT GOD PREFERRED PROPERTY ON THE UPPER EAST SIDE.

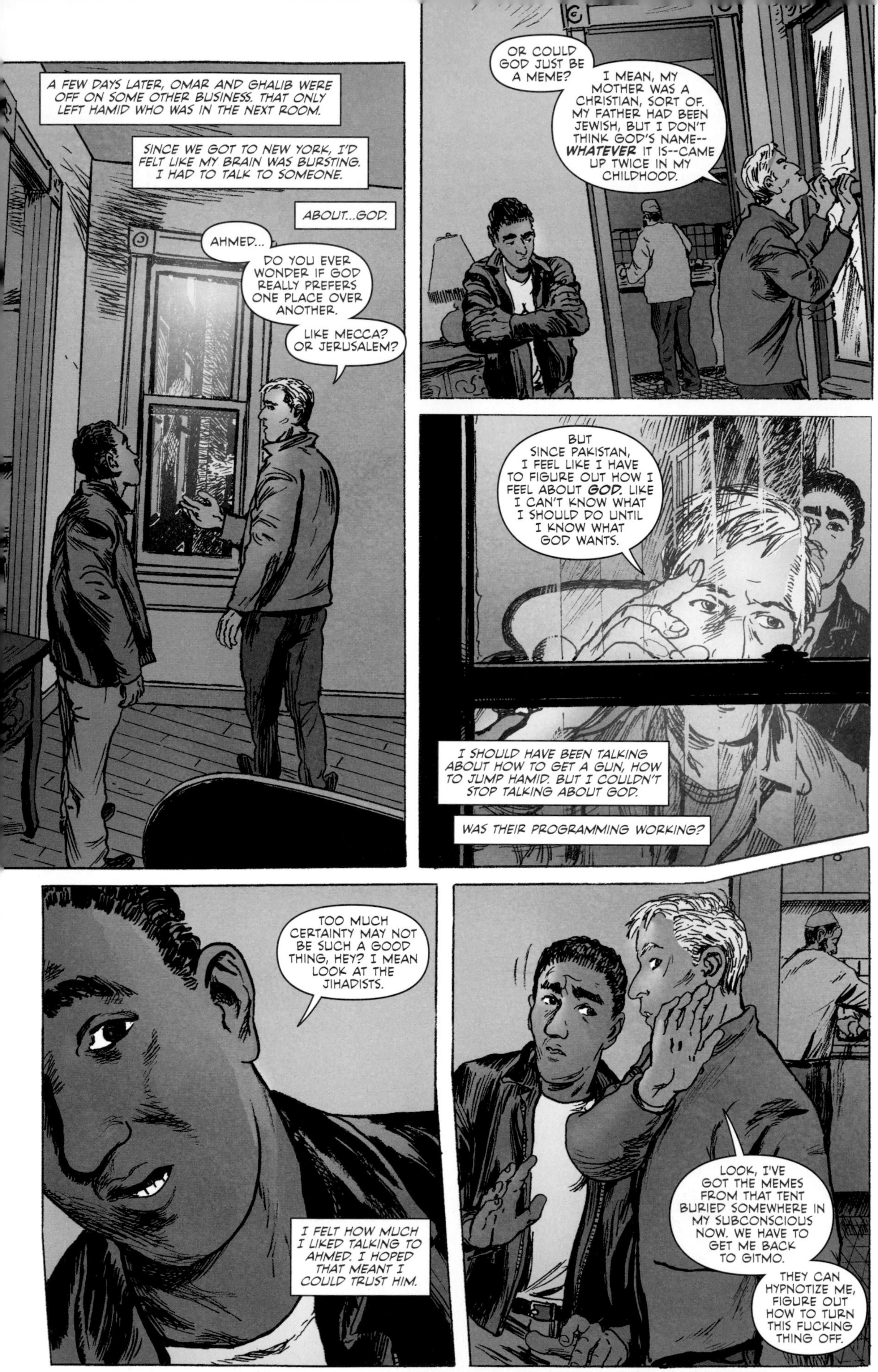
A FEW DAYS LATER, OMAR AND GHALIB WERE OFF ON SOME OTHER BUSINESS. THAT ONLY LEFT HAMID WHO WAS IN THE NEXT ROOM.
SINCE WE GOT TO NEW YORK, I'D FELT LIKE MY BRAIN WAS BURSTING. I HAD TO TALK TO SOMEONE.
ABOUT...GOD.
AHMED...
DO YOU EVER WONDER IF GOD REALLY PREFERS ONE PLACE OVER ANOTHER.
LIKE MECCA? OR JERUSALEM?
OR COULD GOD JUST BE A MEME?
I MEAN, MY MOTHER WAS A CHRISTIAN, SORT OF. MY FATHER HAD BEEN JEWISH, BUT I DON'T THINK GOD'S NAME--*WHATEVER* IT IS--CAME UP TWICE IN MY CHILDHOOD.
BUT SINCE PAKISTAN, I FEEL LIKE I HAVE TO FIGURE OUT HOW I FEEL ABOUT *GOD*. LIKE I CAN'T KNOW WHAT I SHOULD DO UNTIL I KNOW WHAT GOD WANTS.
I SHOULD HAVE BEEN TALKING ABOUT HOW TO GET A GUN, HOW TO JUMP HAMID. BUT I COULDN'T STOP TALKING ABOUT GOD.
WAS THEIR PROGRAMMING WORKING?
TOO MUCH CERTAINTY MAY NOT BE SUCH A GOOD THING, HEY? I MEAN LOOK AT THE JIHADISTS.
I FELT HOW MUCH I LIKED TALKING TO AHMED. I HOPED THAT MEANT I COULD TRUST HIM.
LOOK, I'VE GOT THE MEMES FROM THAT TENT BURIED SOMEWHERE IN MY SUBCONSCIOUS NOW. WE HAVE TO GET ME BACK TO GITMO.
THEY CAN HYPNOTIZE ME, FIGURE OUT HOW TO TURN THIS FUCKING THING OFF.

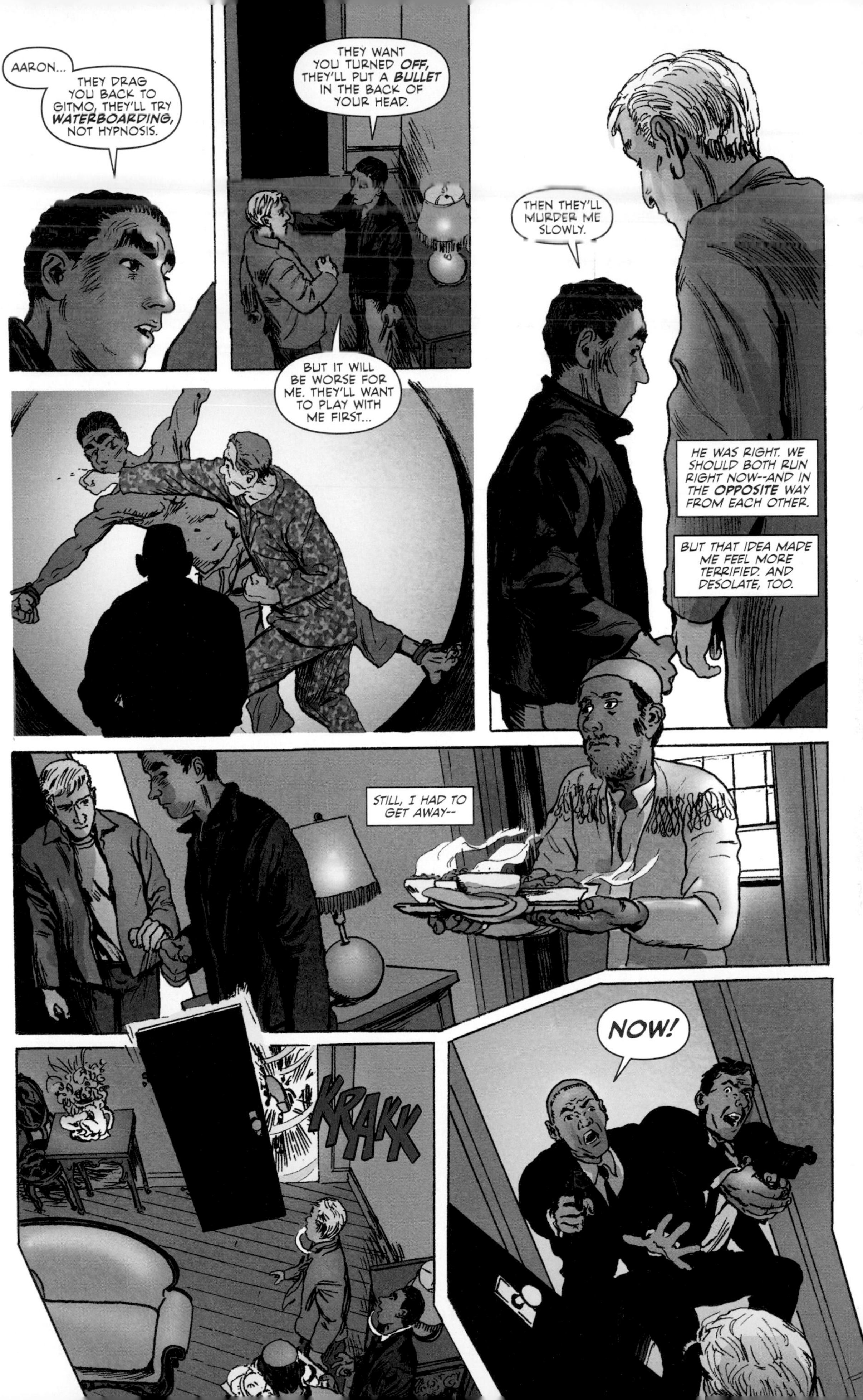
AARON...
THEY DRAG YOU BACK TO GITMO, THEY'LL TRY WATERBOARDING, NOT HYPNOSIS.
THEY WANT YOU TURNED OFF, THEY'LL PUT A BULLET IN THE BACK OF YOUR HEAD.
BUT IT WILL BE WORSE FOR ME. THEY'LL WANT TO PLAY WITH ME FIRST...
THEN THEY'LL MURDER ME SLOWLY.
HE WAS RIGHT. WE SHOULD BOTH RUN RIGHT NOW--AND IN THE OPPOSITE WAY FROM EACH OTHER.
BUT THAT IDEA MADE ME FEEL MORE TERRIFIED. AND DESOLATE, TOO.
STILL, I HAD TO GET AWAY--
KRAKK
NOW!

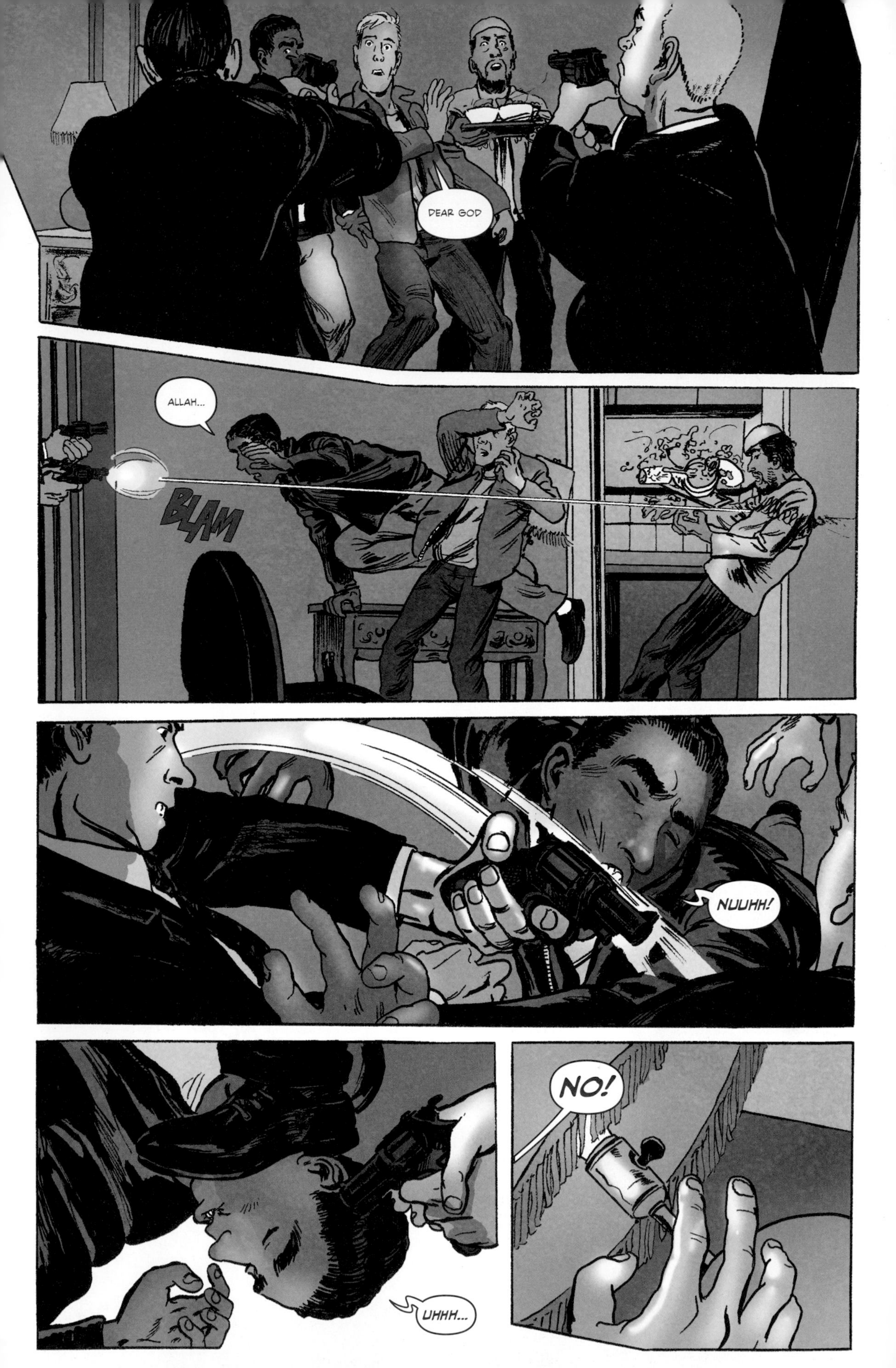
DEAR GOD
ALLAH...
BLAM
NUUHH!
UHHH...
NO!

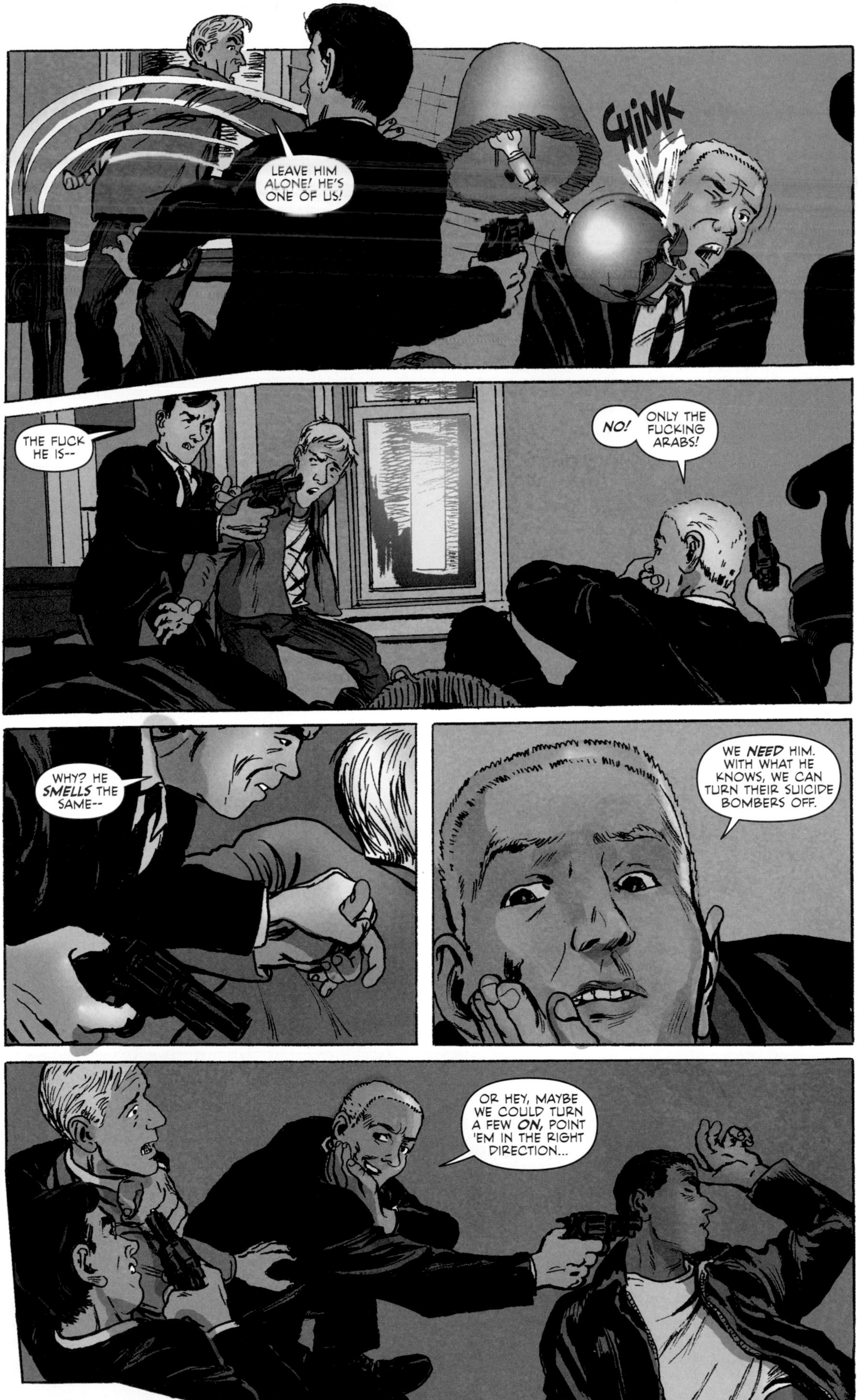
LEAVE HIM ALONE! HE'S ONE OF US!
CHINK
THE FUCK HE IS--
NO!
ONLY THE FUCKING ARABS!
WHY? HE SMELLS THE SAME--
WE NEED HIM. WITH WHAT HE KNOWS, WE CAN TURN THEIR SUICIDE BOMBERS OFF.
OR HEY, MAYBE WE COULD TURN A FEW ON, POINT 'EM IN THE RIGHT DIRECTION...

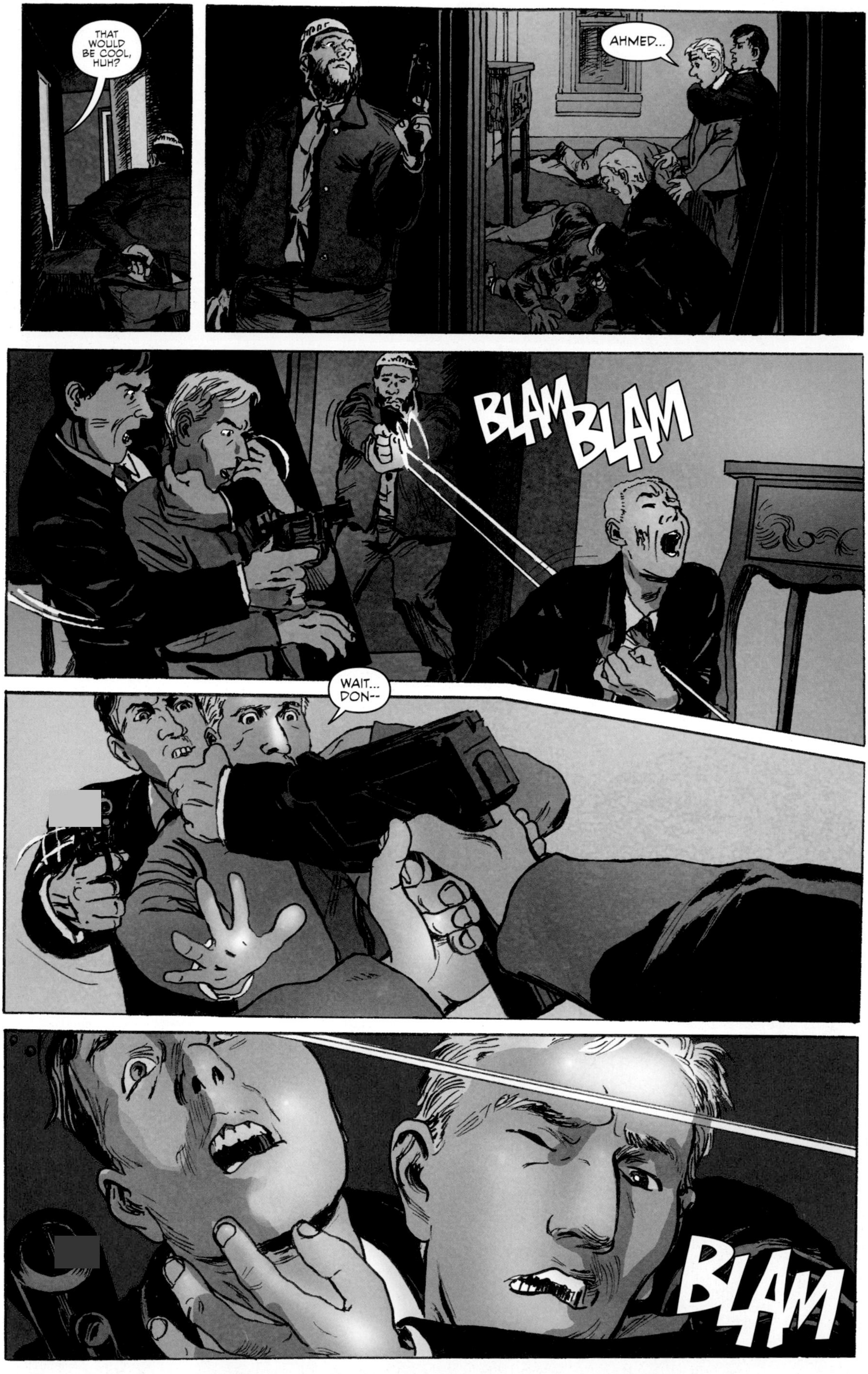
THAT WOULD BE COOL, HUH?
AHMED...
BLAM BLAM
WAIT... DON--
BLAM

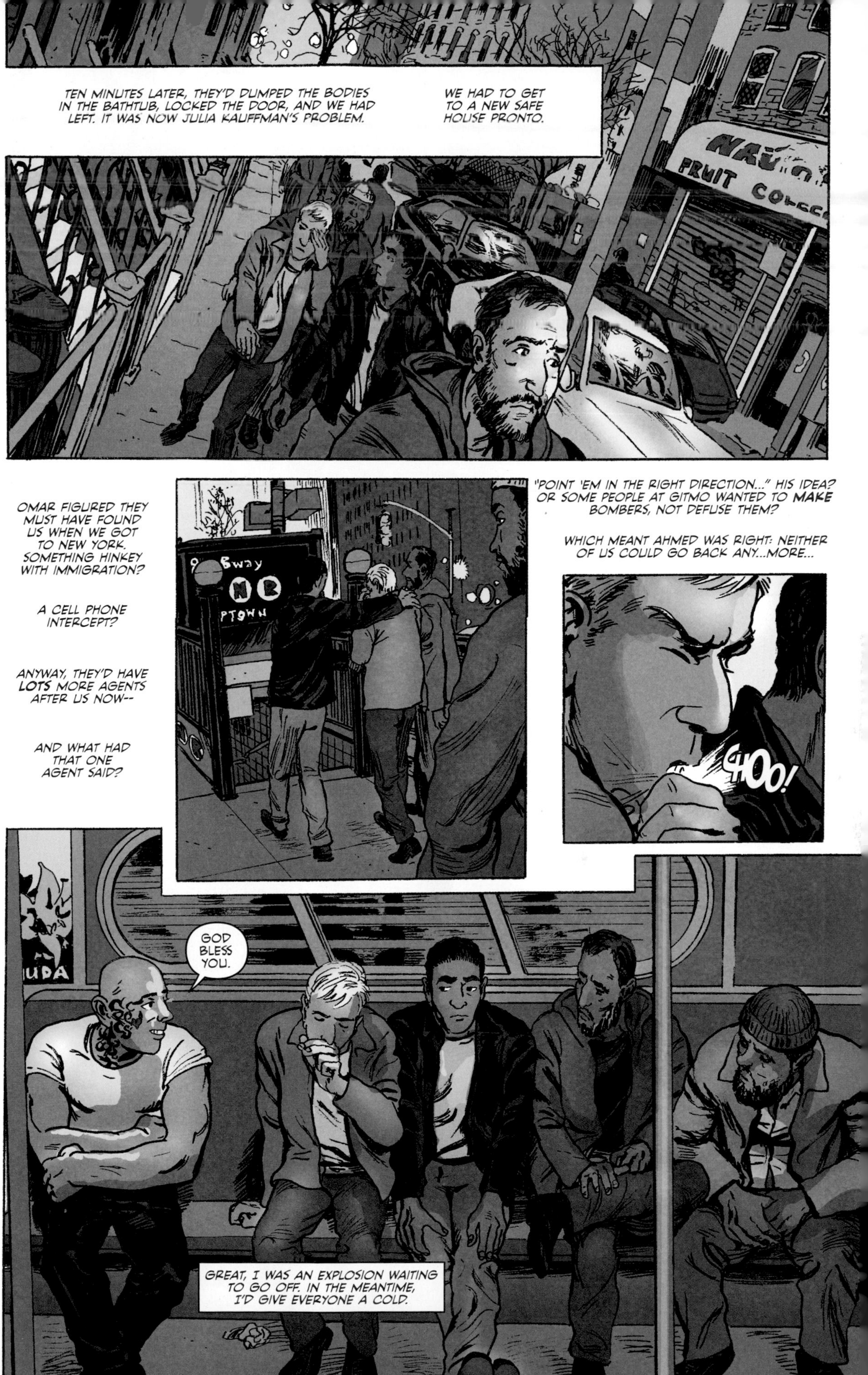
TEN MINUTES LATER, THEY'D DUMPED THE BODIES IN THE BATHTUB, LOCKED THE DOOR, AND WE HAD LEFT. IT WAS NOW JULIA KAUFFMAN'S PROBLEM.
WE HAD TO GET TO A NEW SAFE HOUSE PRONTO.
FRUIT
OMAR FIGURED THEY MUST HAVE FOUND US WHEN WE GOT TO NEW YORK. SOMETHING HINKEY WITH IMMIGRATION?
A CELL PHONE INTERCEPT?
ANYWAY, THEY'D HAVE **LOTS** MORE AGENTS AFTER US NOW--
AND WHAT HAD THAT ONE AGENT SAID?
Bway
N R
PTOWN
"POINT 'EM IN THE RIGHT DIRECTION..." HIS IDEA? OR SOME PEOPLE AT GITMO WANTED TO **MAKE** BOMBERS, NOT DEFUSE THEM?
WHICH MEANT AHMED WAS RIGHT: NEITHER OF US COULD GO BACK ANY...MORE...
CHOO!
GOD BLESS YOU.
GREAT, I WAS AN EXPLOSION WAITING TO GO OFF. IN THE MEANTIME, I'D GIVE EVERYONE A COLD.

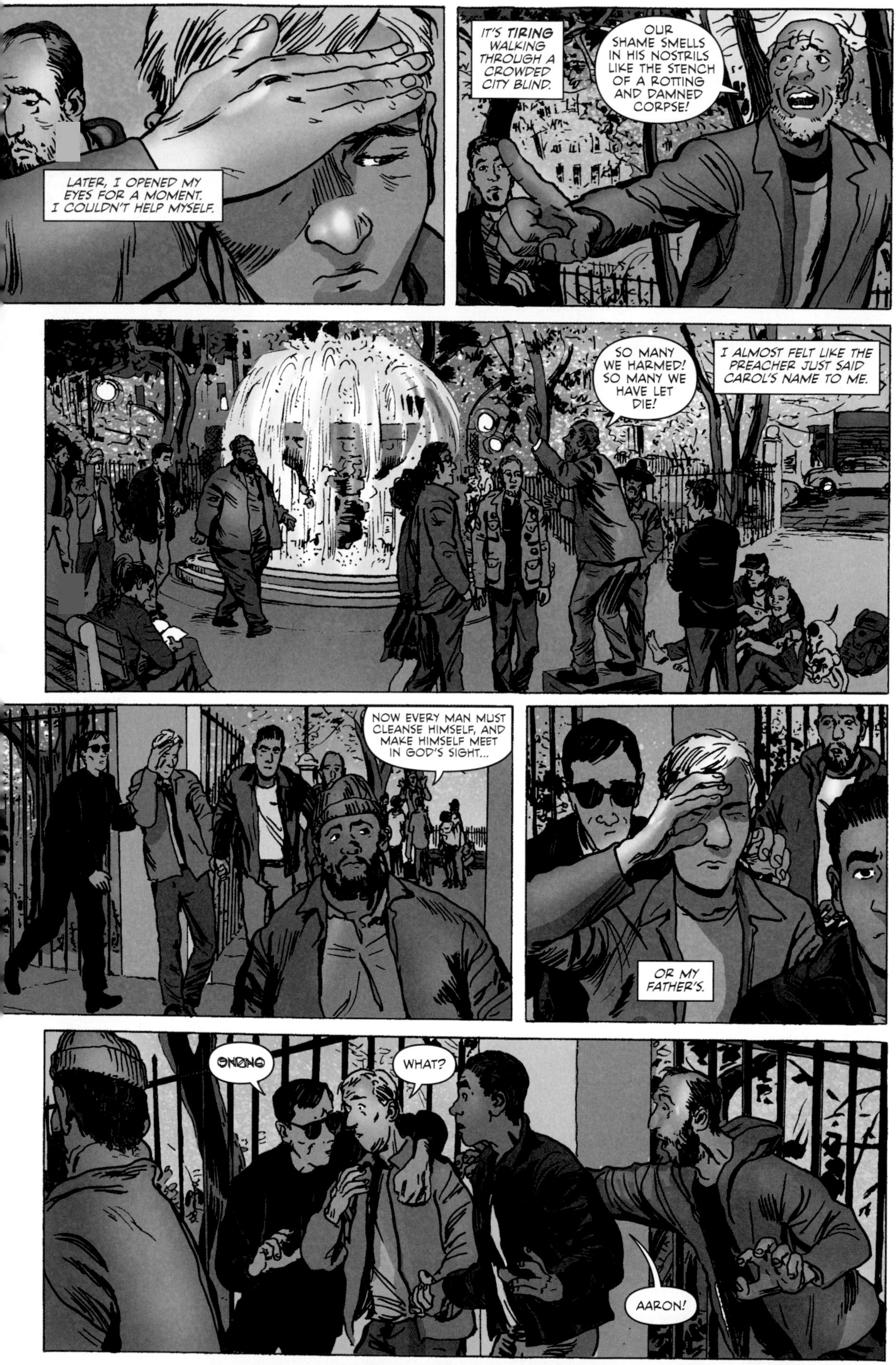
LATER, I OPENED MY EYES FOR A MOMENT. I COULDN'T HELP MYSELF.
IT'S TIRING WALKING THROUGH A CROWDED CITY BLIND.
OUR SHAME SMELLS IN HIS NOSTRILS LIKE THE STENCH OF A ROTTING AND DAMNED CORPSE!
SO MANY WE HARMED! SO MANY WE HAVE LET DIE!
I ALMOST FELT LIKE THE PREACHER JUST SAID CAROL'S NAME TO ME.
NOW EVERY MAN MUST CLEANSE HIMSELF, AND MAKE HIMSELF MEET IN GOD'S SIGHT...
OR MY FATHER'S.
WHAT?
AARON!

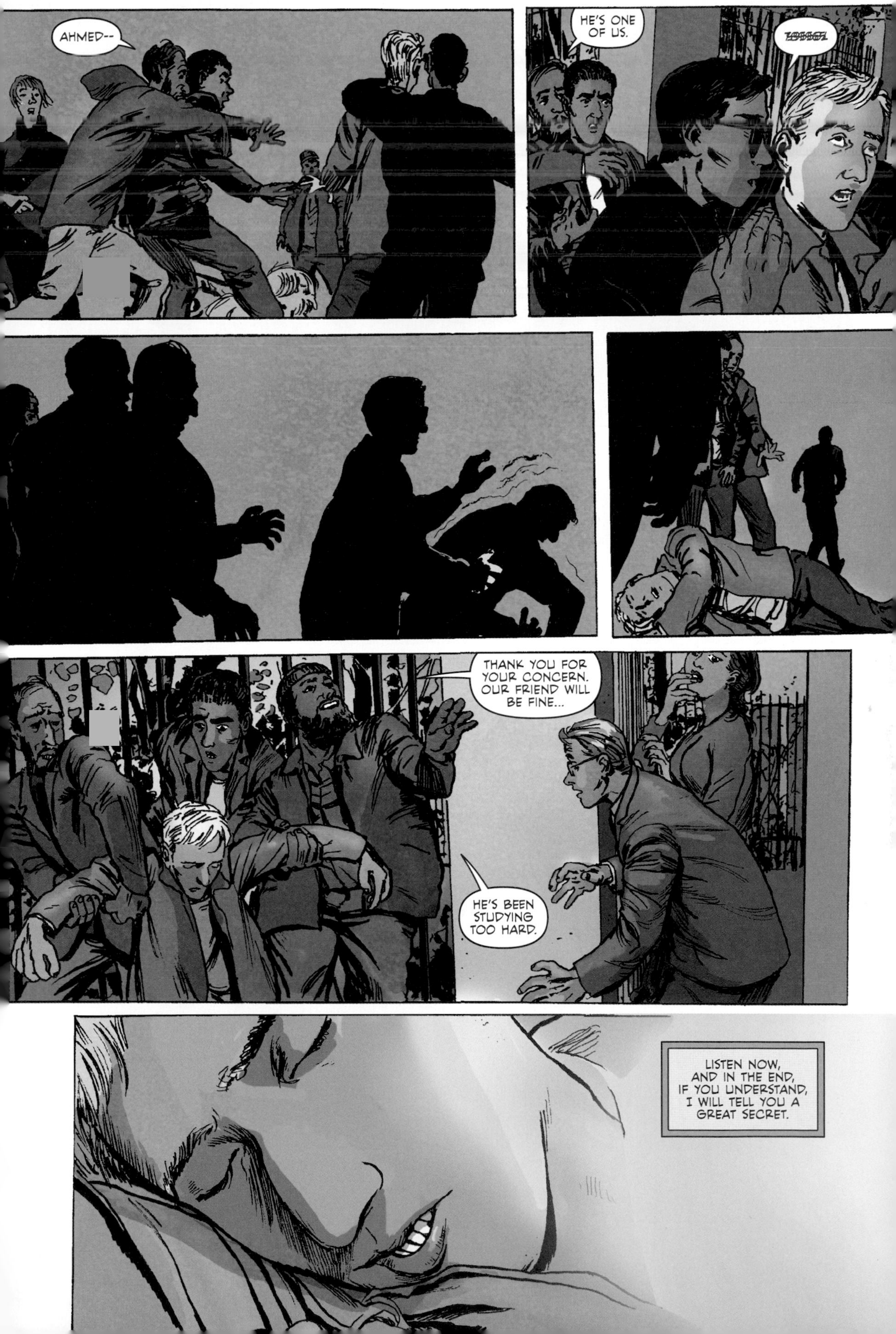
AHMED--
HE'S ONE OF US.
THANK YOU FOR YOUR CONCERN. OUR FRIEND WILL BE FINE...
HE'S BEEN STUDYING TOO HARD.
LISTEN NOW, AND IN THE END, IF YOU UNDERSTAND, I WILL TELL YOU A GREAT SECRET.

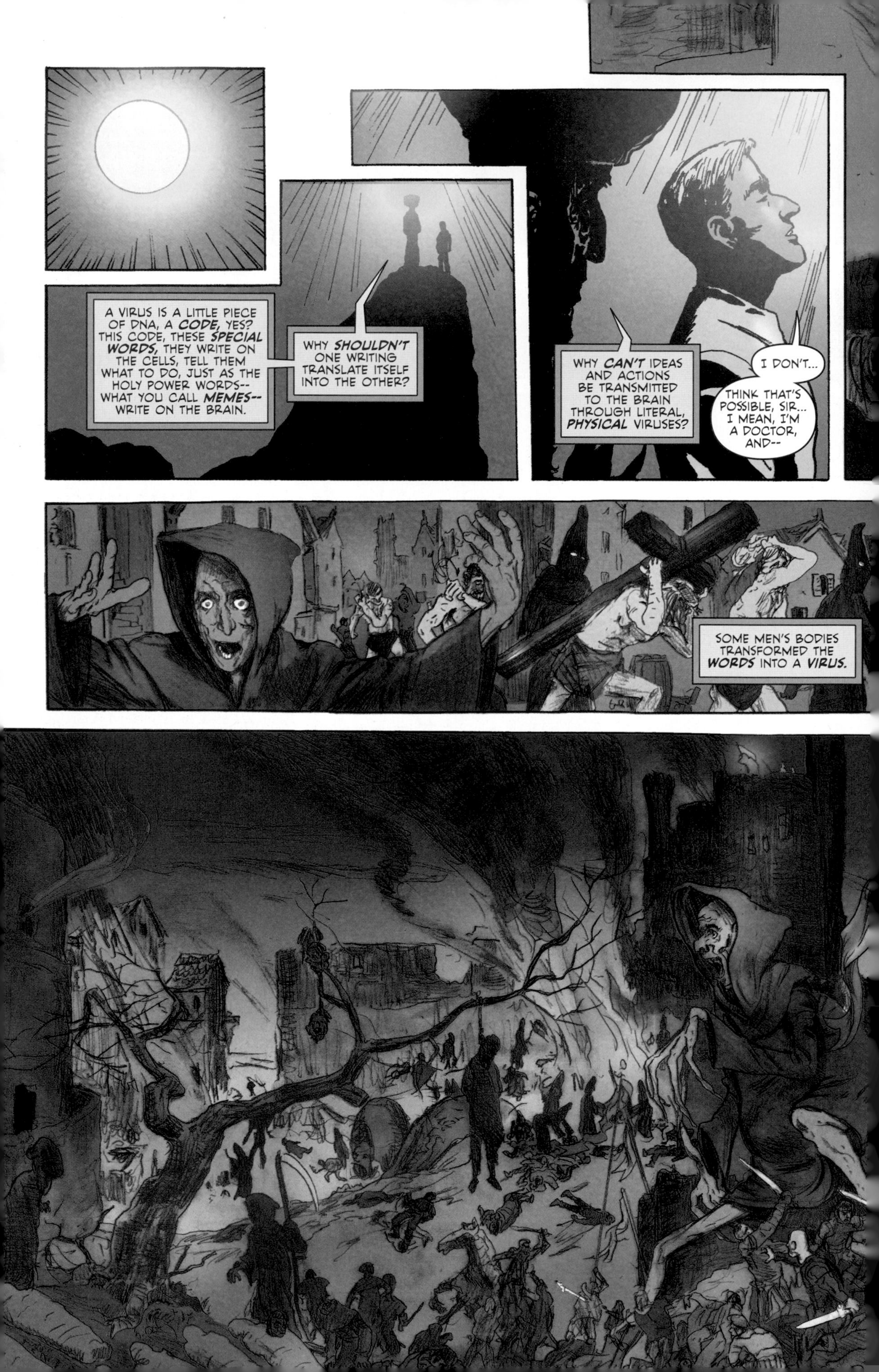
A VIRUS IS A LITTLE PIECE OF DNA, A CODE, YES? THIS CODE, THESE SPECIAL WORDS, THEY WRITE ON THE CELLS, TELL THEM WHAT TO DO, JUST AS THE HOLY POWER WORDS-- WHAT YOU CALL MEMES-- WRITE ON THE BRAIN.
WHY SHOULDN'T ONE WRITING TRANSLATE ITSELF INTO THE OTHER?
WHY CAN'T IDEAS AND ACTIONS BE TRANSMITTED TO THE BRAIN THROUGH LITERAL, PHYSICAL VIRUSES?
I DON'T...
THINK THAT'S POSSIBLE, SIR... I MEAN, I'M A DOCTOR, AND--
SOME MEN'S BODIES TRANSFORMED THE WORDS INTO A VIRUS.

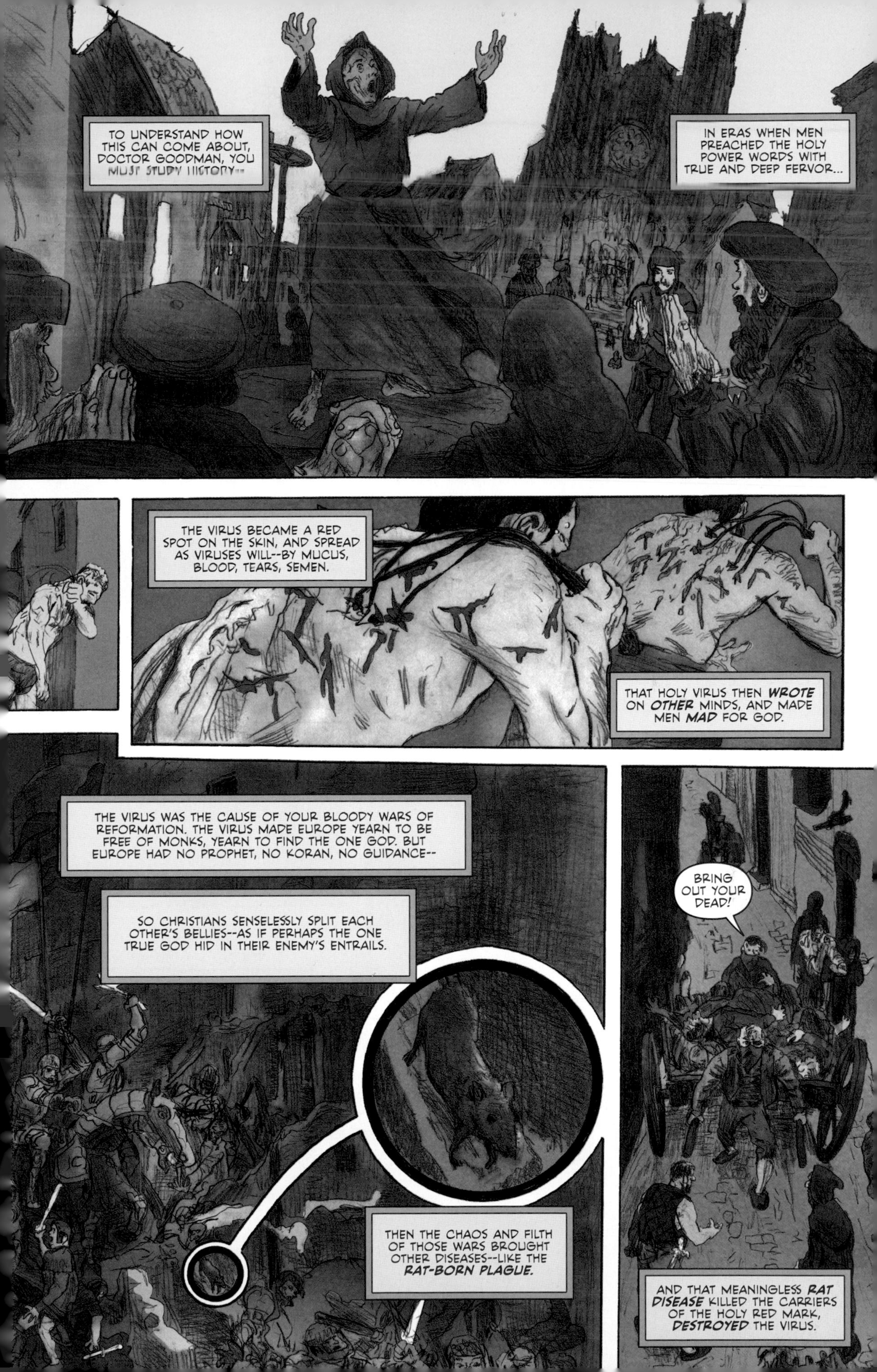
TO UNDERSTAND HOW THIS CAN COME ABOUT, DOCTOR GOODMAN, YOU MUST STUDY HISTORY--
IN ERAS WHEN MEN PREACHED THE HOLY POWER WORDS WITH TRUE AND DEEP FERVOR...
THE VIRUS BECAME A RED SPOT ON THE SKIN, AND SPREAD AS VIRUSES WILL--BY MUCUS, BLOOD, TEARS, SEMEN.
THAT HOLY VIRUS THEN WROTE ON OTHER MINDS, AND MADE MEN MAD FOR GOD.
THE VIRUS WAS THE CAUSE OF YOUR BLOODY WARS OF REFORMATION. THE VIRUS MADE EUROPE YEARN TO BE FREE OF MONKS, YEARN TO FIND THE ONE GOD. BUT EUROPE HAD NO PROPHET, NO KORAN, NO GUIDANCE--
SO CHRISTIANS SENSELESSLY SPLIT EACH OTHER'S BELLIES--AS IF PERHAPS THE ONE TRUE GOD HID IN THEIR ENEMY'S ENTRAILS.
THEN THE CHAOS AND FILTH OF THOSE WARS BROUGHT OTHER DISEASES--LIKE THE RAT-BORN PLAGUE.
BRING OUT YOUR DEAD!
AND THAT MEANINGLESS RAT DISEASE KILLED THE CARRIERS OF THE HOLY RED MARK, DESTROYED THE VIRUS.

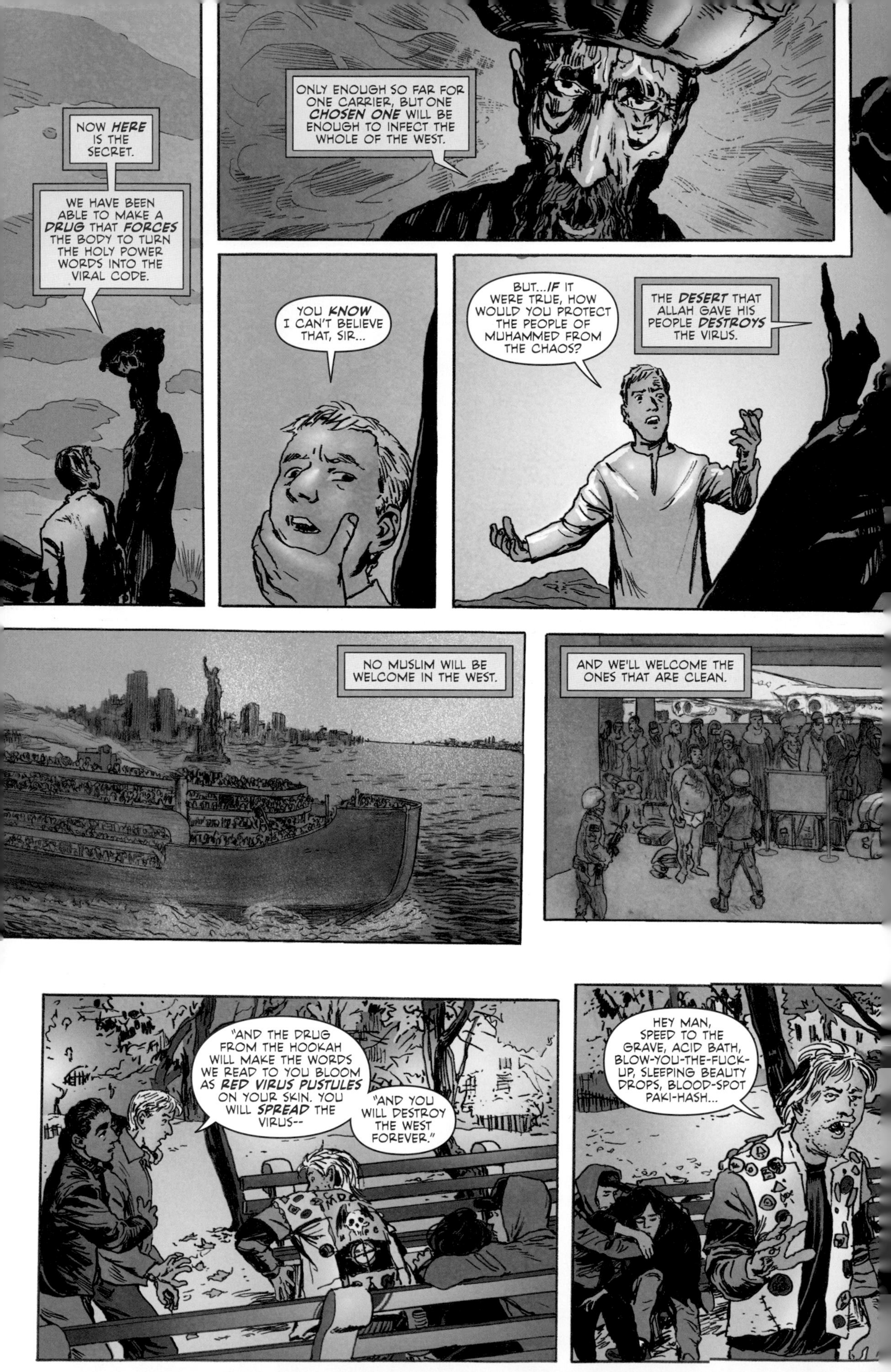
NOW HERE IS THE SECRET.
WE HAVE BEEN ABLE TO MAKE A DRUG THAT FORCES THE BODY TO TURN THE HOLY POWER WORDS INTO THE VIRAL CODE.
ONLY ENOUGH SO FAR FOR ONE CARRIER, BUT ONE CHOSEN ONE WILL BE ENOUGH TO INFECT THE WHOLE OF THE WEST.
YOU KNOW I CAN'T BELIEVE THAT, SIR...
BUT...IF IT WERE TRUE, HOW WOULD YOU PROTECT THE PEOPLE OF MUHAMMED FROM THE CHAOS?
THE DESERT THAT ALLAH GAVE HIS PEOPLE DESTROYS THE VIRUS.
NO MUSLIM WILL BE WELCOME IN THE WEST.
AND WE'LL WELCOME THE ONES THAT ARE CLEAN.
"AND THE DRUG FROM THE HOOKAH WILL MAKE THE WORDS WE READ TO YOU BLOOM AS RED VIRUS PUSTULES ON YOUR SKIN. YOU WILL SPREAD THE VIRUS--
"AND YOU WILL DESTROY THE WEST FOREVER."
HEY MAN, SPEED TO THE GRAVE, ACID BATH, BLOW-YOU-THE-FUCK-UP, SLEEPING BEAUTY DROPS, BLOOD-SPOT PAKI-HASH...

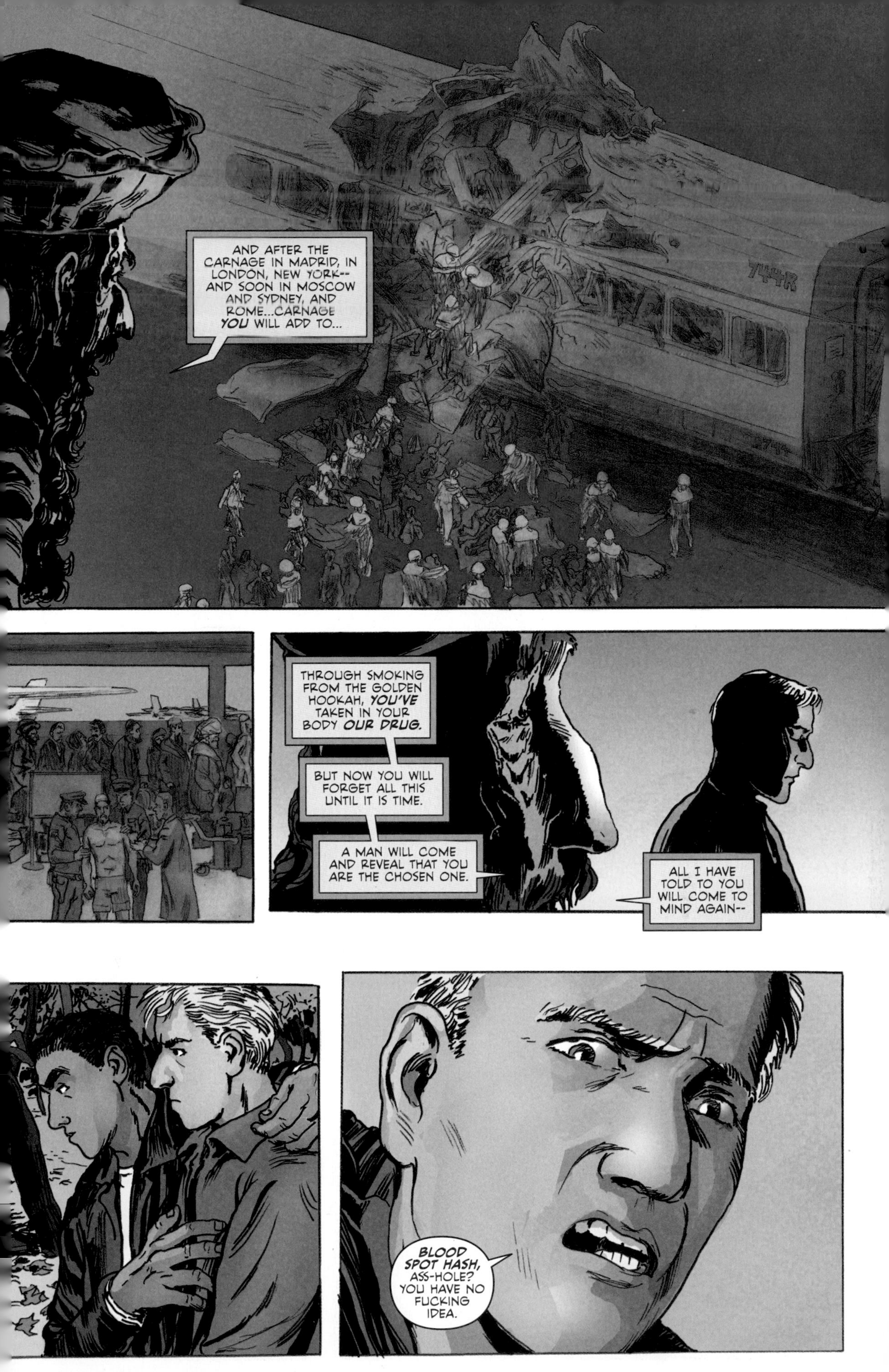
AND AFTER THE CARNAGE IN MADRID, IN LONDON, NEW YORK-- AND SOON IN MOSCOW AND SYDNEY, AND ROME...CARNAGE YOU WILL ADD TO...
744R
THROUGH SMOKING FROM THE GOLDEN HOOKAH, YOU'VE TAKEN IN YOUR BODY OUR DRUG.
BUT NOW YOU WILL FORGET ALL THIS UNTIL IT IS TIME.
A MAN WILL COME AND REVEAL THAT YOU ARE THE CHOSEN ONE.
ALL I HAVE TOLD TO YOU WILL COME TO MIND AGAIN--
BLOOD SPOT HASH, ASS-HOLE? YOU HAVE NO FUCKING IDEA.

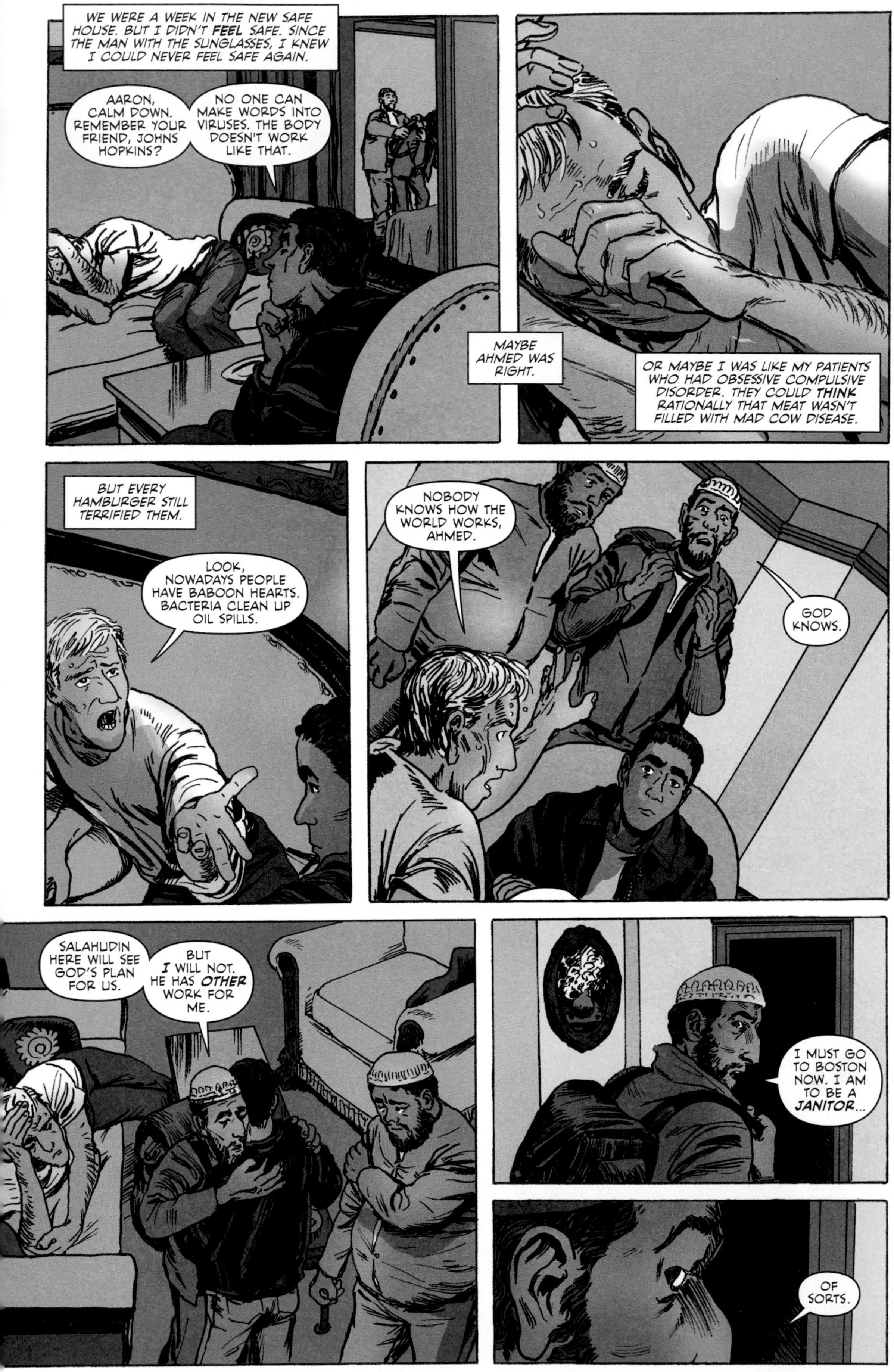
WE WERE A WEEK IN THE NEW SAFE HOUSE. BUT I DIDN'T **FEEL** SAFE. SINCE THE MAN WITH THE SUNGLASSES, I KNEW I COULD NEVER FEEL SAFE AGAIN.
AARON, CALM DOWN. REMEMBER YOUR FRIEND, JOHNS HOPKINS?
NO ONE CAN MAKE WORDS INTO VIRUSES. THE BODY DOESN'T WORK LIKE THAT.
MAYBE AHMED WAS RIGHT.
OR MAYBE I WAS LIKE MY PATIENTS WHO HAD OBSESSIVE COMPULSIVE DISORDER. THEY COULD **THINK** RATIONALLY THAT MEAT WASN'T FILLED WITH MAD COW DISEASE.
BUT EVERY HAMBURGER STILL TERRIFIED THEM.
LOOK, NOWADAYS PEOPLE HAVE BABOON HEARTS. BACTERIA CLEAN UP OIL SPILLS.
NOBODY KNOWS HOW THE WORLD WORKS, AHMED.
GOD KNOWS.
SALAHUDIN HERE WILL SEE GOD'S PLAN FOR US.
BUT *I* WILL NOT. HE HAS ***OTHER*** WORK FOR ME.
I MUST GO TO BOSTON NOW. I AM TO BE A ***JANITOR***...
OF SORTS.

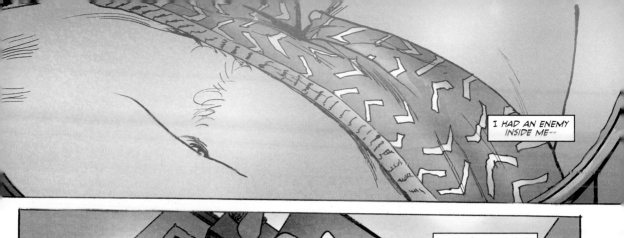

I HAD AN ENEMY INSIDE ME--

A VIRUS THAT WOULD PROGRAM MY BRAIN.

WORSE, IT WOULD BUILD PUSTULES ON MY ARMS AND LEGS--

AND THEN ESCAPE TO INFECT OTHERS.

I DON'T GET THIS VIRUS STORY.

IT DOESN'T FIT THEIR USUAL M.O.

ANYWAY, YOU'RE NOT *PRIMED* YET. YOU'RE TOO CALM.

DO I *LOOK* CALM, AHMED?

LYING IN MY UNDERWEAR, COMBING OVER MY BODY LIKE IT WAS A *CRIME SCENE* ON CSI?

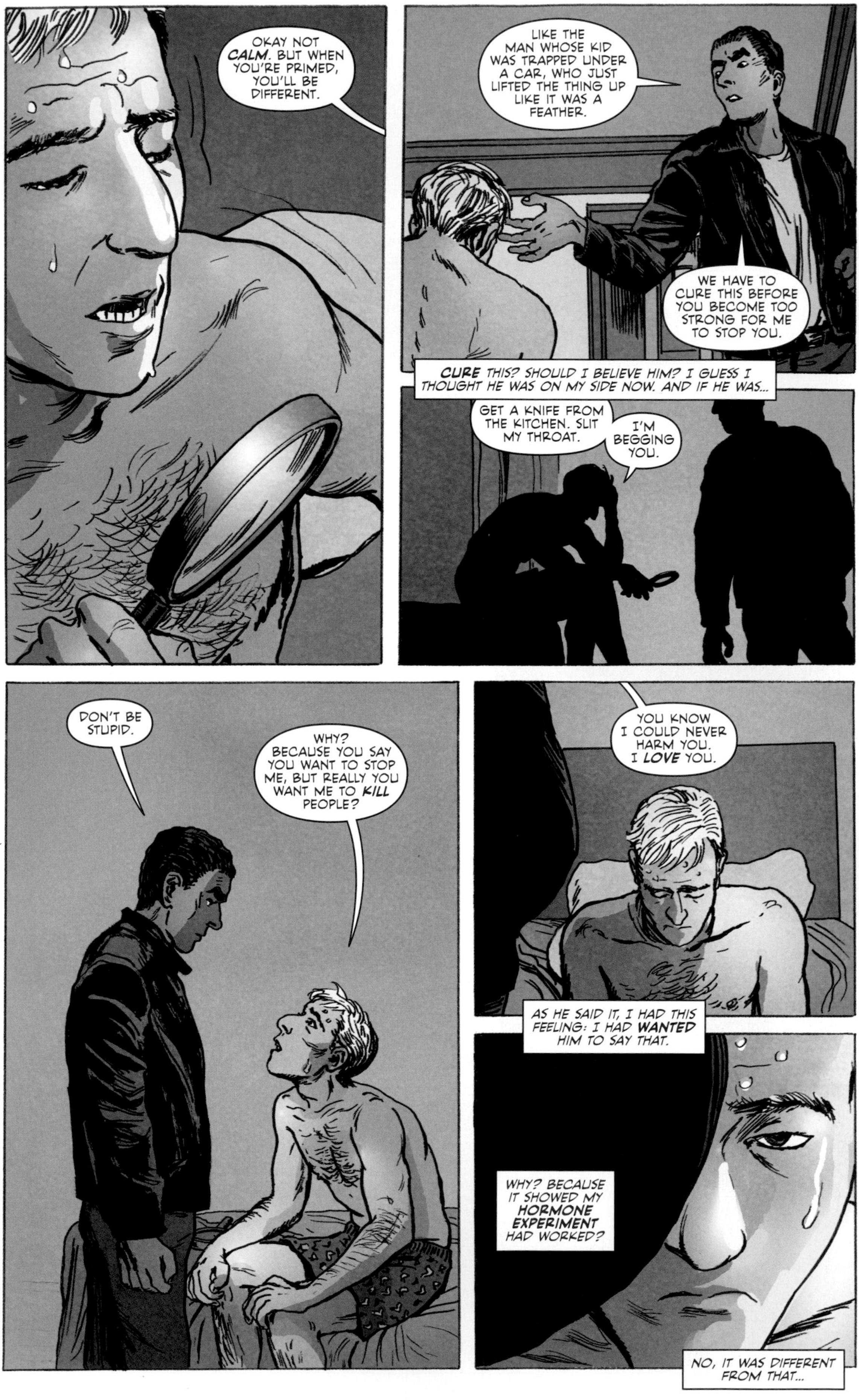
OKAY NOT CALM. BUT WHEN YOU'RE PRIMED, YOU'LL BE DIFFERENT.
LIKE THE MAN WHOSE KID WAS TRAPPED UNDER A CAR, WHO JUST LIFTED THE THING UP LIKE IT WAS A FEATHER.
WE HAVE TO CURE THIS BEFORE YOU BECOME TOO STRONG FOR ME TO STOP YOU.
CURE THIS? SHOULD I BELIEVE HIM? I GUESS I THOUGHT HE WAS ON MY SIDE NOW. AND IF HE WAS...
GET A KNIFE FROM THE KITCHEN. SLIT MY THROAT.
I'M BEGGING YOU.
DON'T BE STUPID.
WHY? BECAUSE YOU SAY YOU WANT TO STOP ME, BUT REALLY YOU WANT ME TO KILL PEOPLE?
YOU KNOW I COULD NEVER HARM YOU. I LOVE YOU.
AS HE SAID IT, I HAD THIS FEELING: I HAD WANTED HIM TO SAY THAT.
WHY? BECAUSE IT SHOWED MY HORMONE EXPERIMENT HAD WORKED?
NO, IT WAS DIFFERENT FROM THAT...

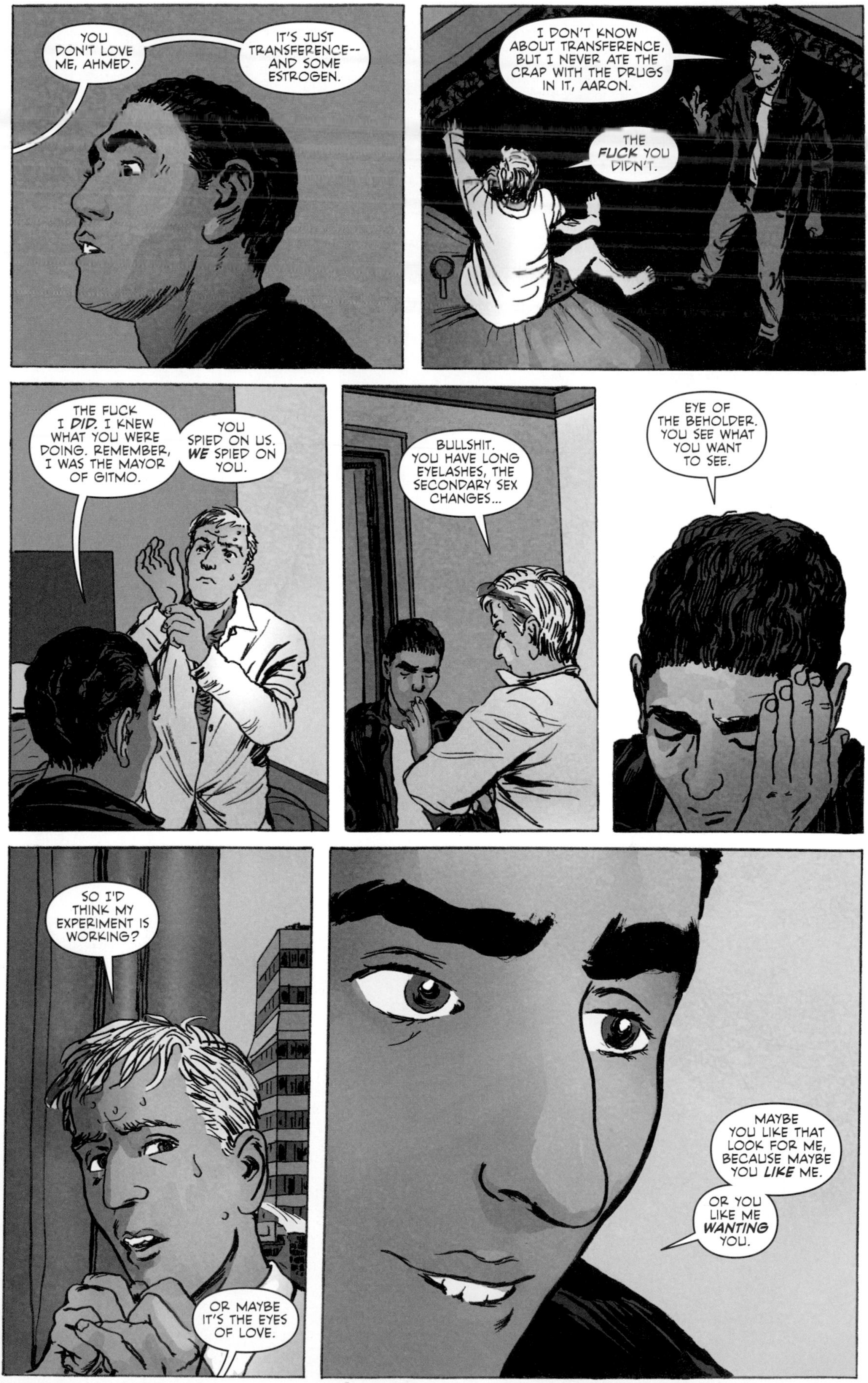
YOU DON'T LOVE ME, AHMED.
IT'S JUST TRANSFERENCE-- AND SOME ESTROGEN.
I DON'T KNOW ABOUT TRANSFERENCE, BUT I NEVER ATE THE CRAP WITH THE DRUGS IN IT, AARON.
THE FUCK YOU DIDN'T.
THE FUCK I DID. I KNEW WHAT YOU WERE DOING. REMEMBER, I WAS THE MAYOR OF GITMO.
YOU SPIED ON US. WE SPIED ON YOU.
BULLSHIT. YOU HAVE LONG EYELASHES, THE SECONDARY SEX CHANGES...
EYE OF THE BEHOLDER. YOU SEE WHAT YOU WANT TO SEE.
SO I'D THINK MY EXPERIMENT IS WORKING?
OR MAYBE IT'S THE EYES OF LOVE.
MAYBE YOU LIKE THAT LOOK FOR ME, BECAUSE MAYBE YOU LIKE ME.
OR YOU LIKE ME WANTING YOU.

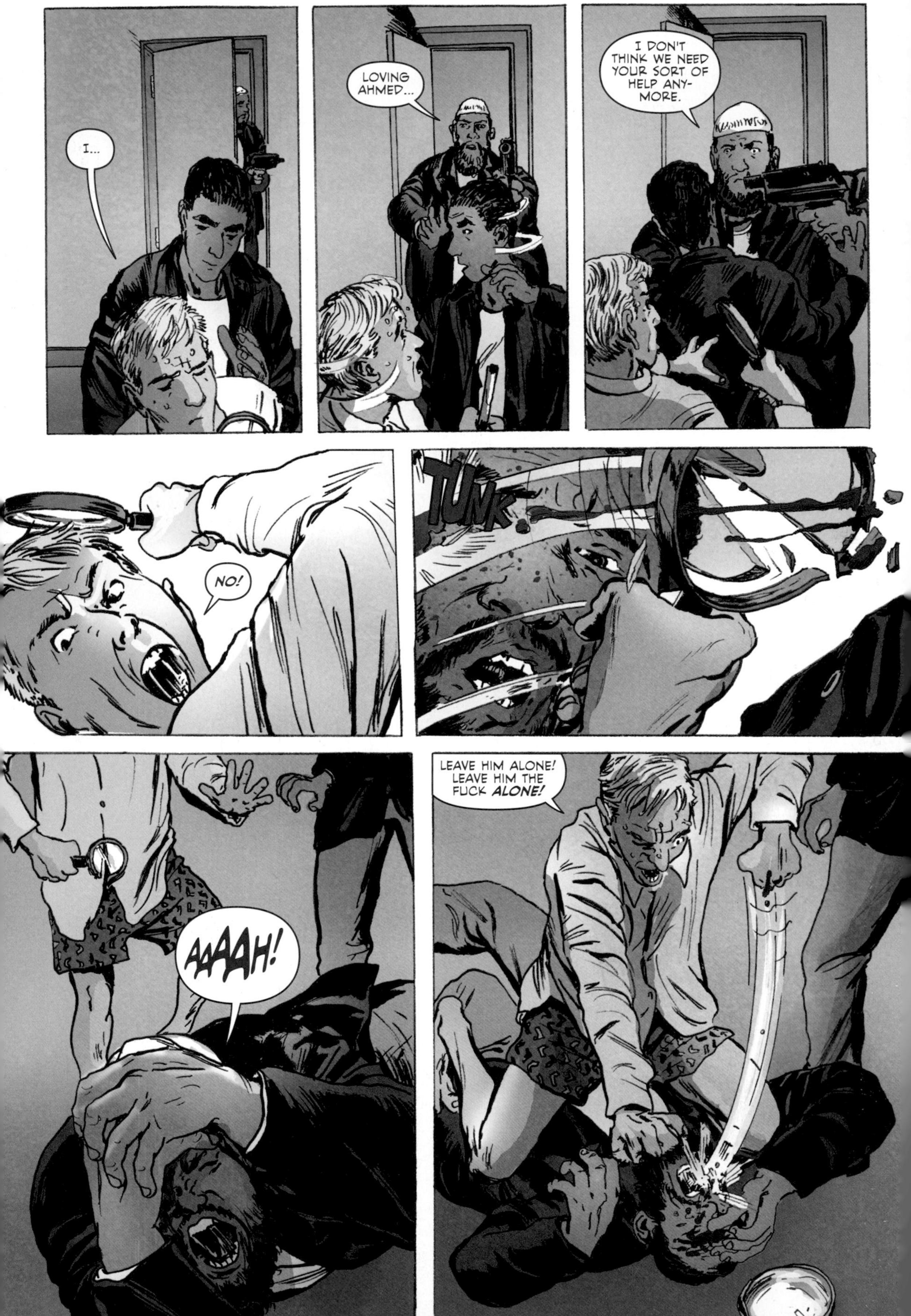
I...
LOVING AHMED...
I DON'T THINK WE NEED YOUR SORT OF HELP ANY-MORE.
NO!
TUNK
AAAAH!
LEAVE HIM ALONE! LEAVE HIM THE FUCK *ALONE!*

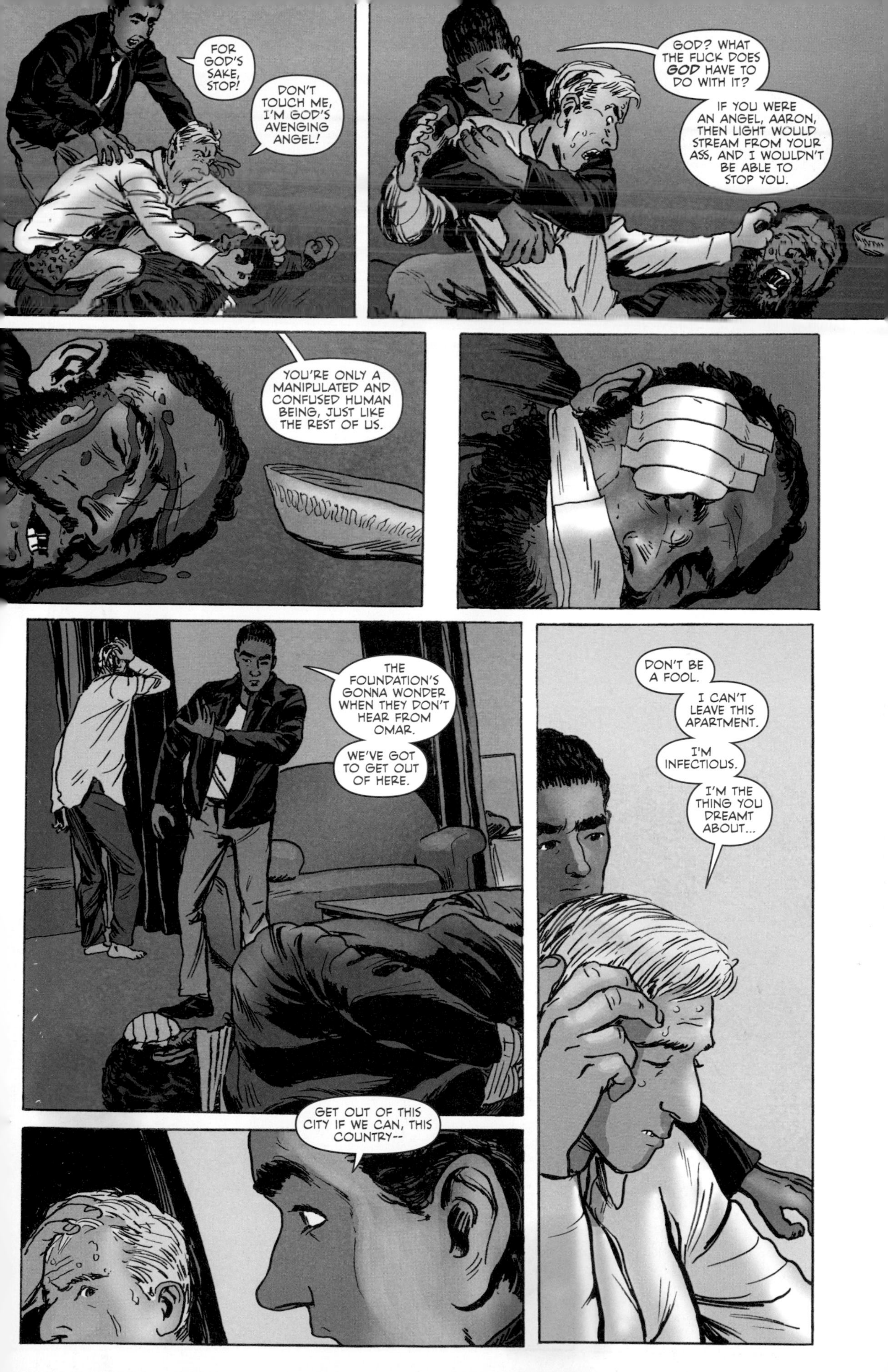
FOR GOD'S SAKE, STOP!
DON'T TOUCH ME, I'M GOD'S AVENGING ANGEL!
GOD? WHAT THE FUCK DOES GOD HAVE TO DO WITH IT?
IF YOU WERE AN ANGEL, AARON, THEN LIGHT WOULD STREAM FROM YOUR ASS, AND I WOULDN'T BE ABLE TO STOP YOU.
YOU'RE ONLY A MANIPULATED AND CONFUSED HUMAN BEING, JUST LIKE THE REST OF US.
THE FOUNDATION'S GONNA WONDER WHEN THEY DON'T HEAR FROM OMAR.
WE'VE GOT TO GET OUT OF HERE.
GET OUT OF THIS CITY IF WE CAN, THIS COUNTRY--
DON'T BE A FOOL.
I CAN'T LEAVE THIS APARTMENT.
I'M INFECTIOUS.
I'M THE THING YOU DREAMT ABOUT...

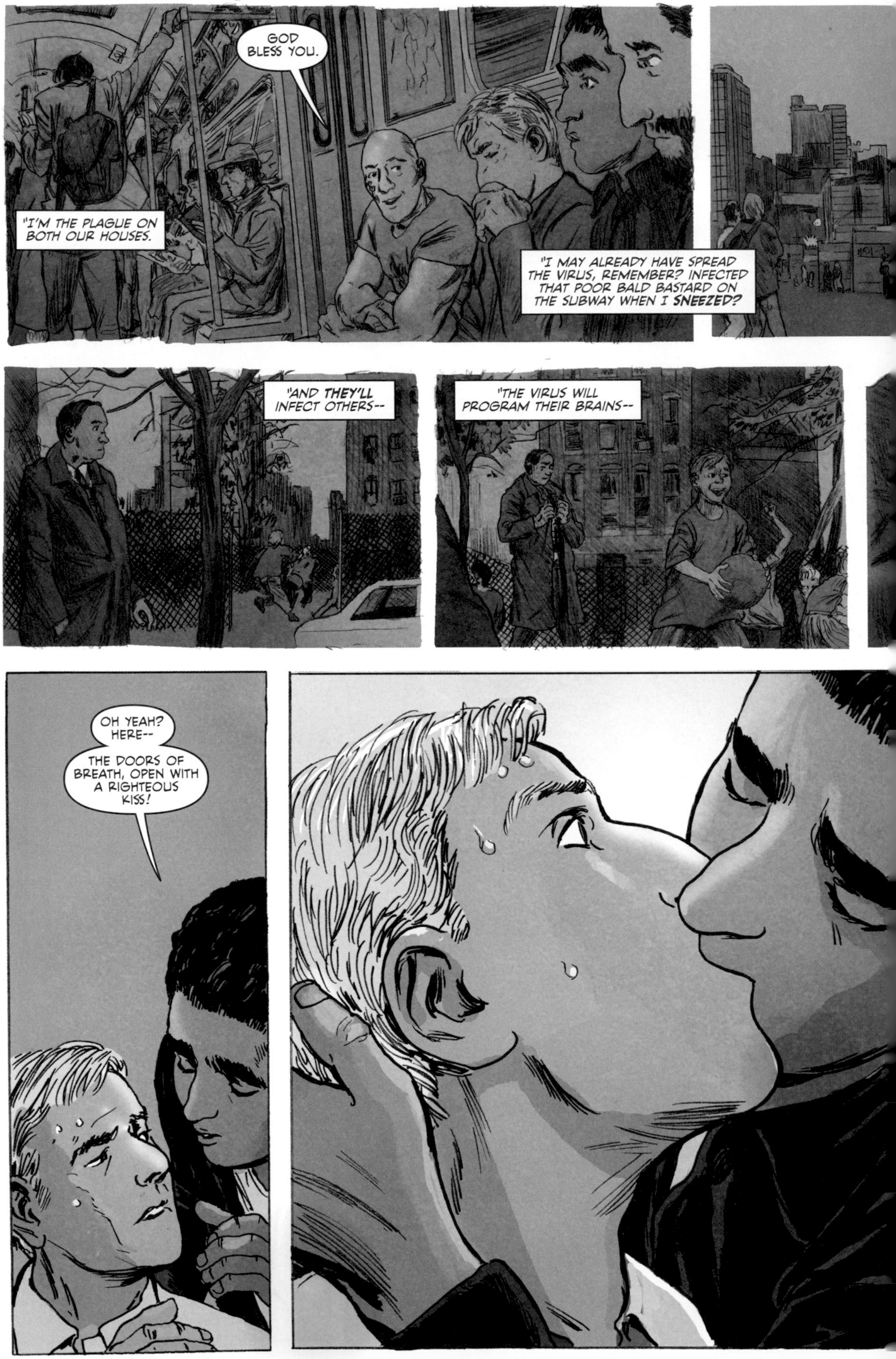
"I'M THE PLAGUE ON BOTH OUR HOUSES.
GOD BLESS YOU.
"I MAY ALREADY HAVE SPREAD THE VIRUS, REMEMBER? INFECTED THAT POOR BALD BASTARD ON THE SUBWAY WHEN I SNEEZED?
"AND THEY'LL INFECT OTHERS--
"THE VIRUS WILL PROGRAM THEIR BRAINS--
OH YEAH? HERE--
THE DOORS OF BREATH, OPEN WITH A RIGHTEOUS KISS!

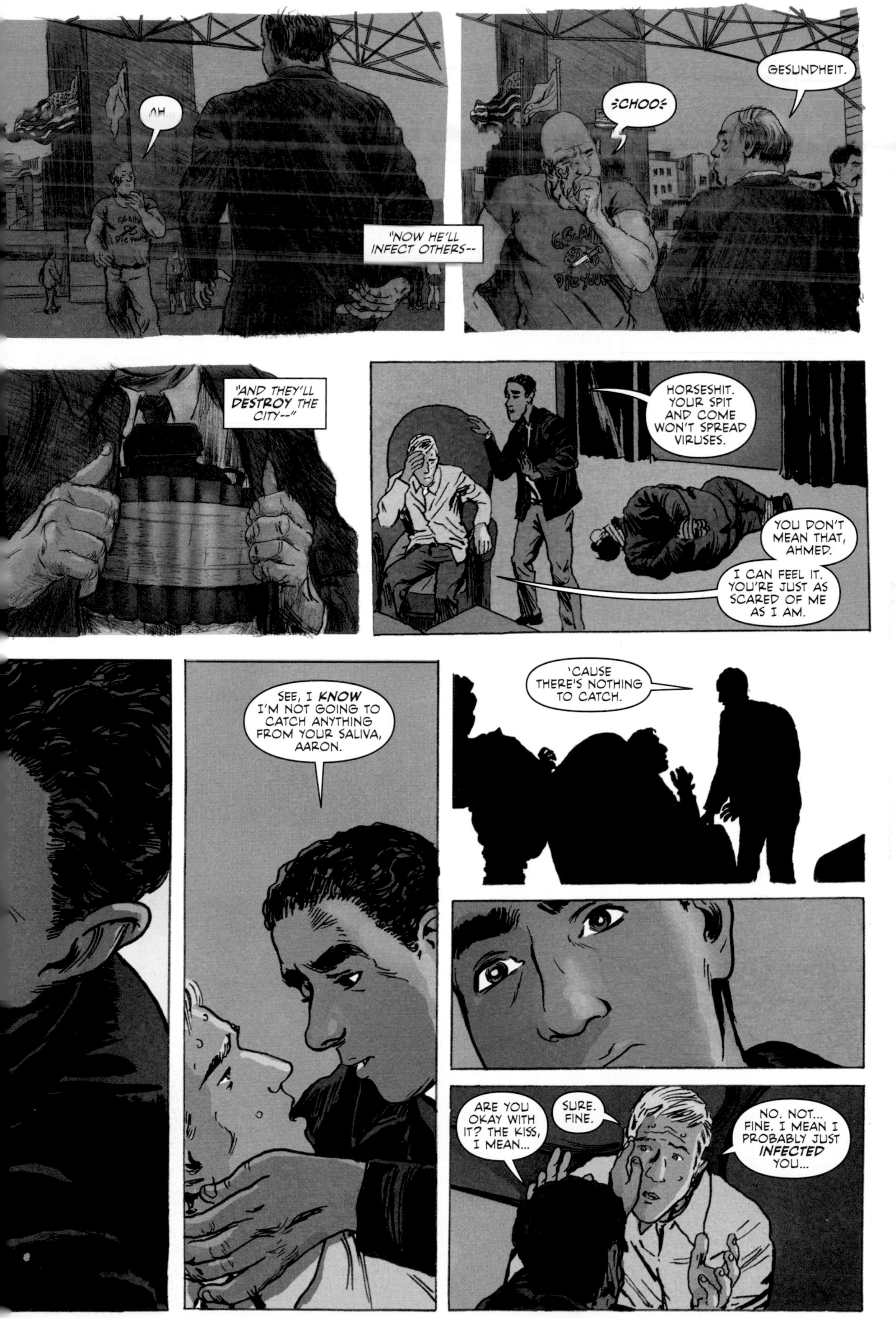
AH
"NOW HE'LL INFECT OTHERS--
CHOO
GESUNDHEIT.
"AND THEY'LL DESTROY THE CITY--"
HORSESHIT. YOUR SPIT AND COME WON'T SPREAD VIRUSES.
YOU DON'T MEAN THAT, AHMED.
I CAN FEEL IT. YOU'RE JUST AS SCARED OF ME AS I AM.
SEE, I KNOW I'M NOT GOING TO CATCH ANYTHING FROM YOUR SALIVA, AARON.
'CAUSE THERE'S NOTHING TO CATCH.
ARE YOU OKAY WITH IT? THE KISS, I MEAN...
SURE. FINE.
NO. NOT... FINE. I MEAN I PROBABLY JUST INFECTED YOU...

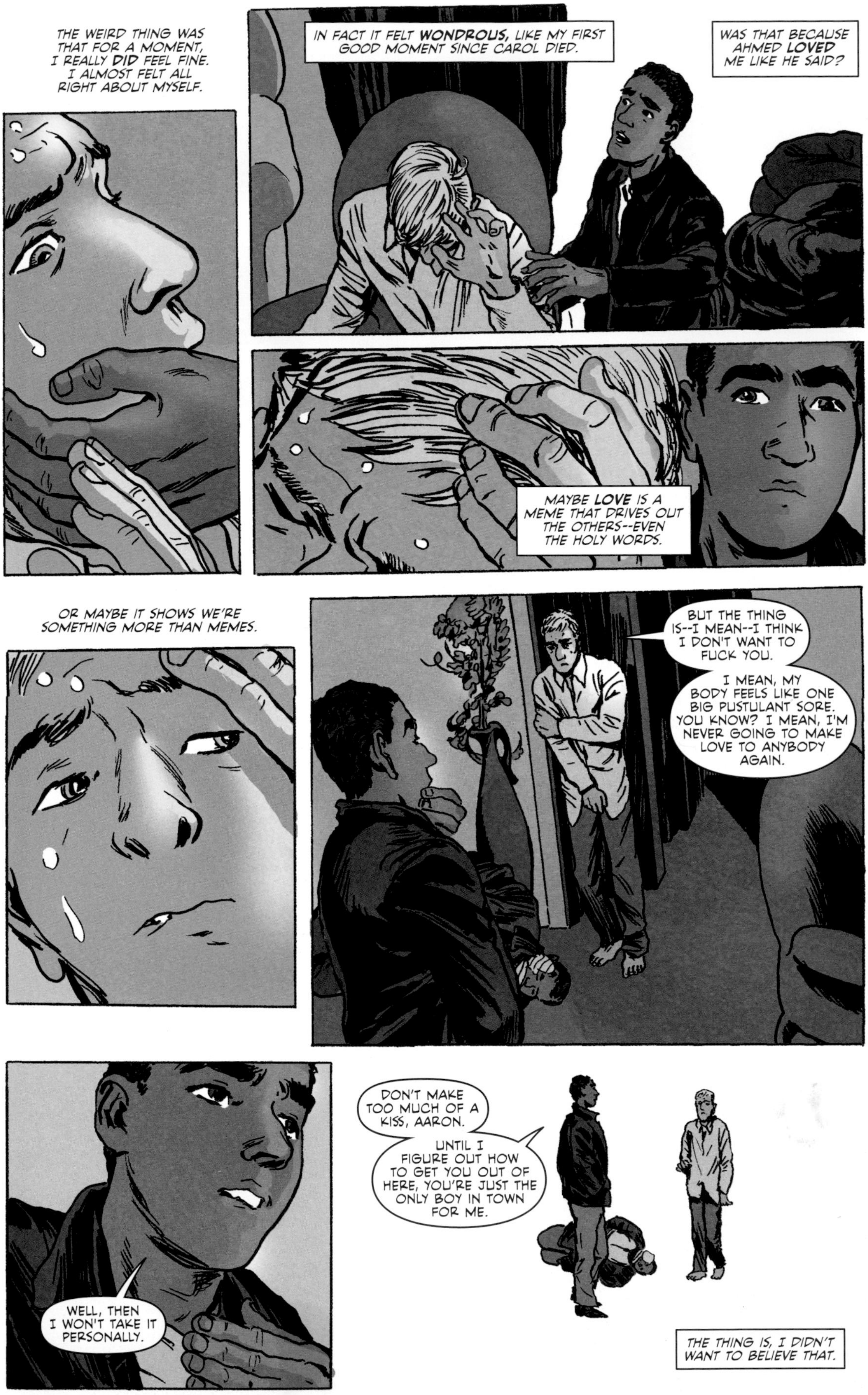
THE WEIRD THING WAS THAT FOR A MOMENT, I REALLY DID FEEL FINE. I ALMOST FELT ALL RIGHT ABOUT MYSELF.
IN FACT IT FELT WONDROUS, LIKE MY FIRST GOOD MOMENT SINCE CAROL DIED.
WAS THAT BECAUSE AHMED LOVED ME LIKE HE SAID?
MAYBE LOVE IS A MEME THAT DRIVES OUT THE OTHERS--EVEN THE HOLY WORDS.
OR MAYBE IT SHOWS WE'RE SOMETHING MORE THAN MEMES.
BUT THE THING IS--I MEAN--I THINK I DON'T WANT TO FUCK YOU.
I MEAN, MY BODY FEELS LIKE ONE BIG PUSTULANT SORE. YOU KNOW? I MEAN, I'M NEVER GOING TO MAKE LOVE TO ANYBODY AGAIN.
WELL, THEN I WON'T TAKE IT PERSONALLY.
DON'T MAKE TOO MUCH OF A KISS, AARON.
UNTIL I FIGURE OUT HOW TO GET YOU OUT OF HERE, YOU'RE JUST THE ONLY BOY IN TOWN FOR ME.
THE THING IS, I DIDN'T WANT TO BELIEVE THAT.

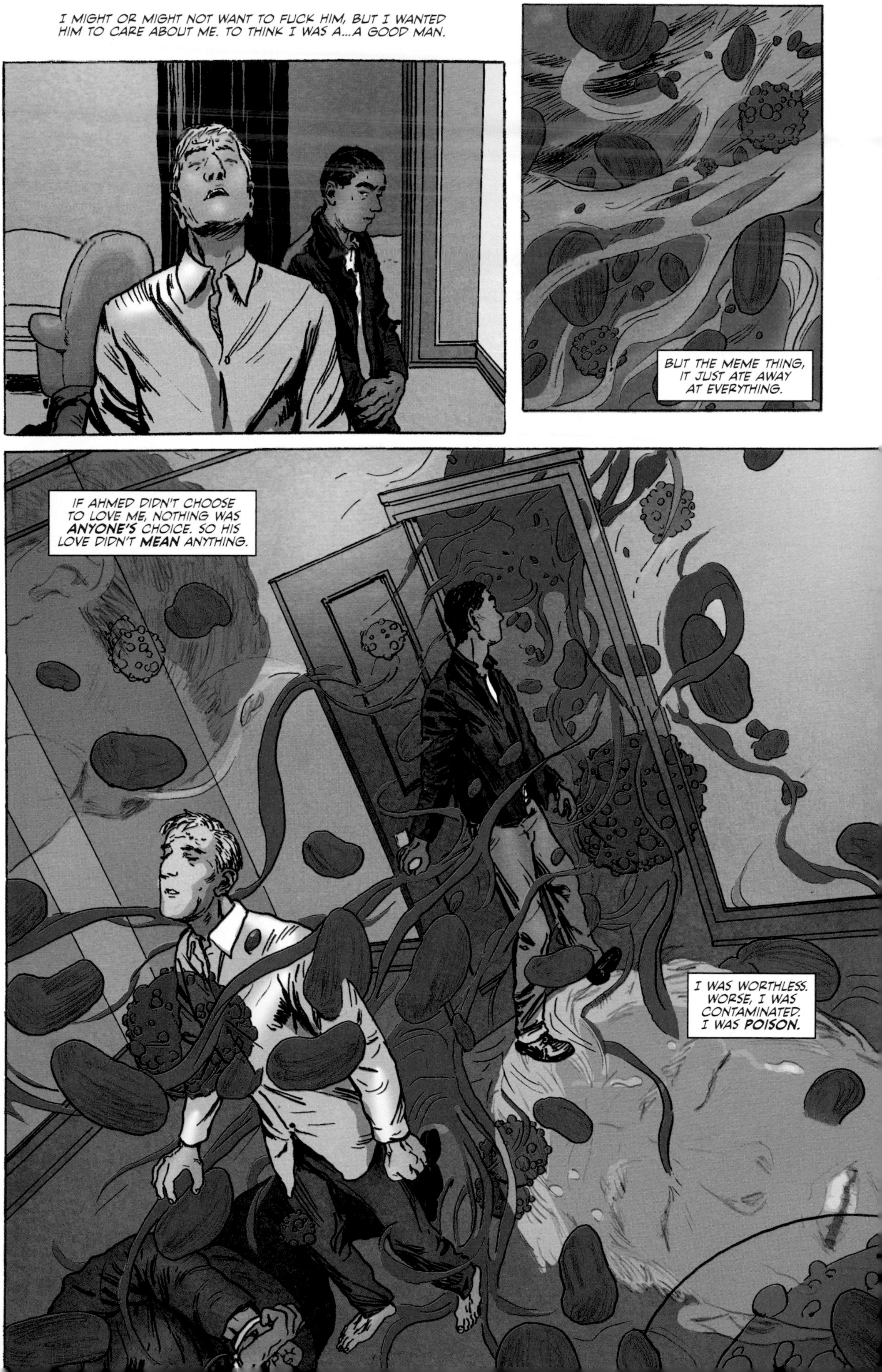
I MIGHT OR MIGHT NOT WANT TO FUCK HIM, BUT I WANTED HIM TO CARE ABOUT ME. TO THINK I WAS A...A GOOD MAN.
BUT THE MEME THING, IT JUST ATE AWAY AT EVERYTHING.
IF AHMED DIDN'T CHOOSE TO LOVE ME, NOTHING WAS ANYONE'S CHOICE. SO HIS LOVE DIDN'T MEAN ANYTHING.
I WAS WORTHLESS. WORSE, I WAS CONTAMINATED. I WAS POISON.

...AND SO WE LET THEM CROSS THE BORDER AND INFECT OUR COUNTRY WITH THEIR-- POISONOUS...

MAYBE IF I PLAYED THE RADIO LOUD ENOUGH, AND IF I DRANK ENOUGH-- I COULD FORGET FOR A SECOND--

...IDEAS THAT POLLUTE OUR KIDS'...

...FOOD, WATER...

...YOU KNOW ALL THAT COULD BE MADE IMPURE BY...

...PEOPLE BRING FILTH LIKE THAT...

...ACROSS OUR BORDERS EVERY SINGLE...

I KEPT CHANGING STATIONS.

I DON'T KNOW WHAT I WAS LOOKING FOR.

A CURE FOR THE TERROR-VIRUS?

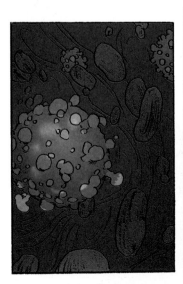

I'VE GOT TO GO FIND SOMETHING FOR YOU THAT WORKS BETTER THAN BOURBON, SO YOU'LL *LEAVE* THIS DEATH TRAP.

YOU BETTER TIE ME UP BEFORE YOU GO.

IF THE VIRUS BLOOMS IN MY MIND, I MIGHT-- I MIGHT--

HELL, I DON'T KNOW *WHAT* I MIGHT DO.

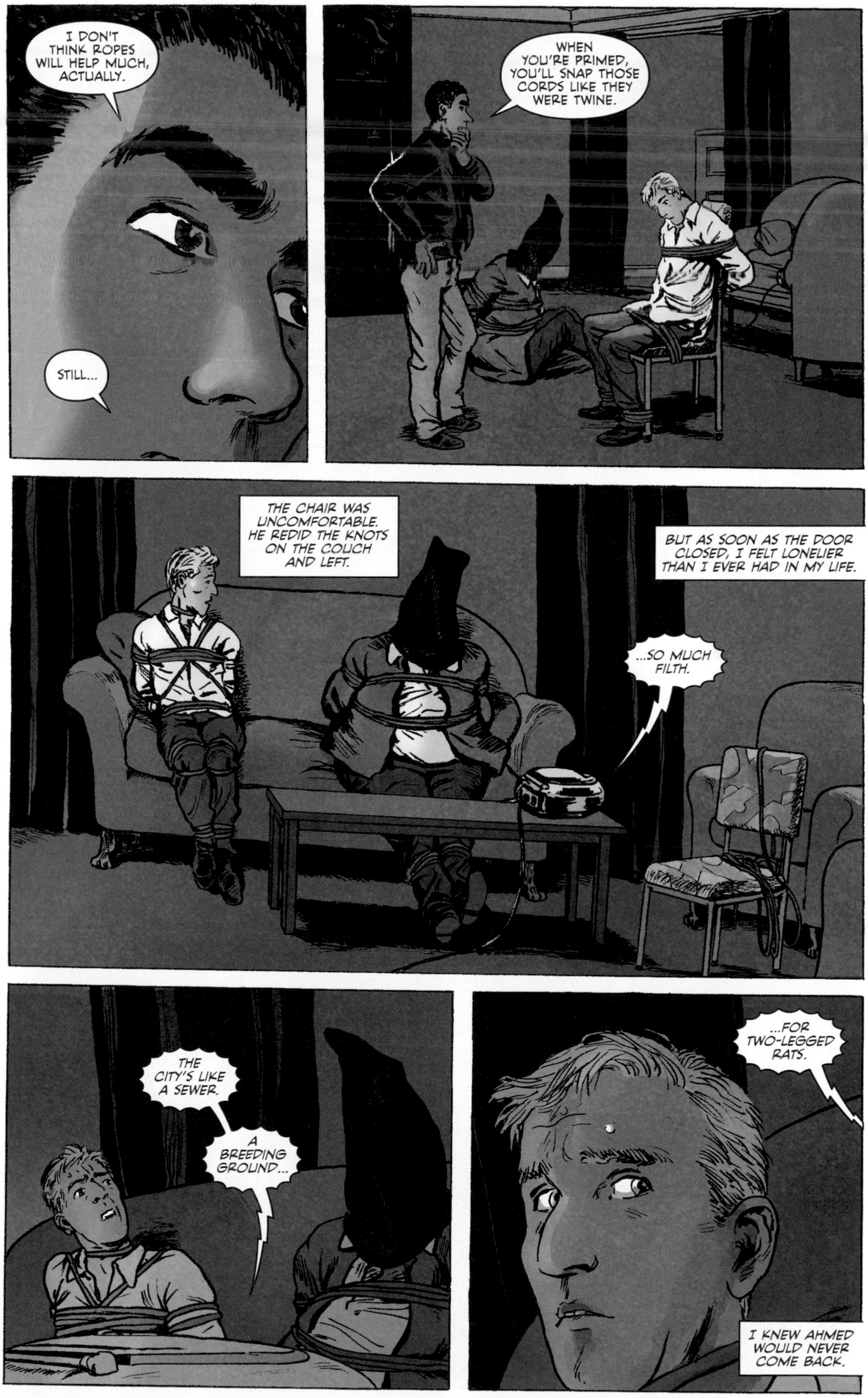
I DON'T THINK ROPES WILL HELP MUCH, ACTUALLY.
STILL...
WHEN YOU'RE PRIMED, YOU'LL SNAP THOSE CORDS LIKE THEY WERE TWINE.
THE CHAIR WAS UNCOMFORTABLE. HE REDID THE KNOTS ON THE COUCH AND LEFT.
BUT AS SOON AS THE DOOR CLOSED, I FELT LONELIER THAN I EVER HAD IN MY LIFE.
...SO MUCH FILTH.
THE CITY'S LIKE A SEWER.
A BREEDING GROUND...
...FOR TWO-LEGGED RATS.
I KNEW AHMED WOULD NEVER COME BACK.

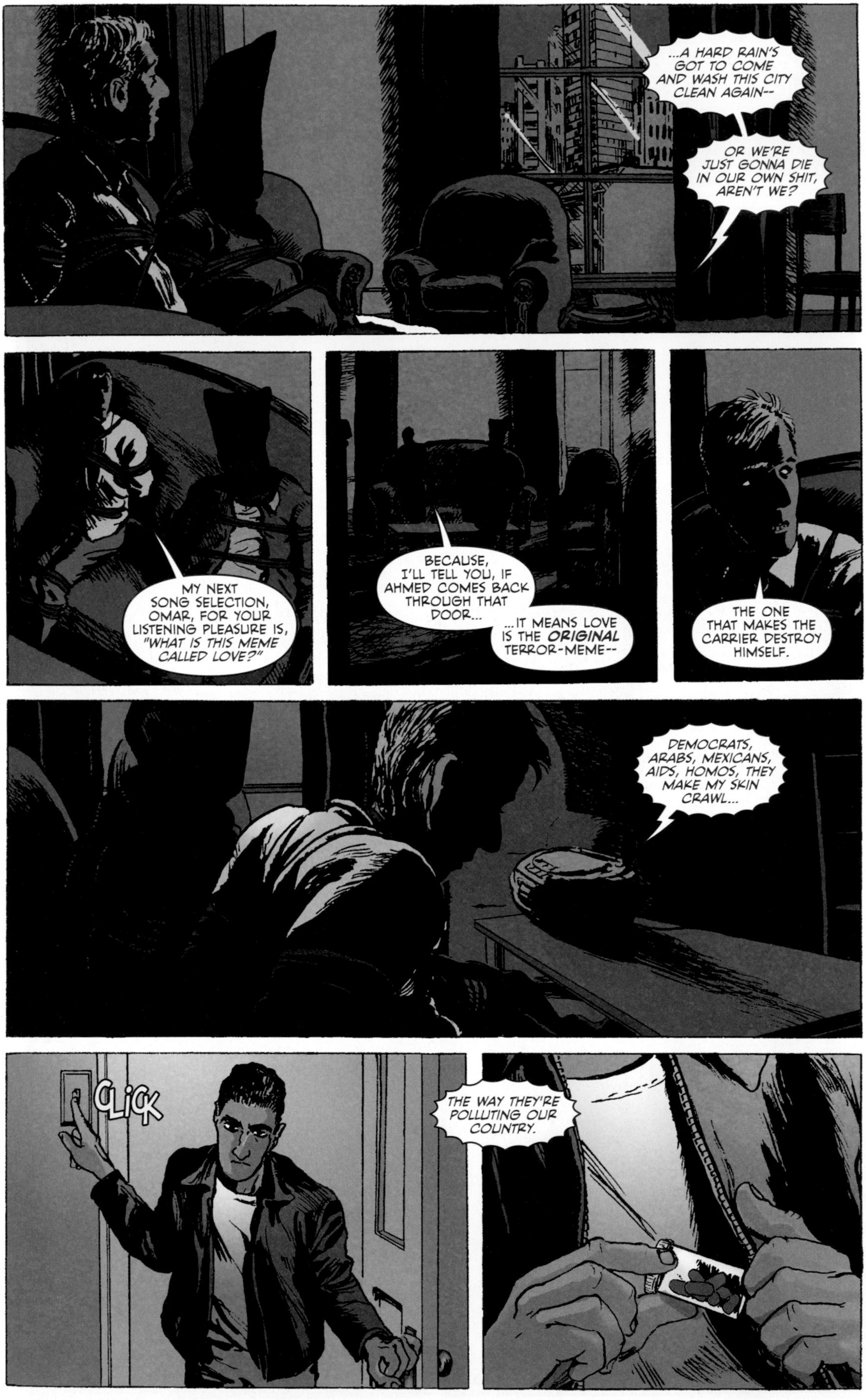
...A HARD RAIN'S GOT TO COME AND WASH THIS CITY CLEAN AGAIN--
OR WE'RE JUST GONNA DIE IN OUR OWN SHIT, AREN'T WE?
MY NEXT SONG SELECTION, OMAR, FOR YOUR LISTENING PLEASURE IS, "WHAT IS THIS MEME CALLED LOVE?"
BECAUSE, I'LL TELL YOU, IF AHMED COMES BACK THROUGH THAT DOOR...
...IT MEANS LOVE IS THE ORIGINAL TERROR-MEME--
THE ONE THAT MAKES THE CARRIER DESTROY HIMSELF.
DEMOCRATS, ARABS, MEXICANS, AIDS, HOMOS, THEY MAKE MY SKIN CRAWL...
CLICK
THE WAY THEY'RE POLLUTING OUR COUNTRY.

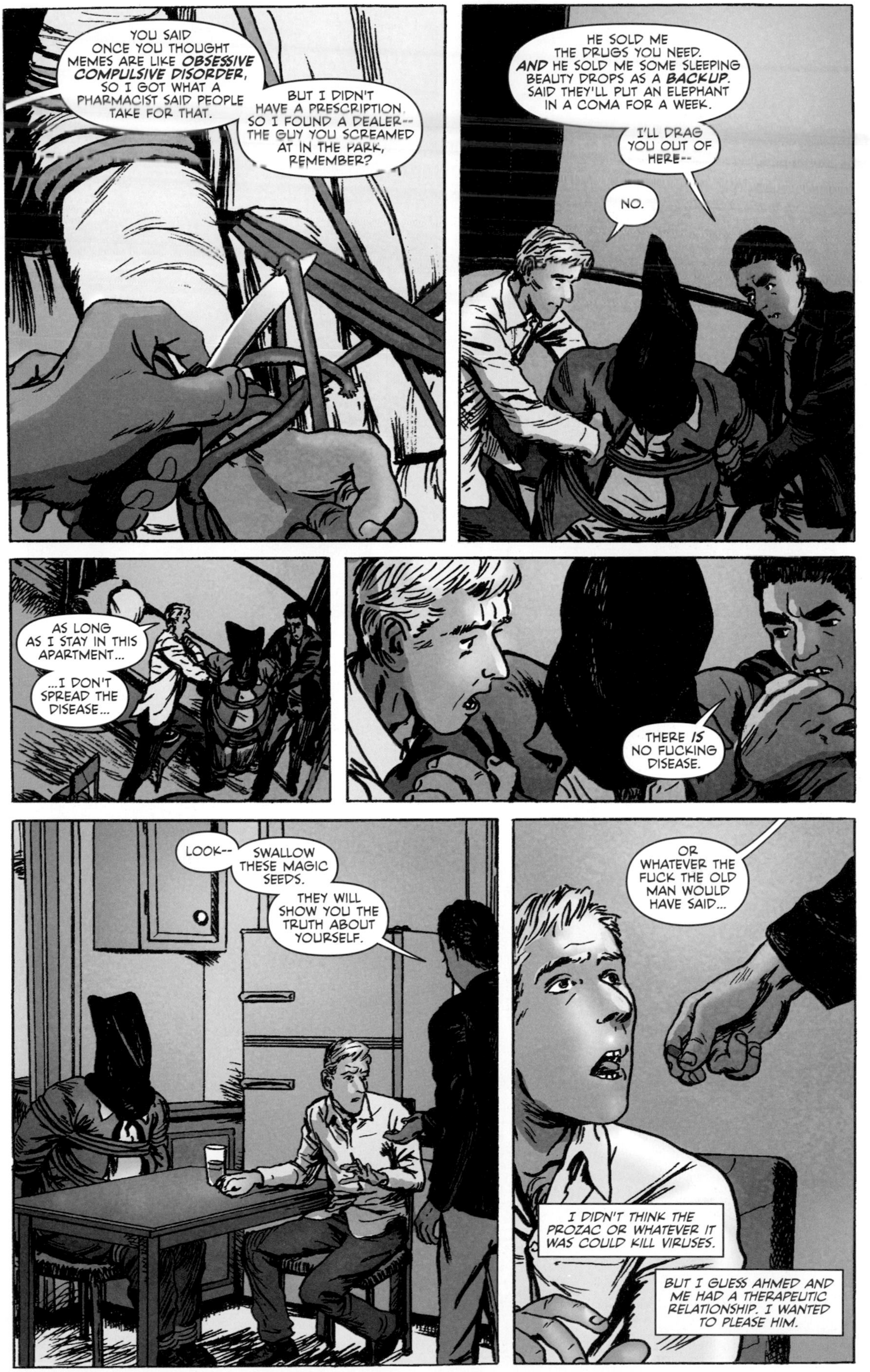
YOU SAID ONCE YOU THOUGHT MEMES ARE LIKE OBSESSIVE COMPULSIVE DISORDER, SO I GOT WHAT A PHARMACIST SAID PEOPLE TAKE FOR THAT.
BUT I DIDN'T HAVE A PRESCRIPTION. SO I FOUND A DEALER-- THE GUY YOU SCREAMED AT IN THE PARK, REMEMBER?
HE SOLD ME THE DRUGS YOU NEED. AND HE SOLD ME SOME SLEEPING BEAUTY DROPS AS A BACKUP. SAID THEY'LL PUT AN ELEPHANT IN A COMA FOR A WEEK.
I'LL DRAG YOU OUT OF HERE--
NO.
AS LONG AS I STAY IN THIS APARTMENT...
...I DON'T SPREAD THE DISEASE...
THERE IS NO FUCKING DISEASE.
LOOK--
SWALLOW THESE MAGIC SEEDS.
THEY WILL SHOW YOU THE TRUTH ABOUT YOURSELF.
OR WHATEVER THE FUCK THE OLD MAN WOULD HAVE SAID...
I DIDN'T THINK THE PROZAC OR WHATEVER IT WAS COULD KILL VIRUSES.
BUT I GUESS AHMED AND ME HAD A THERAPEUTIC RELATIONSHIP. I WANTED TO PLEASE HIM.

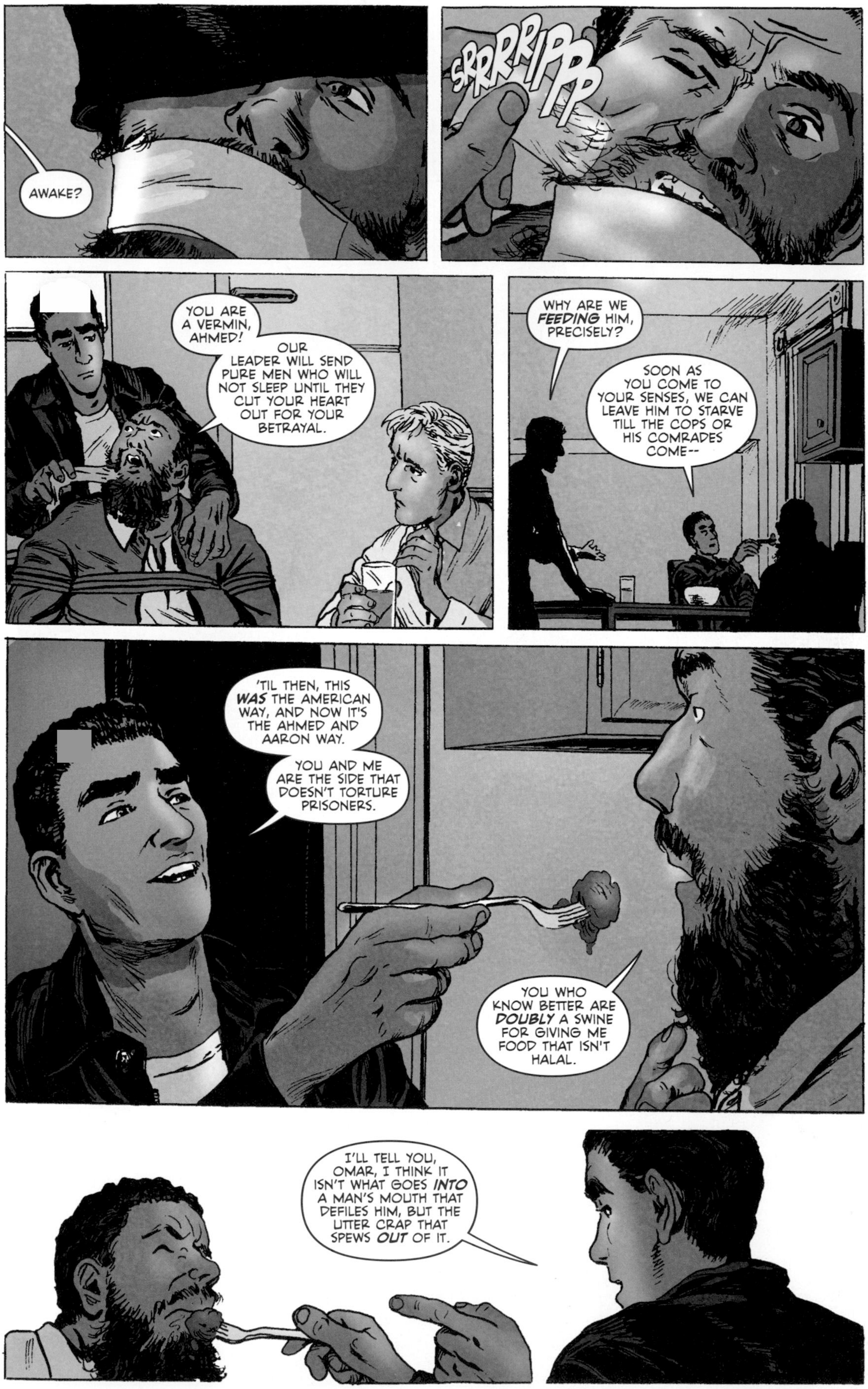
AWAKE?
SRRRRIPPP
YOU ARE A VERMIN, AHMED!
OUR LEADER WILL SEND PURE MEN WHO WILL NOT SLEEP UNTIL THEY CUT YOUR HEART OUT FOR YOUR BETRAYAL.
WHY ARE WE FEEDING HIM, PRECISELY?
SOON AS YOU COME TO YOUR SENSES, WE CAN LEAVE HIM TO STARVE TILL THE COPS OR HIS COMRADES COME--
'TIL THEN, THIS WAS THE AMERICAN WAY, AND NOW IT'S THE AHMED AND AARON WAY.
YOU AND ME ARE THE SIDE THAT DOESN'T TORTURE PRISONERS.
YOU WHO KNOW BETTER ARE DOUBLY A SWINE FOR GIVING ME FOOD THAT ISN'T HALAL.
I'LL TELL YOU, OMAR, I THINK IT ISN'T WHAT GOES INTO A MAN'S MOUTH THAT DEFILES HIM, BUT THE UTTER CRAP THAT SPEWS OUT OF IT.

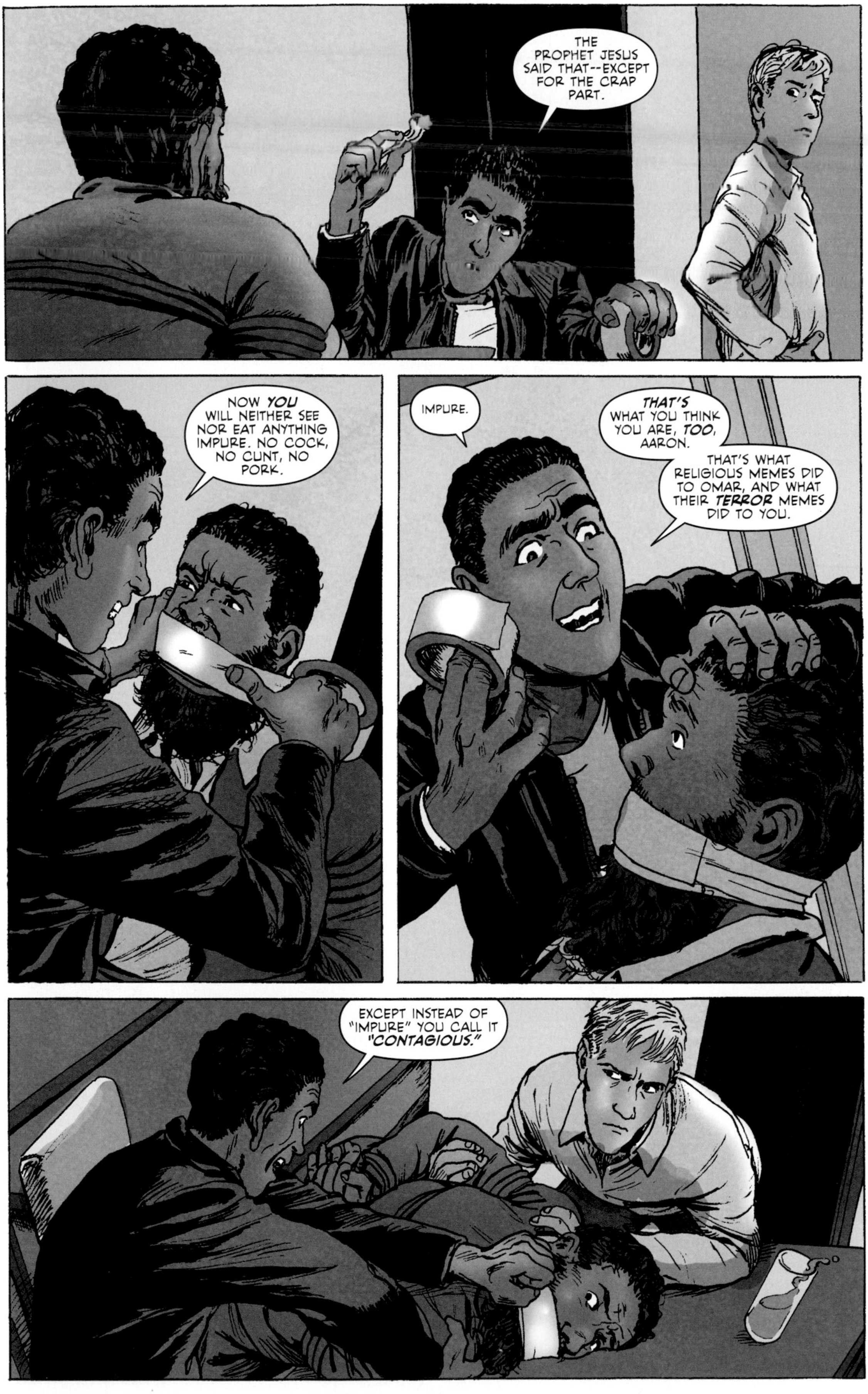
THE PROPHET JESUS SAID THAT--EXCEPT FOR THE CRAP PART.
NOW *YOU* WILL NEITHER SEE NOR EAT ANYTHING IMPURE. NO COCK, NO CUNT, NO PORK.
IMPURE.
THAT'S WHAT YOU THINK YOU ARE, *TOO*, AARON.
THAT'S WHAT RELIGIOUS MEMES DID TO OMAR, AND WHAT THEIR *TERROR* MEMES DID TO YOU.
EXCEPT INSTEAD OF "IMPURE" YOU CALL IT *"CONTAGIOUS."*

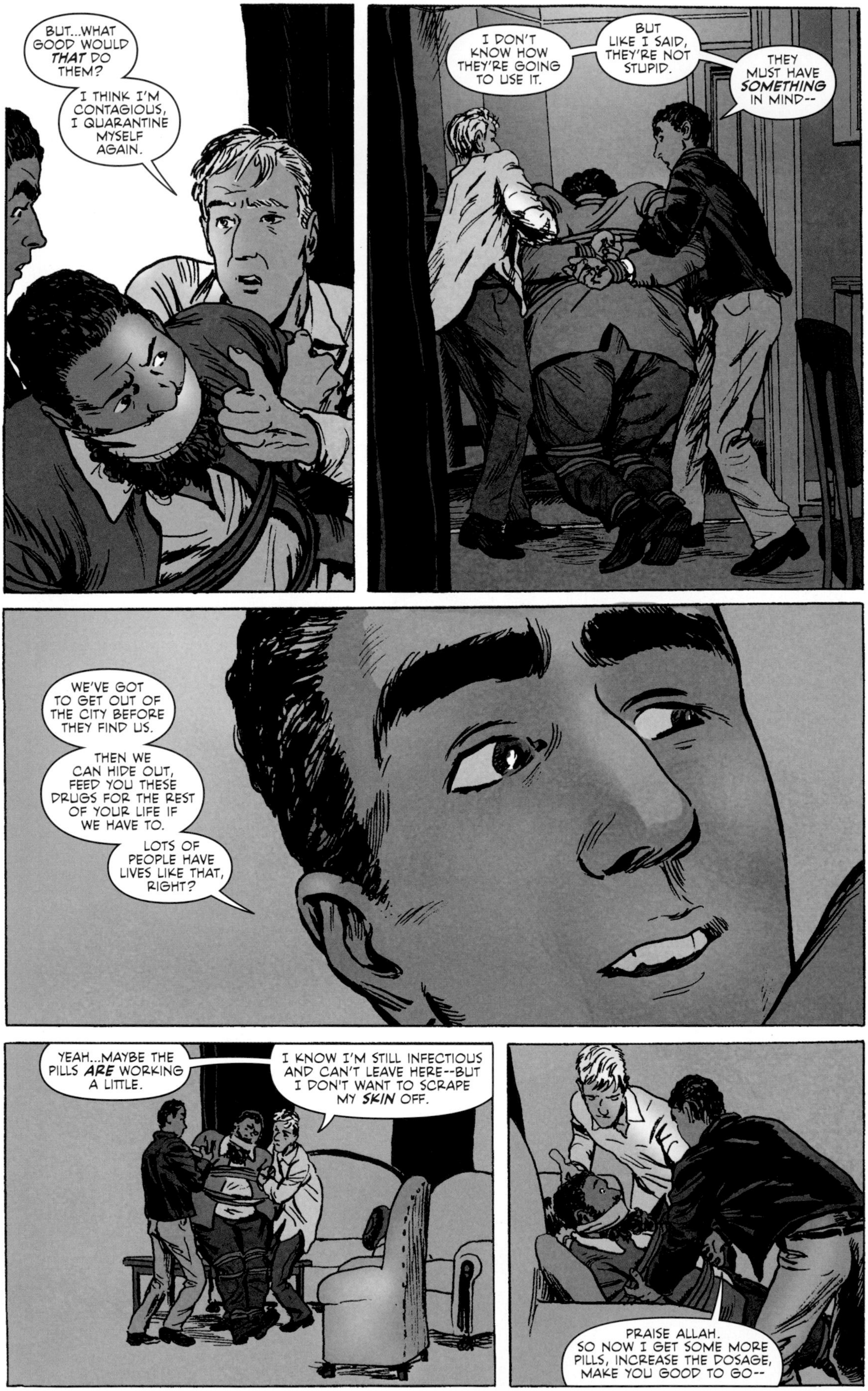
BUT...WHAT GOOD WOULD *THAT* DO THEM?
I THINK I'M CONTAGIOUS, I QUARANTINE MYSELF AGAIN.
I DON'T KNOW HOW THEY'RE GOING TO USE IT.
BUT LIKE I SAID, THEY'RE NOT STUPID.
THEY MUST HAVE *SOMETHING* IN MIND--
WE'VE GOT TO GET OUT OF THE CITY BEFORE THEY FIND US.
THEN WE CAN HIDE OUT, FEED YOU THESE DRUGS FOR THE REST OF YOUR LIFE IF WE HAVE TO.
LOTS OF PEOPLE HAVE LIVES LIKE THAT, RIGHT?
YEAH...MAYBE THE PILLS *ARE* WORKING A LITTLE.
I KNOW I'M STILL INFECTIOUS AND CAN'T LEAVE HERE--BUT I DON'T WANT TO SCRAPE MY *SKIN* OFF.
PRAISE ALLAH. SO NOW I GET SOME MORE PILLS, INCREASE THE DOSAGE, MAKE YOU GOOD TO GO--

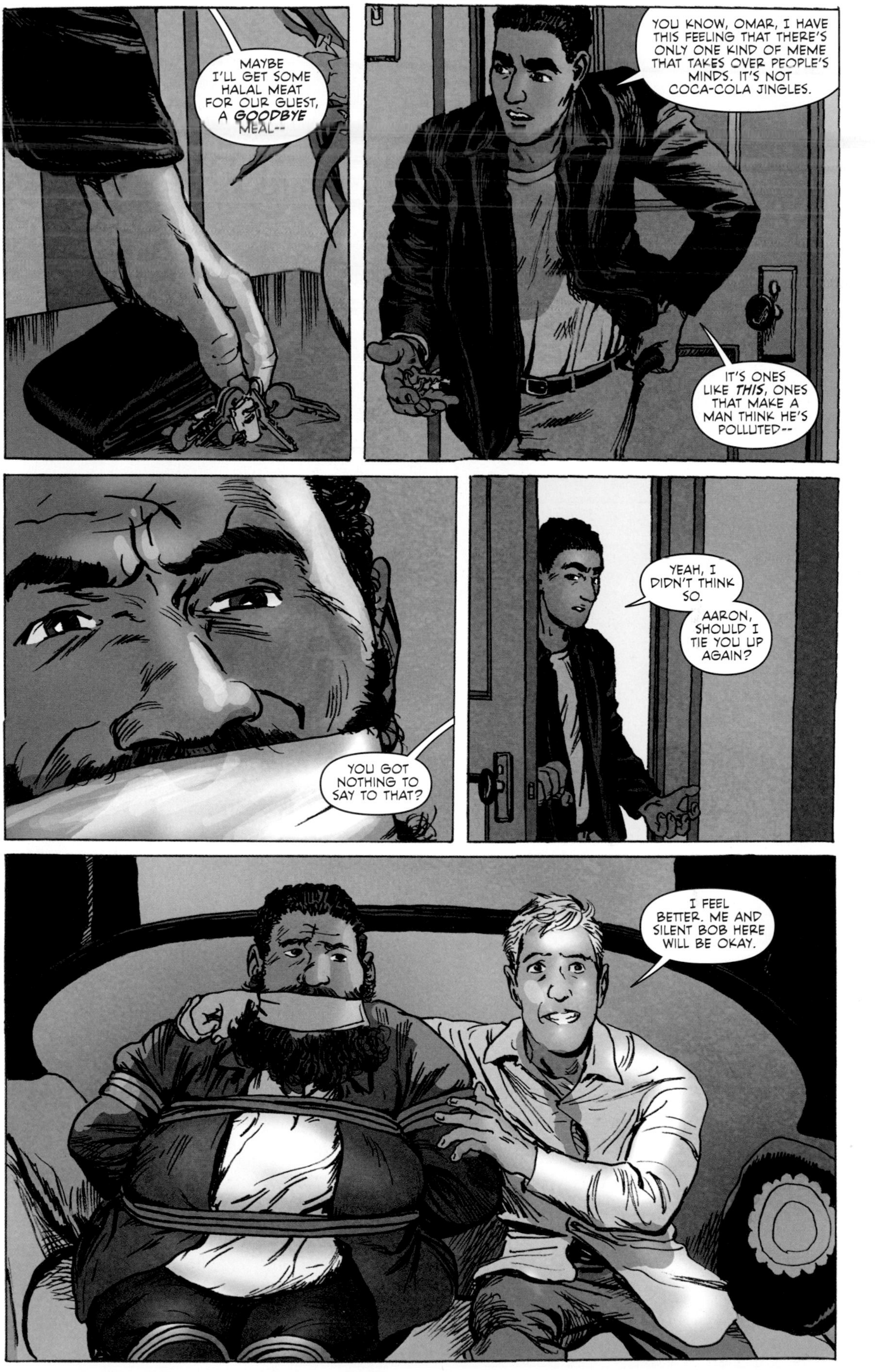
MAYBE I'LL GET SOME HALAL MEAT FOR OUR GUEST, A *GOODBYE* MEAL--
YOU KNOW, OMAR, I HAVE THIS FEELING THAT THERE'S ONLY ONE KIND OF MEME THAT TAKES OVER PEOPLE'S MINDS. IT'S NOT COCA-COLA JINGLES.
IT'S ONES LIKE *THIS*, ONES THAT MAKE A MAN THINK HE'S POLLUTED--
YOU GOT NOTHING TO SAY TO THAT?
YEAH, I DIDN'T THINK SO.
AARON, SHOULD I TIE YOU UP AGAIN?
I FEEL BETTER. ME AND SILENT BOB HERE WILL BE OKAY.

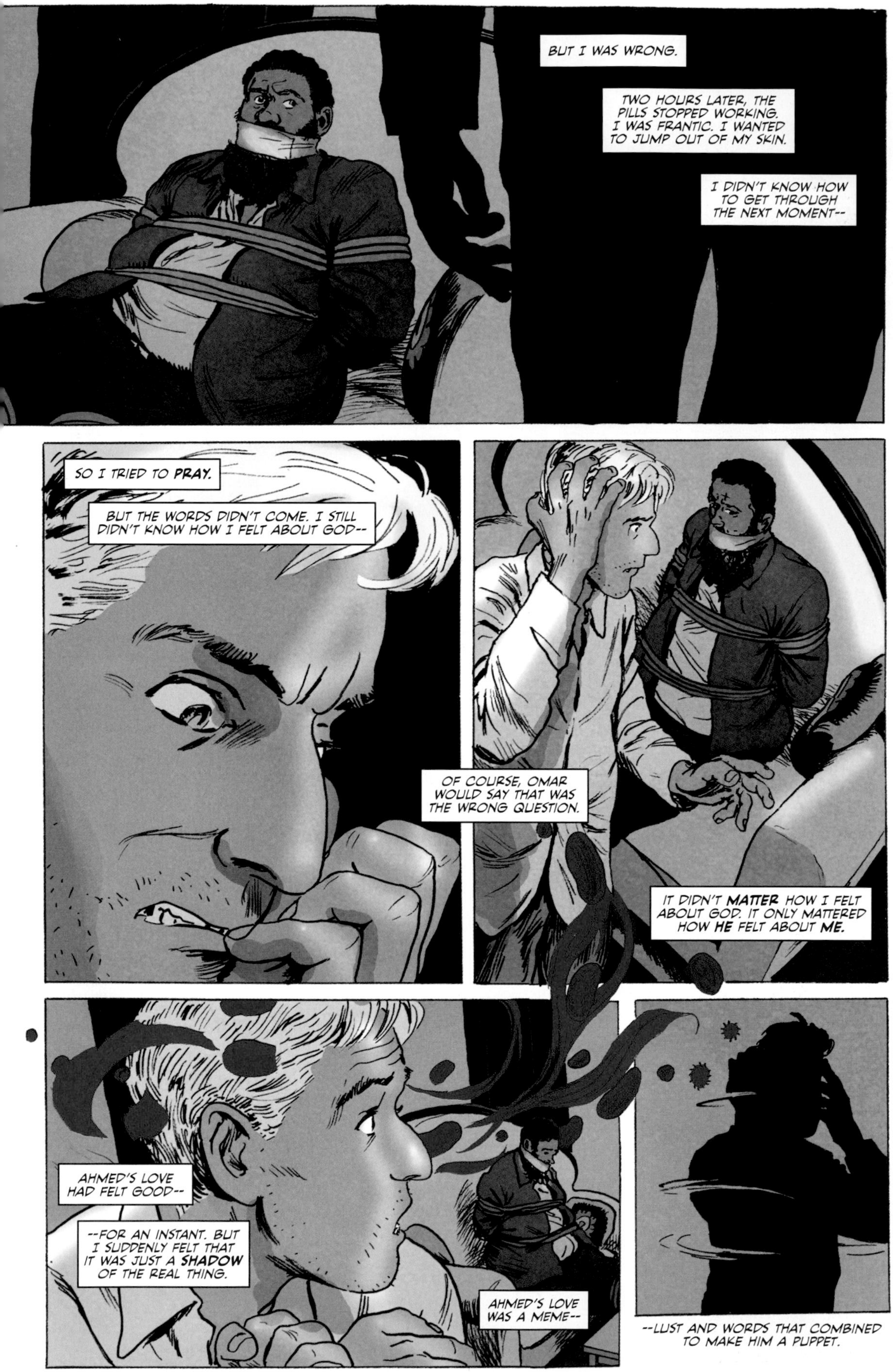
BUT I WAS WRONG.
TWO HOURS LATER, THE PILLS STOPPED WORKING. I WAS FRANTIC. I WANTED TO JUMP OUT OF MY SKIN.
I DIDN'T KNOW HOW TO GET THROUGH THE NEXT MOMENT--
SO I TRIED TO **PRAY.**
BUT THE WORDS DIDN'T COME. I STILL DIDN'T KNOW HOW I FELT ABOUT GOD--
OF COURSE, OMAR WOULD SAY THAT WAS THE WRONG QUESTION.
IT DIDN'T **MATTER** HOW I FELT ABOUT GOD. IT ONLY MATTERED HOW **HE** FELT ABOUT **ME.**
AHMED'S LOVE HAD FELT GOOD--
--FOR AN INSTANT. BUT I SUDDENLY FELT THAT IT WAS JUST A **SHADOW** OF THE REAL THING.
AHMED'S LOVE WAS A MEME--
--LUST AND WORDS THAT COMBINED TO MAKE HIM A PUPPET.

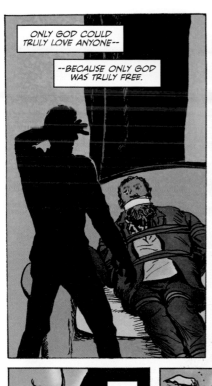

ONLY GOD COULD TRULY LOVE ANYONE--

--BECAUSE ONLY GOD WAS TRULY FREE.

BUT AFTER ALL THE PEOPLE I'D FAILED, WHY WOULD GOD LOVE ME? WHAT HAD I EVER DONE THAT WAS WORTHY OF SUCH LOVE?

I LONGED TO DISTRACT MYSELF FROM THAT ACCUSING VOICE.

BUT THEIR SAFE HOUSE HAD NO DISTRACTIONS. NO TELEVISION. NO IMAGES. ALL I HAD...

WAS

SOME

STALE

GUM...

AS I LOOKED AT THOSE TINY IMAGES, SOMETHING PIERCED MY HEART.

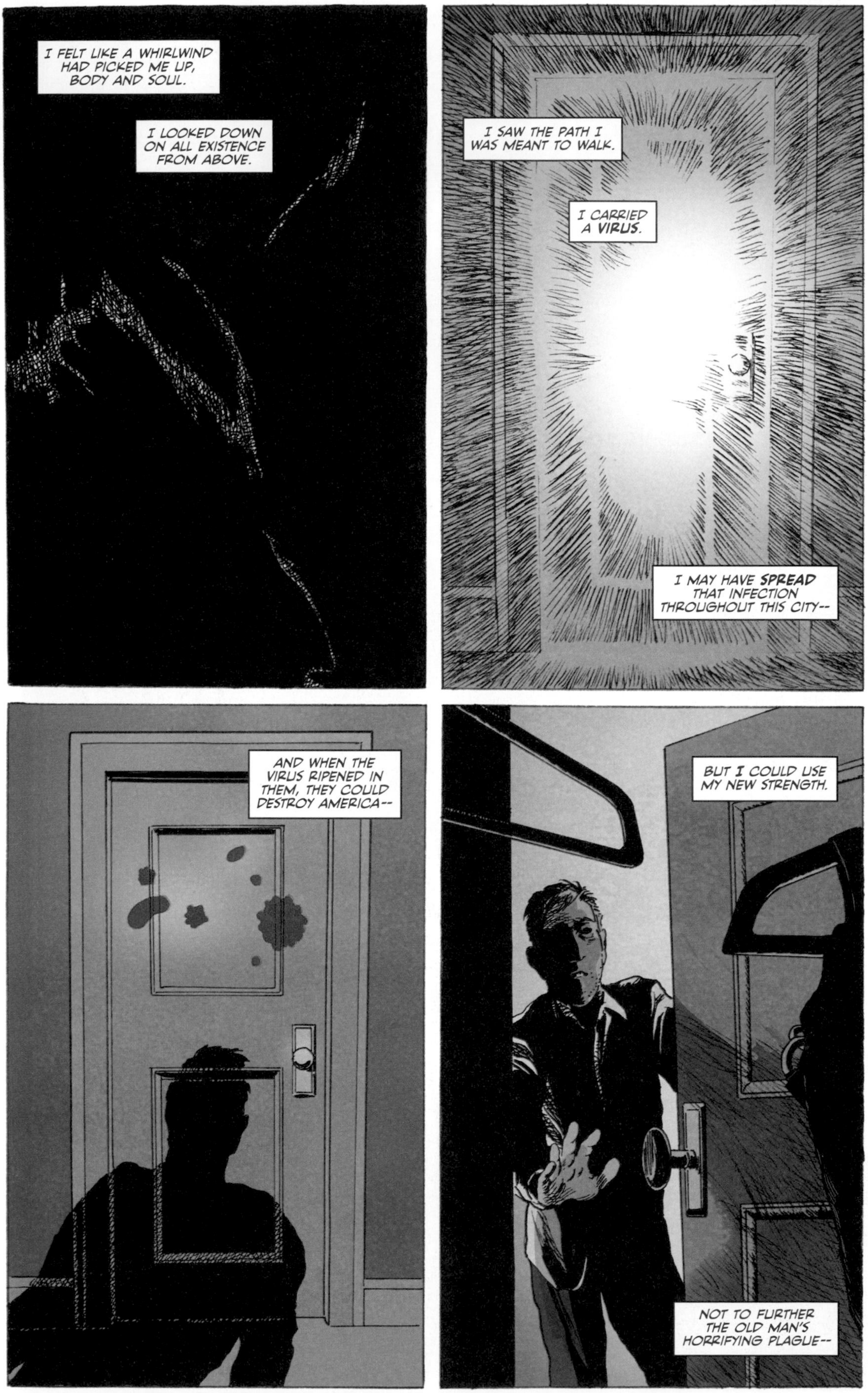
I FELT LIKE A WHIRLWIND HAD PICKED ME UP, BODY AND SOUL.
I LOOKED DOWN ON ALL EXISTENCE FROM ABOVE.
I SAW THE PATH I WAS MEANT TO WALK.
I CARRIED A VIRUS.
I MAY HAVE SPREAD THAT INFECTION THROUGHOUT THIS CITY--
AND WHEN THE VIRUS RIPENED IN THEM, THEY COULD DESTROY AMERICA--
BUT I COULD USE MY NEW STRENGTH.
NOT TO FURTHER THE OLD MAN'S HORRIFYING PLAGUE--

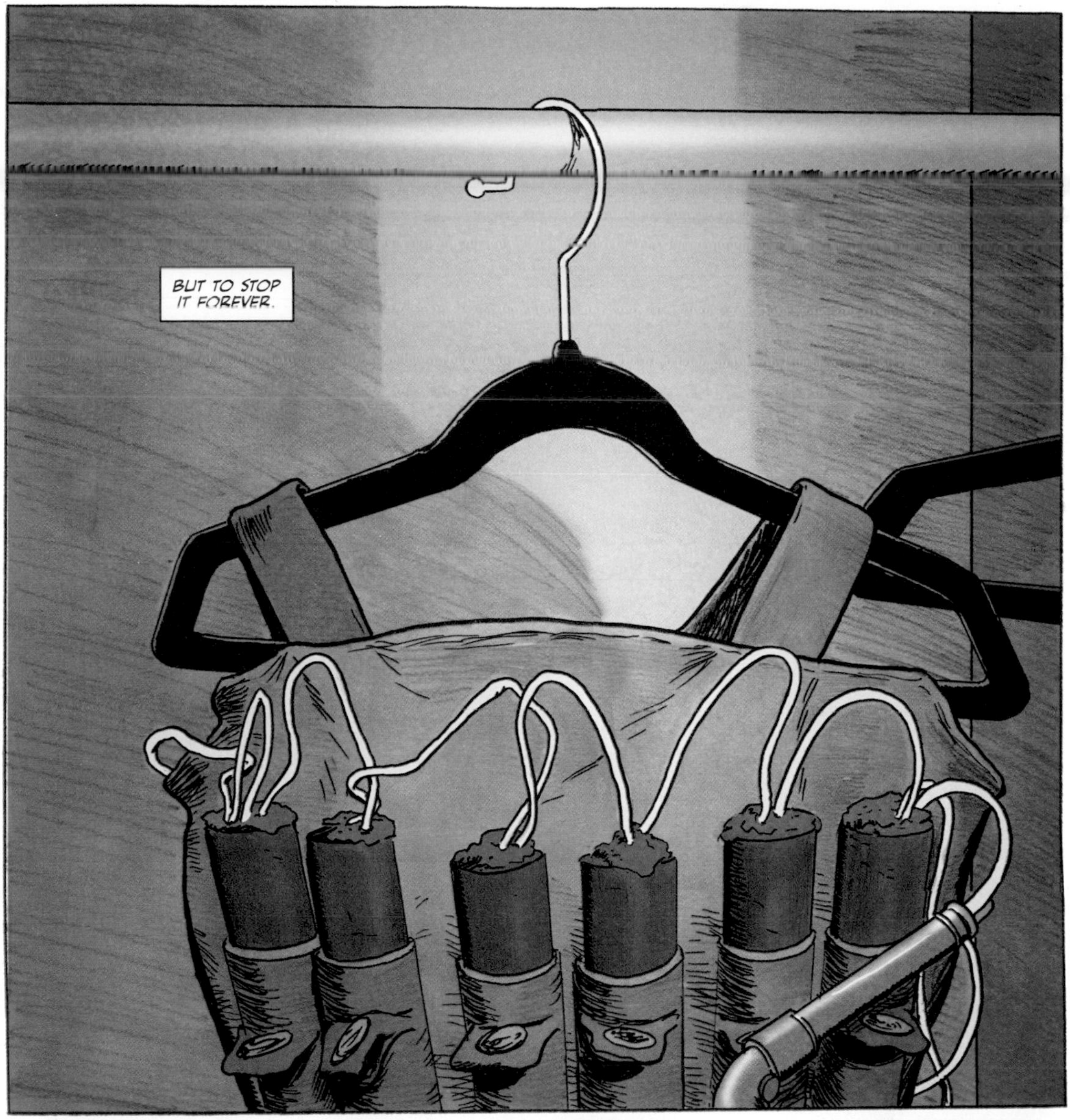
BUT TO STOP
IT FOREVER.

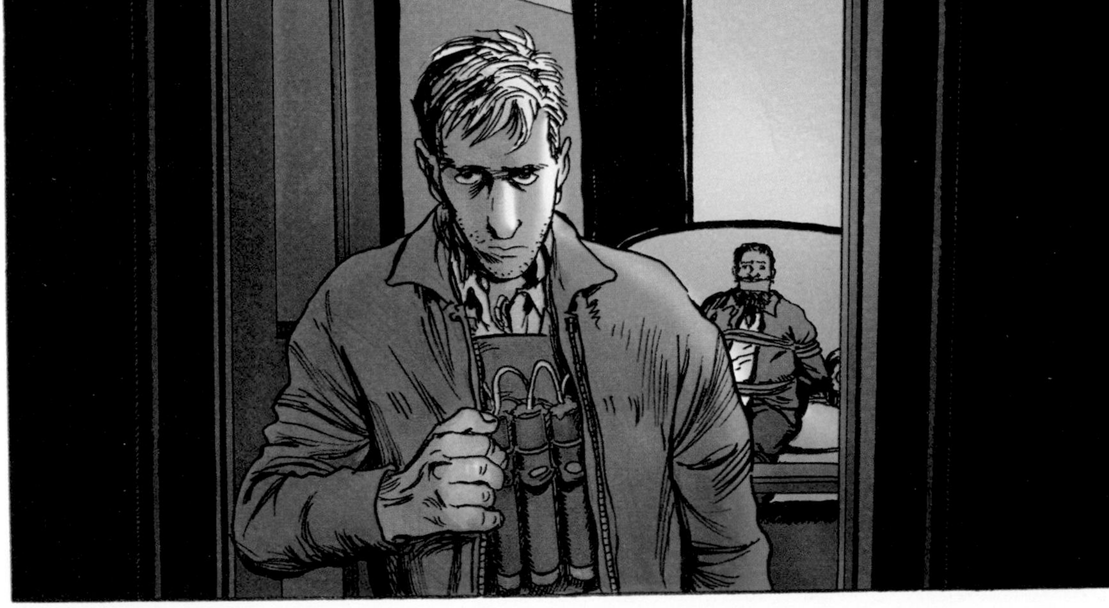

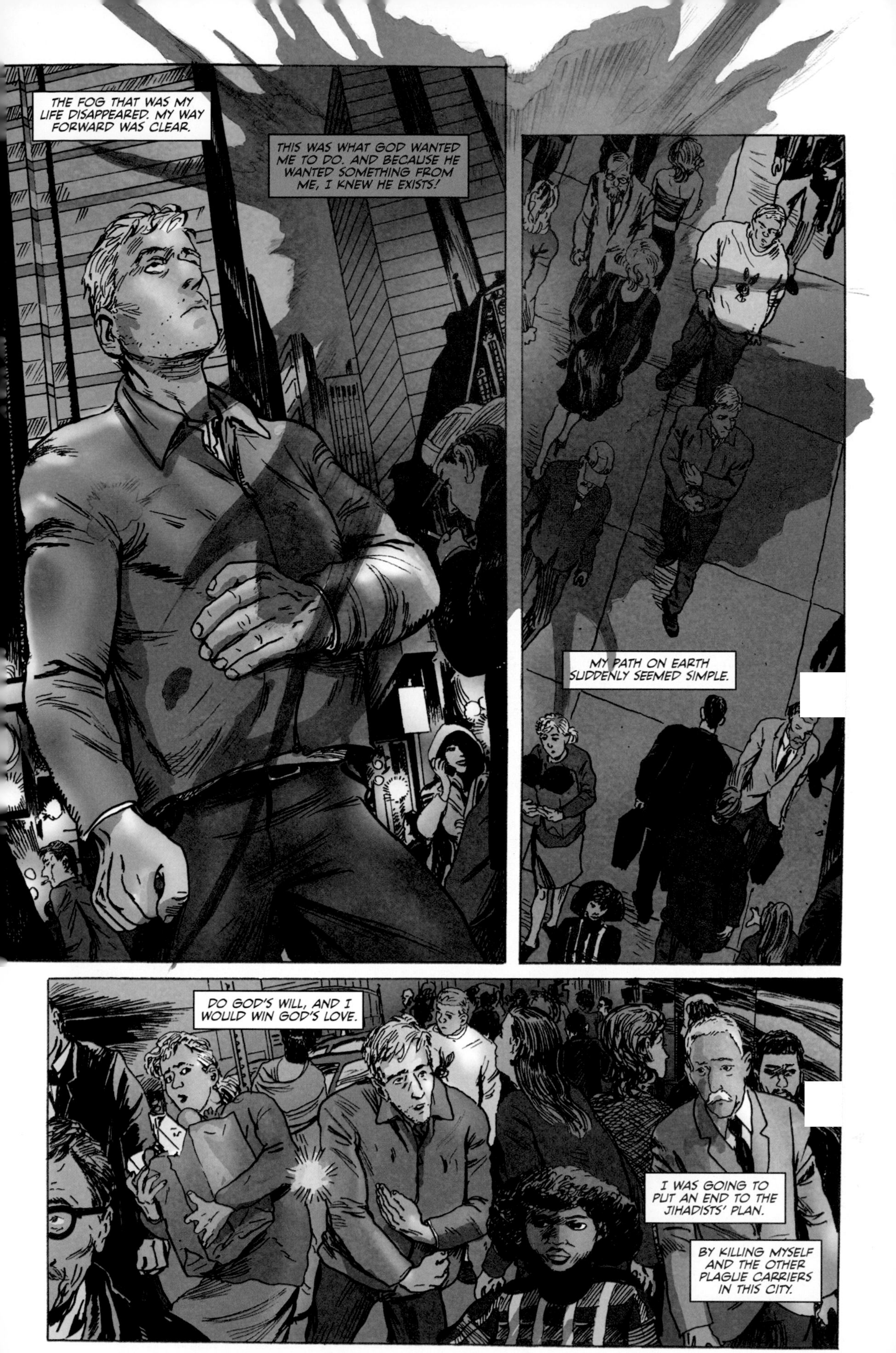
THE FOG THAT WAS MY LIFE DISAPPEARED. MY WAY FORWARD WAS CLEAR.
THIS WAS WHAT GOD WANTED ME TO DO. AND BECAUSE HE WANTED SOMETHING FROM ME, I KNEW HE EXISTS!
MY PATH ON EARTH SUDDENLY SEEMED SIMPLE.
DO GOD'S WILL, AND I WOULD WIN GOD'S LOVE.
I WAS GOING TO PUT AN END TO THE JIHADISTS' PLAN.
BY KILLING MYSELF AND THE OTHER PLAGUE CARRIERS IN THIS CITY.

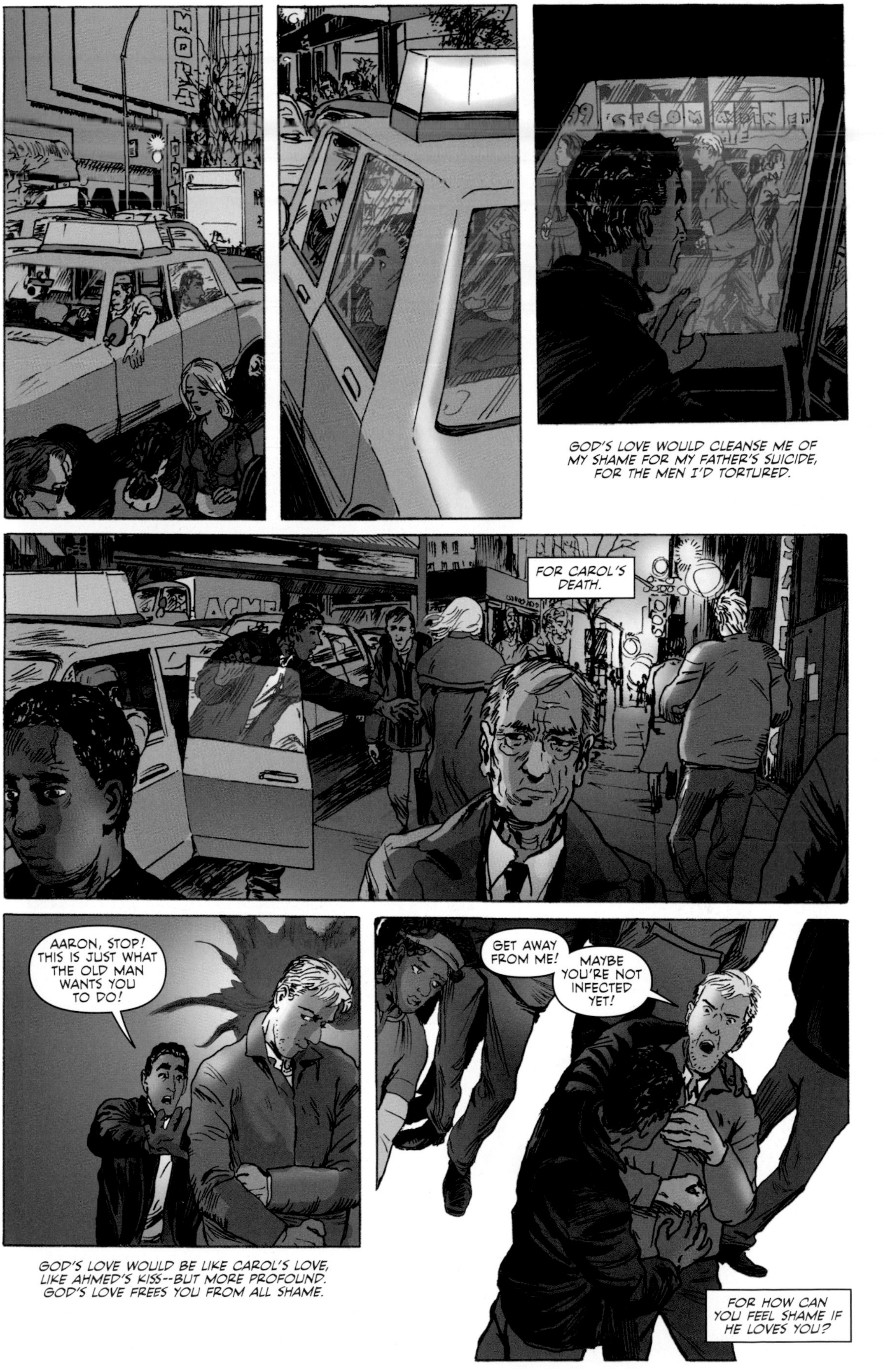
GOD'S LOVE WOULD CLEANSE ME OF MY SHAME FOR MY FATHER'S SUICIDE, FOR THE MEN I'D TORTURED.
FOR CAROL'S DEATH.
AARON, STOP! THIS IS JUST WHAT THE OLD MAN WANTS YOU TO DO!
GOD'S LOVE WOULD BE LIKE CAROL'S LOVE, LIKE AHMED'S KISS--BUT MORE PROFOUND. GOD'S LOVE FREES YOU FROM ALL SHAME.
GET AWAY FROM ME!
MAYBE YOU'RE NOT INFECTED YET!
FOR HOW CAN YOU FEEL SHAME IF HE LOVES YOU?

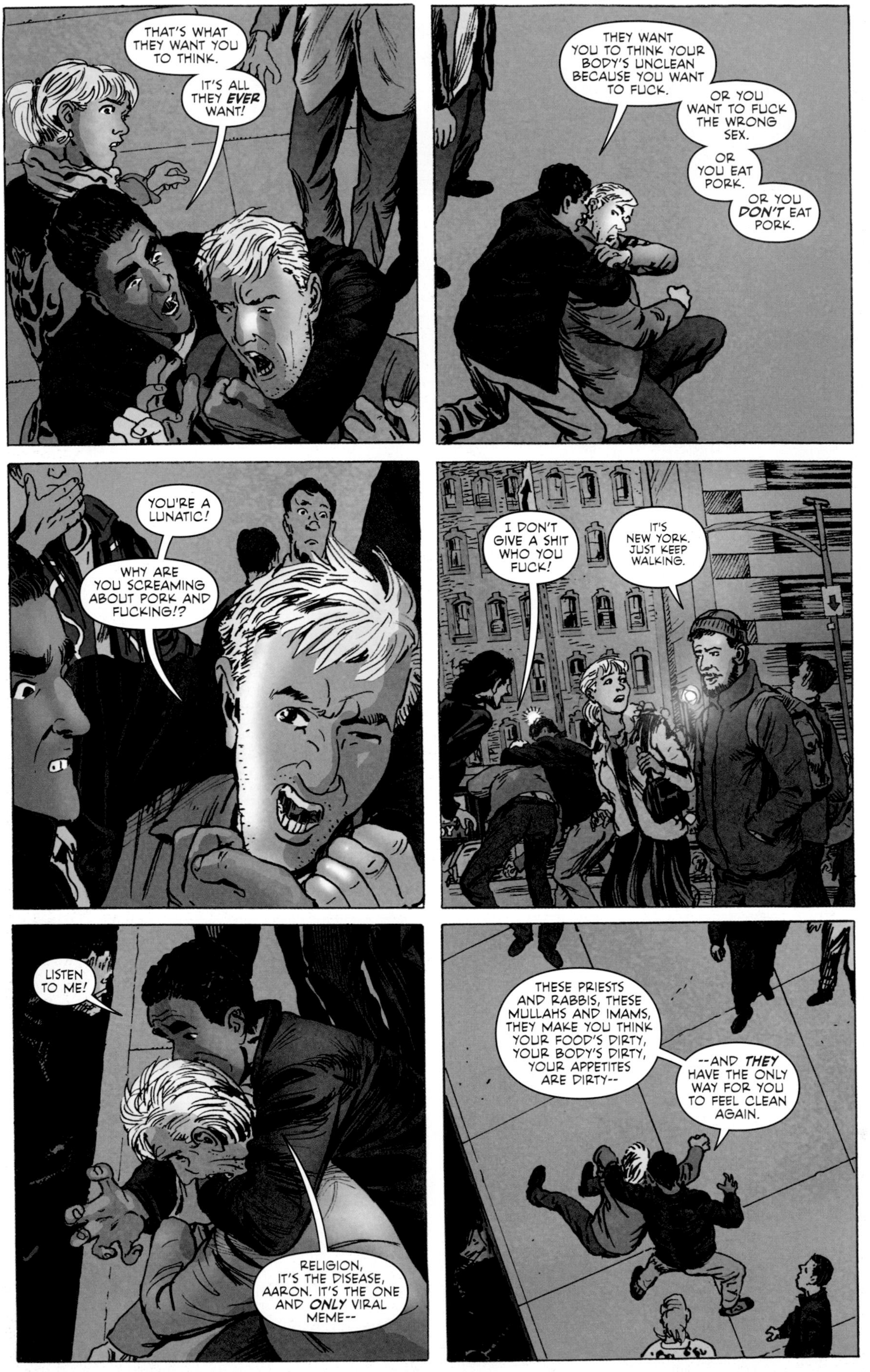
THAT'S WHAT THEY WANT YOU TO THINK.
IT'S ALL THEY *EVER* WANT!
THEY WANT YOU TO THINK YOUR BODY'S UNCLEAN BECAUSE YOU WANT TO FUCK.
OR YOU WANT TO FUCK THE WRONG SEX.
OR YOU EAT PORK.
OR YOU *DON'T* EAT PORK.
YOU'RE A LUNATIC!
WHY ARE YOU SCREAMING ABOUT PORK AND FUCKING!?
I DON'T GIVE A SHIT WHO YOU FUCK!
IT'S NEW YORK. JUST KEEP WALKING.
LISTEN TO ME!
RELIGION, IT'S THE DISEASE, AARON. IT'S THE ONE AND *ONLY* VIRAL MEME--
THESE PRIESTS AND RABBIS, THESE MULLAHS AND IMAMS, THEY MAKE YOU THINK YOUR FOOD'S DIRTY, YOUR BODY'S DIRTY, YOUR APPETITES ARE DIRTY--
--AND *THEY* HAVE THE ONLY WAY FOR YOU TO FEEL CLEAN AGAIN.

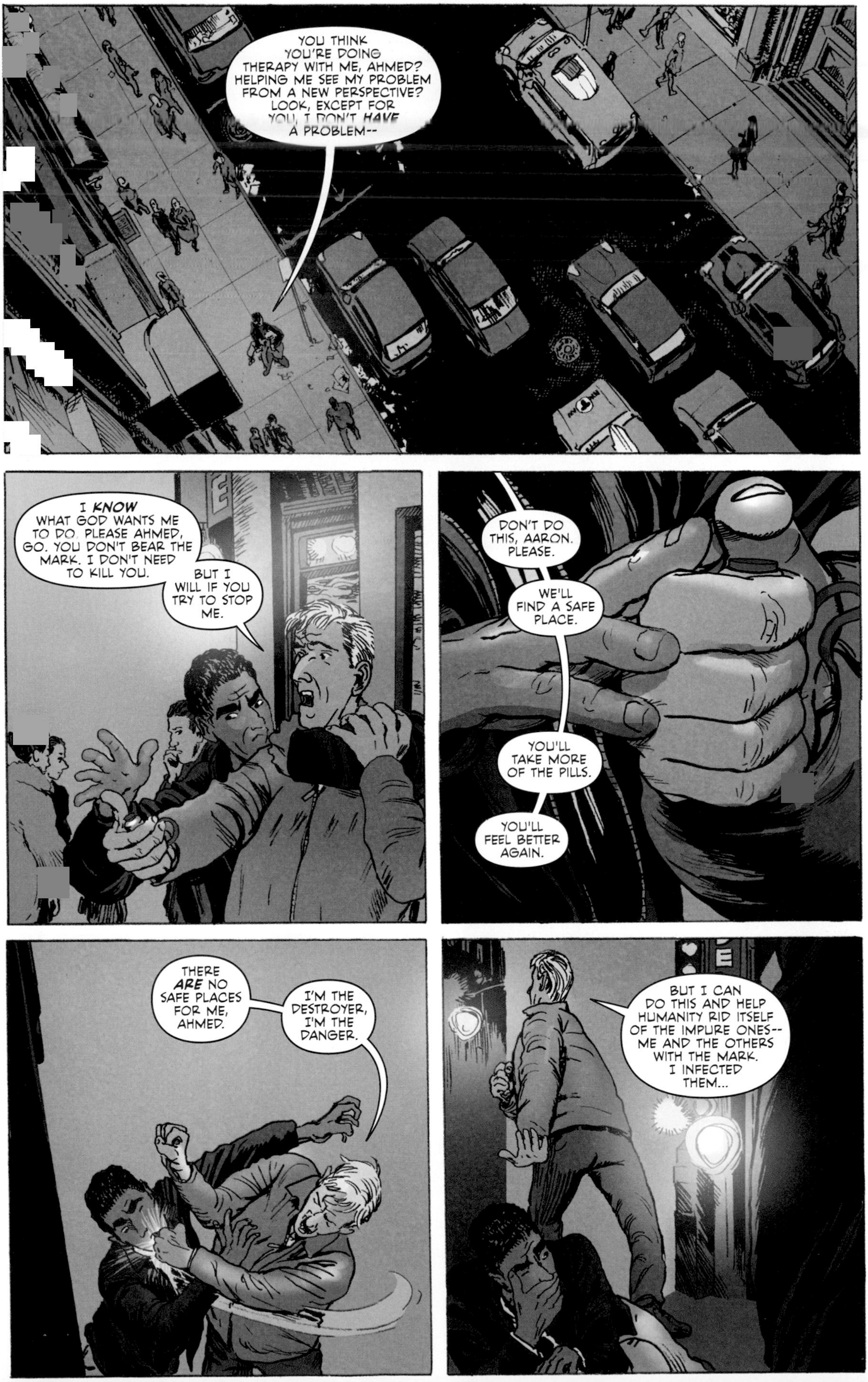

YOU THINK YOU'RE DOING THERAPY WITH ME, AHMED? HELPING ME SEE MY PROBLEM FROM A NEW PERSPECTIVE? LOOK, EXCEPT FOR YOU, I DON'T *HAVE* A PROBLEM--
I *KNOW* WHAT GOD WANTS ME TO DO. PLEASE AHMED, GO. YOU DON'T BEAR THE MARK. I DON'T NEED TO KILL YOU.
BUT I WILL IF YOU TRY TO STOP ME.
DON'T DO THIS, AARON. PLEASE.
WE'LL FIND A SAFE PLACE.
YOU'LL TAKE MORE OF THE PILLS.
YOU'LL FEEL BETTER AGAIN.
THERE *ARE* NO SAFE PLACES FOR ME, AHMED.
I'M THE DESTROYER, I'M THE DANGER.
BUT I CAN DO THIS AND HELP HUMANITY RID ITSELF OF THE IMPURE ONES-- ME AND THE OTHERS WITH THE MARK. I INFECTED THEM...

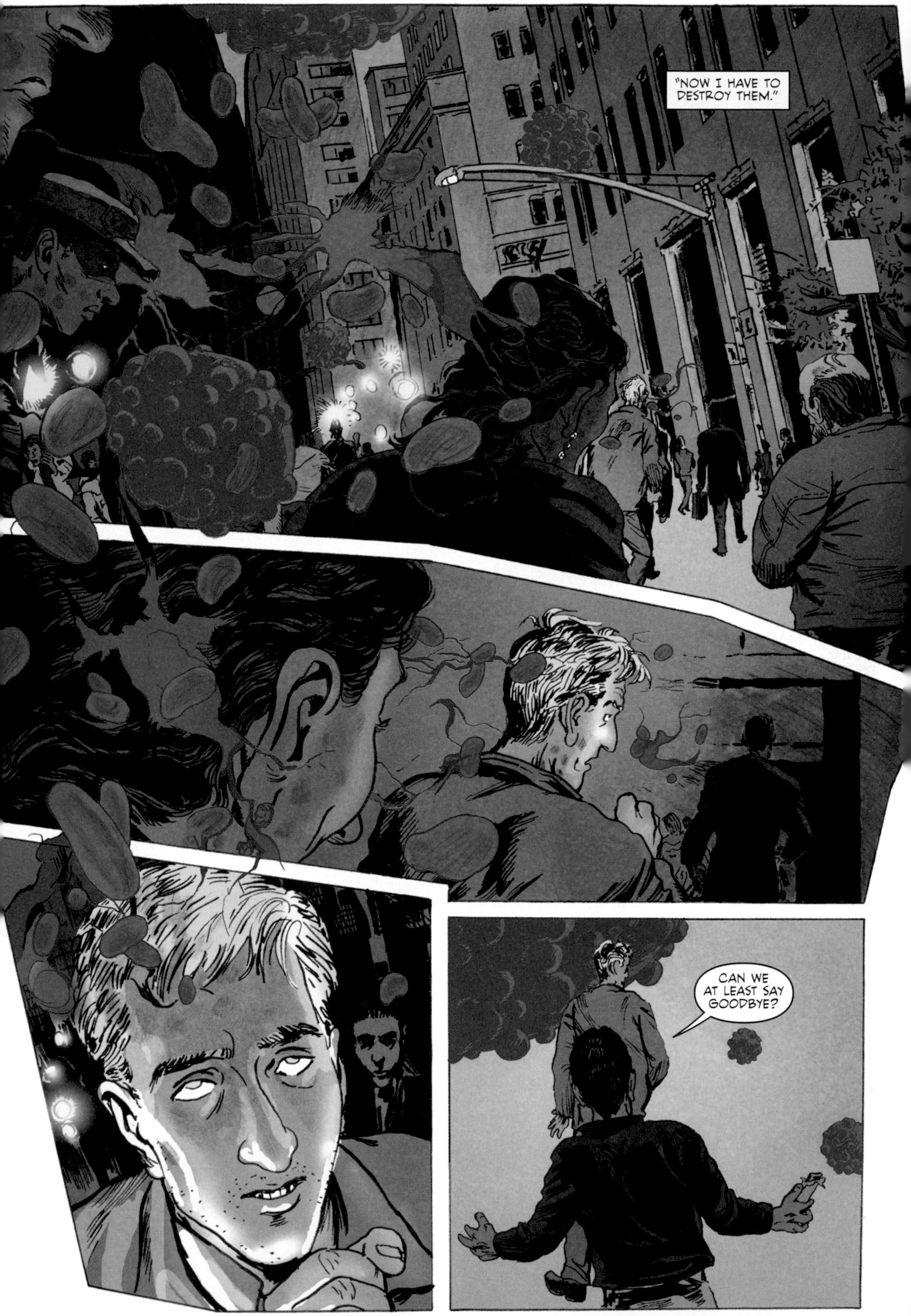
"NOW I HAVE TO DESTROY THEM."
CAN WE AT LEAST SAY GOODBYE?

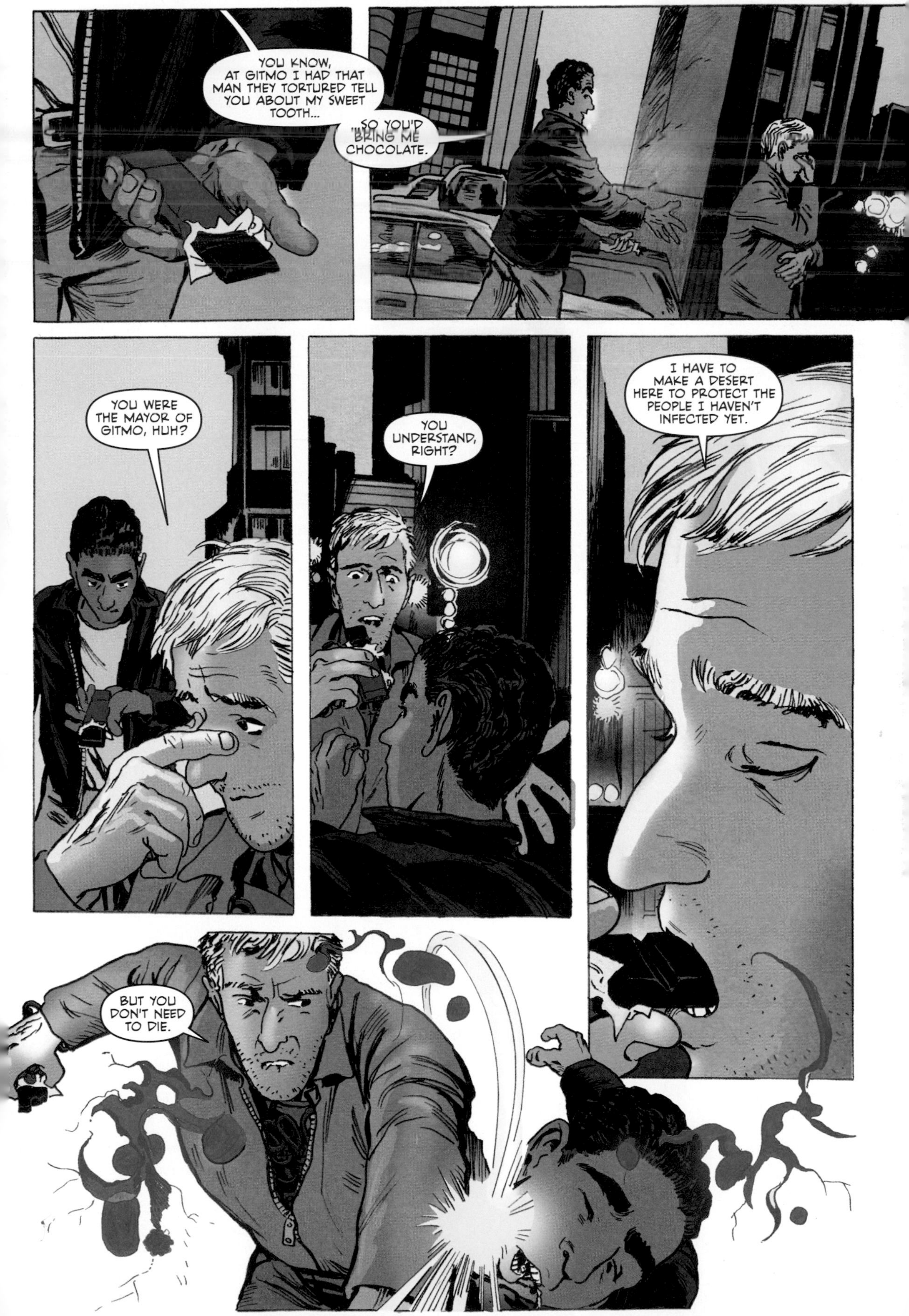
YOU KNOW, AT GITMO I HAD THAT MAN THEY TORTURED TELL YOU ABOUT MY SWEET TOOTH...
...SO YOU'D BRING ME CHOCOLATE.
YOU WERE THE MAYOR OF GITMO, HUH?
YOU UNDERSTAND, RIGHT?
I HAVE TO MAKE A DESERT HERE TO PROTECT THE PEOPLE I HAVEN'T INFECTED YET.
BUT YOU DON'T NEED TO DIE.

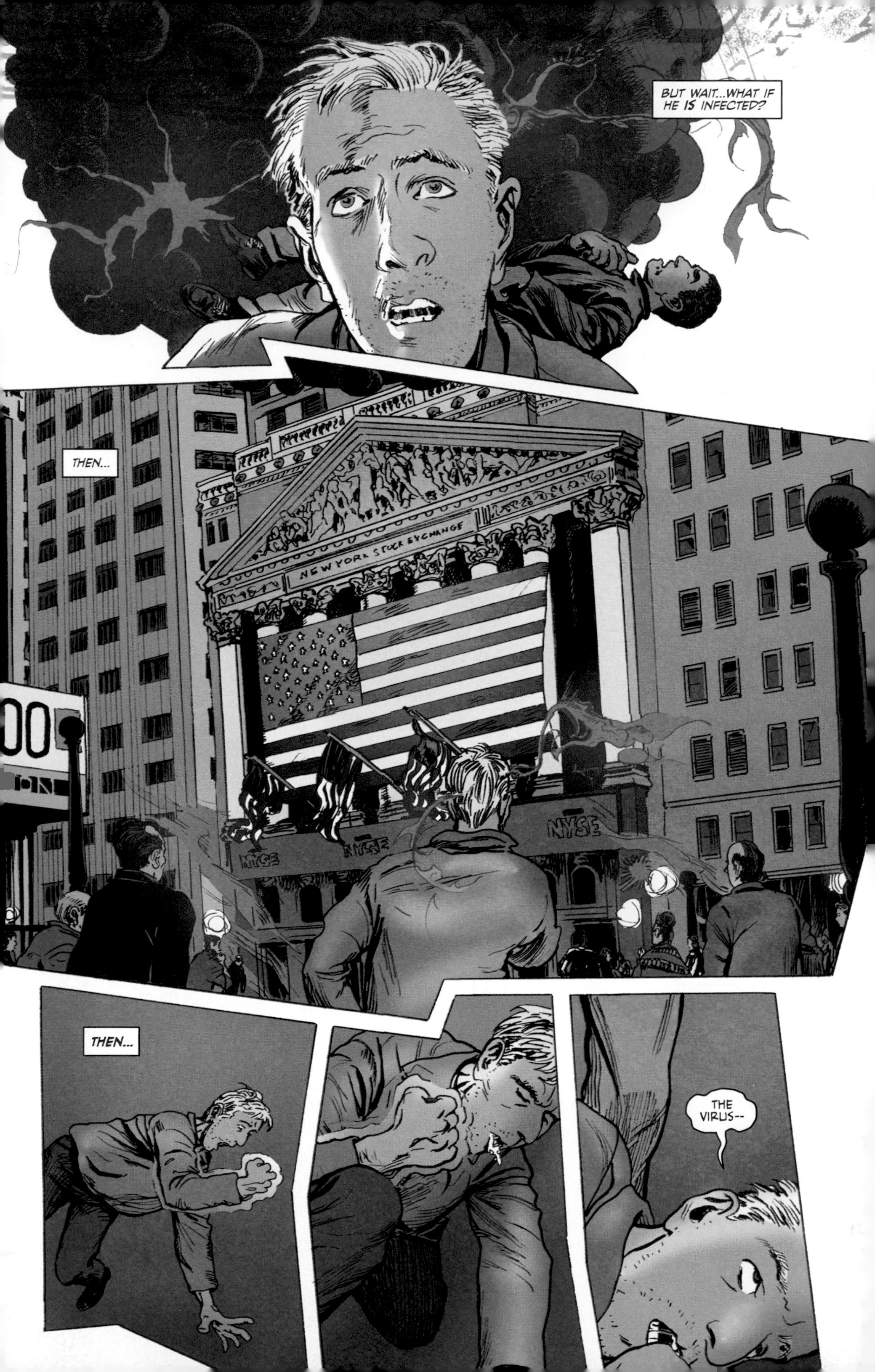
BUT WAIT...WHAT IF HE IS INFECTED?
THEN...
NEW YORK STOCK EXCHANGE
NYSE
NYSE
NYSE
THEN...
THE VIRUS--

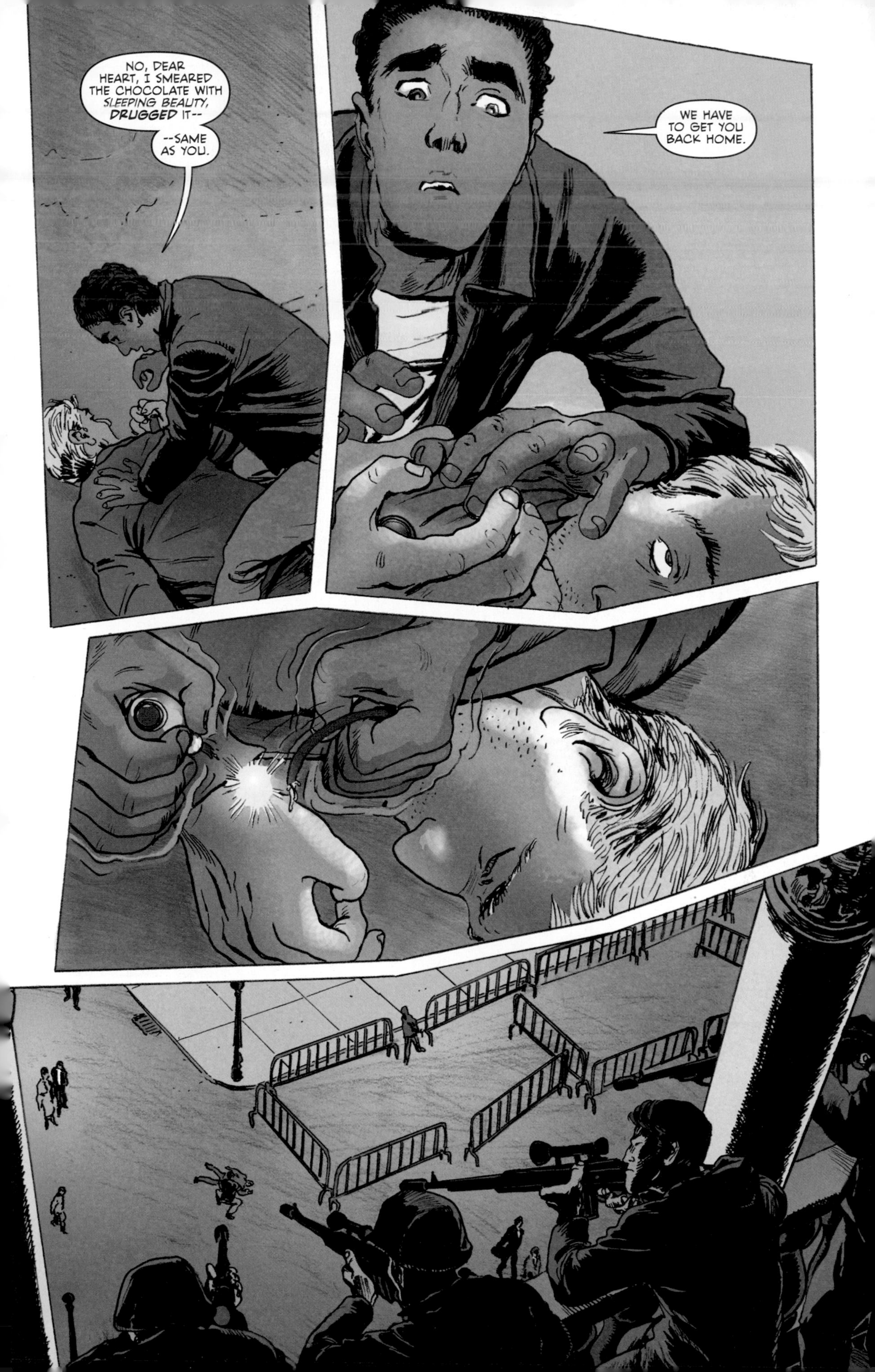
NO, DEAR HEART, I SMEARED THE CHOCOLATE WITH SLEEPING BEAUTY, DRUGGED IT--
--SAME AS YOU.
WE HAVE TO GET YOU BACK HOME.

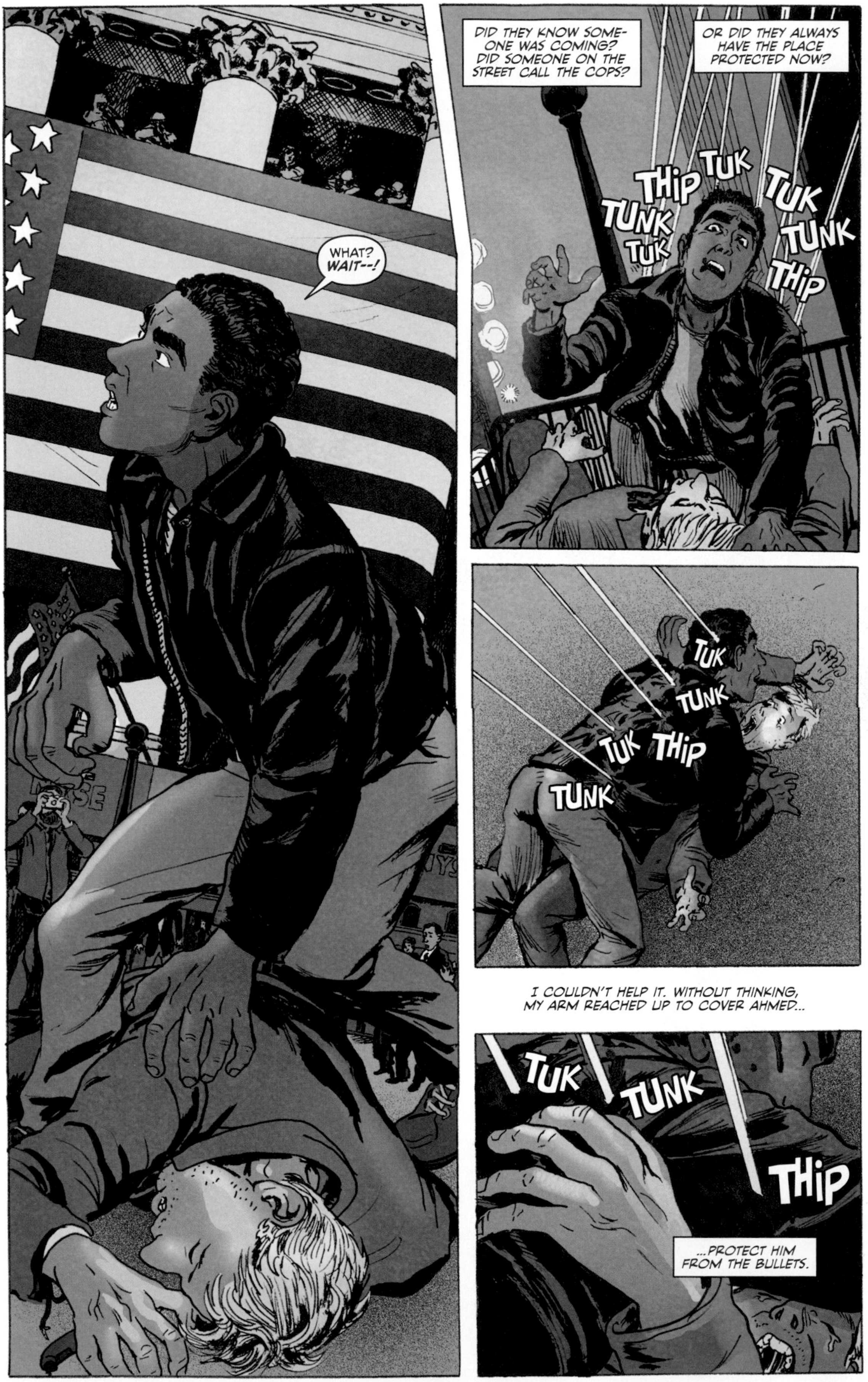
WHAT? WAIT--!
DID THEY KNOW SOMEONE WAS COMING? DID SOMEONE ON THE STREET CALL THE COPS?
OR DID THEY ALWAYS HAVE THE PLACE PROTECTED NOW?
THIP TUK TUK
TUNK TUK
TUNK THIP
TUK
TUNK
TUK THIP
TUNK
I COULDN'T HELP IT. WITHOUT THINKING, MY ARM REACHED UP TO COVER AHMED...
TUK TUNK
THIP
...PROTECT HIM FROM THE BULLETS.

TUK   TUNK

THiP

TUNK

THE THING IS...I HAD A BACKUP DETONATOR.

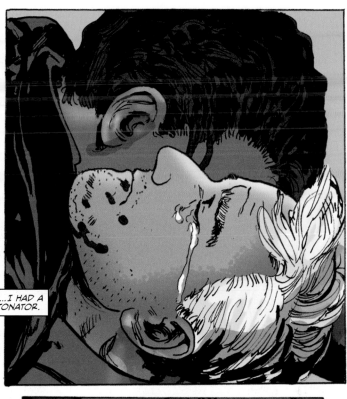

I JUST HAD TO MOVE THE TWO WIRES TOGETHER. BUT I COULDN'T BE SURE IF AHMED HAD BEEN KILLED BY THE SNIPERS--

I COULDN'T TAKE THE CHANCE I'D HURT HIM.

THAT WAS THE SOMETHING STRONGER THAN THE POWER WORDS--

I HAD TO PROTECT THE PERSON I LOVED.

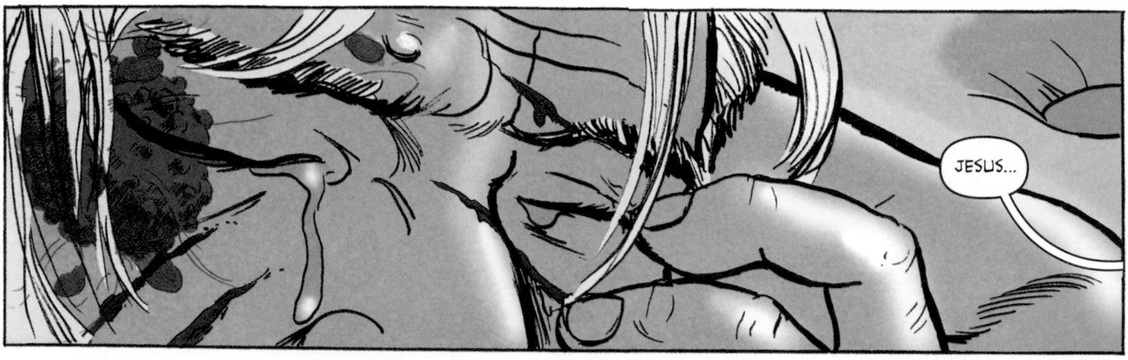
JESUS...

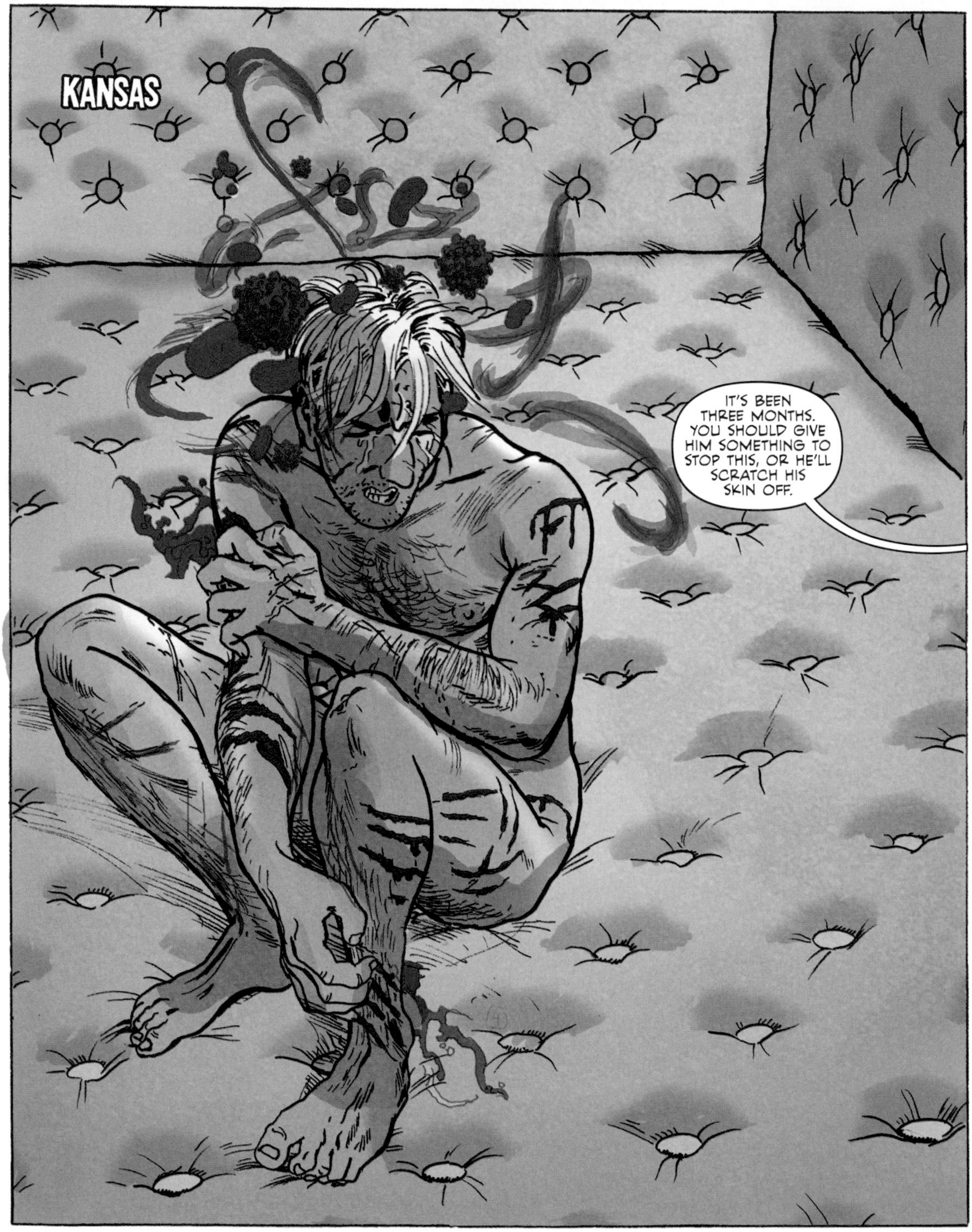
KANSAS
IT'S BEEN THREE MONTHS. YOU SHOULD GIVE HIM SOMETHING TO STOP THIS, OR HE'LL SCRATCH HIS SKIN OFF.

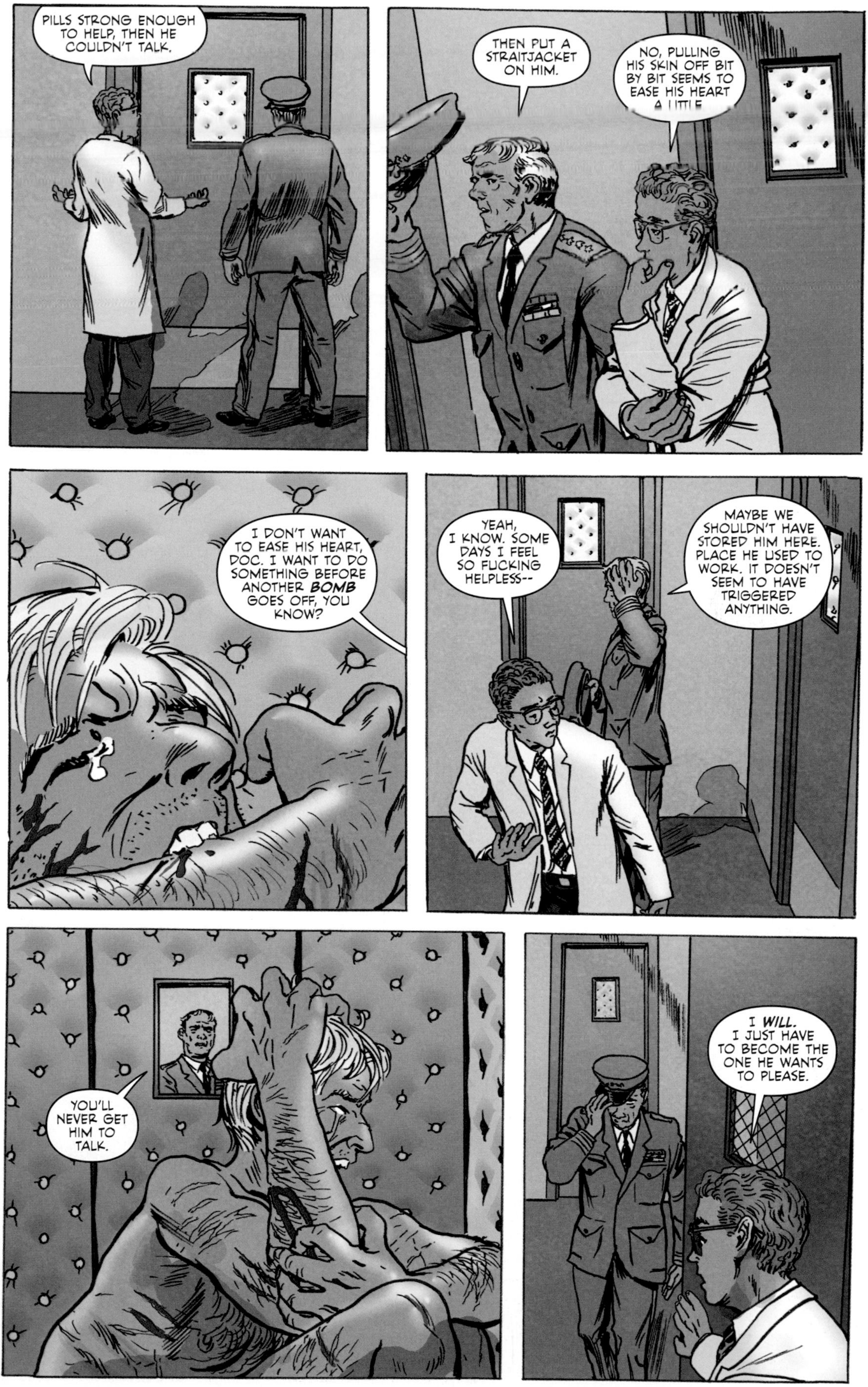
PILLS STRONG ENOUGH TO HELP, THEN HE COULDN'T TALK.
THEN PUT A STRAITJACKET ON HIM.
NO, PULLING HIS SKIN OFF BIT BY BIT SEEMS TO EASE HIS HEART A LITTLE.
I DON'T WANT TO EASE HIS HEART, DOC. I WANT TO DO SOMETHING BEFORE ANOTHER BOMB GOES OFF, YOU KNOW?
YEAH, I KNOW. SOME DAYS I FEEL SO FUCKING HELPLESS--
MAYBE WE SHOULDN'T HAVE STORED HIM HERE. PLACE HE USED TO WORK. IT DOESN'T SEEM TO HAVE TRIGGERED ANYTHING.
YOU'LL NEVER GET HIM TO TALK.
I WILL. I JUST HAVE TO BECOME THE ONE HE WANTS TO PLEASE.

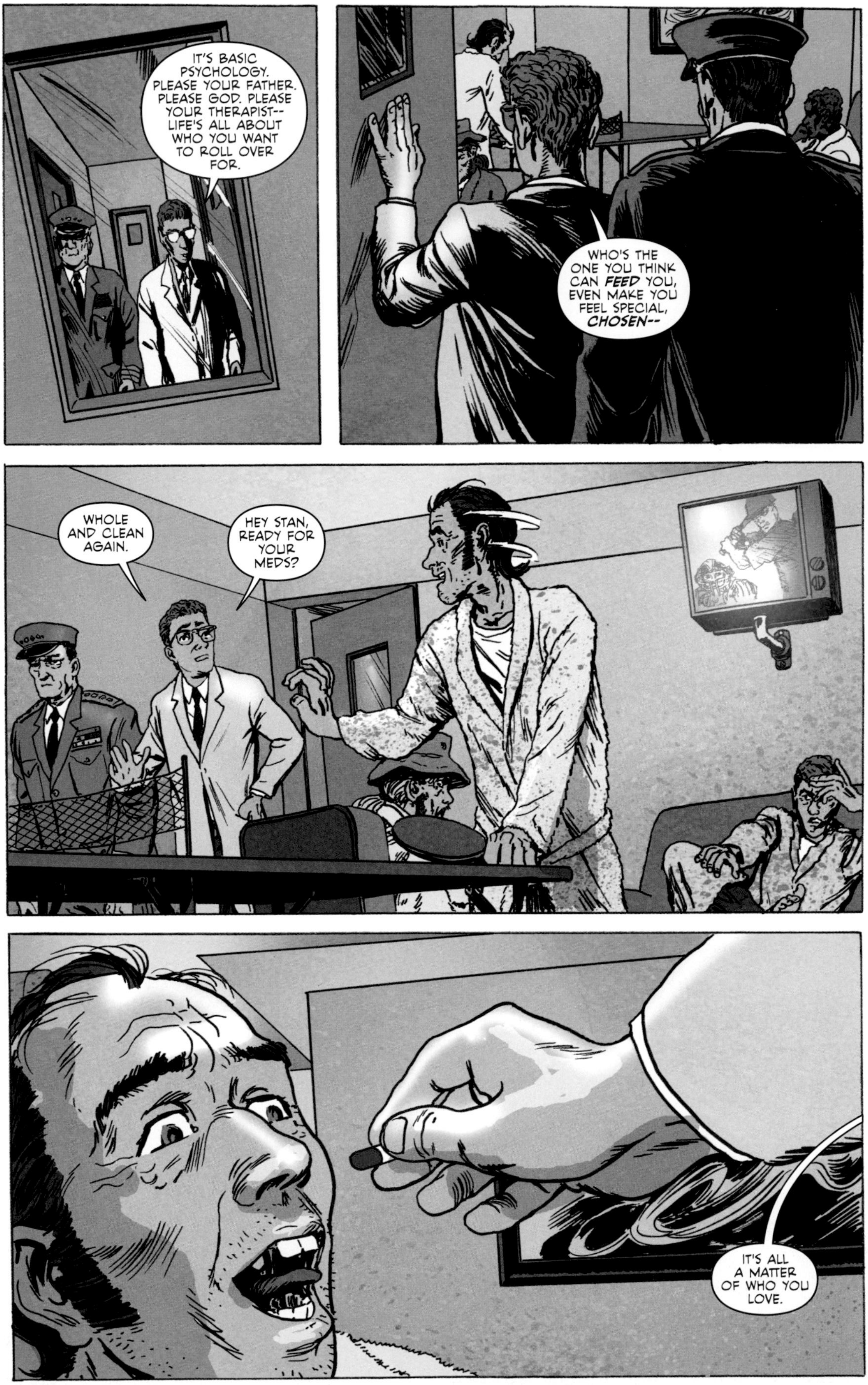
IT'S BASIC PSYCHOLOGY. PLEASE YOUR FATHER. PLEASE GOD. PLEASE YOUR THERAPIST-- LIFE'S ALL ABOUT WHO YOU WANT TO ROLL OVER FOR.
WHO'S THE ONE YOU THINK CAN *FEED* YOU, EVEN MAKE YOU FEEL SPECIAL, ***CHOSEN--***
WHOLE AND CLEAN AGAIN.
HEY STAN, READY FOR YOUR MEDS?
IT'S ALL A MATTER OF WHO YOU LOVE.

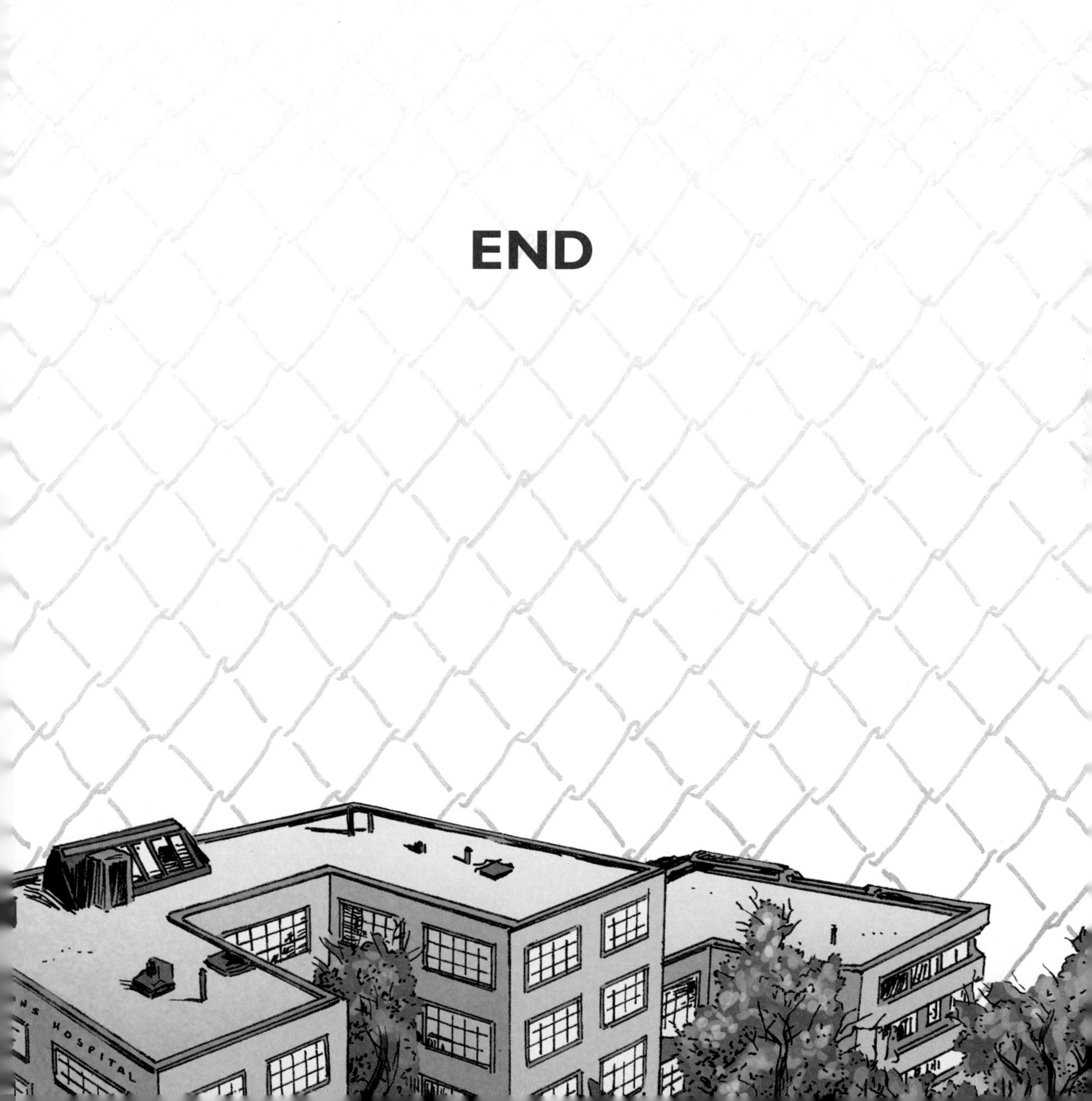
END
HOSPITAL

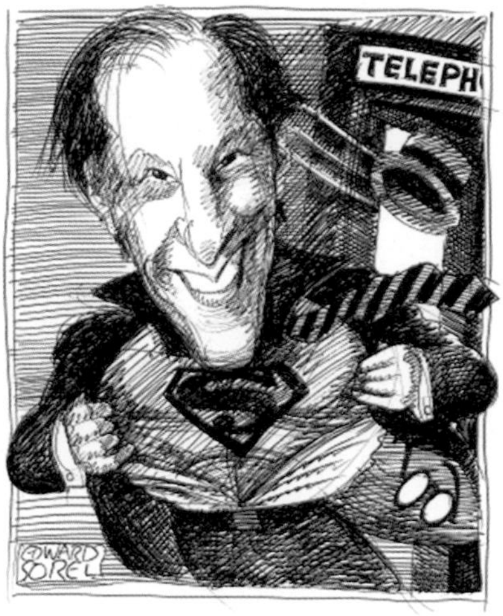
TELEPH
EDWARD SOREL
Illustration by Edward Sorel.

JAY CANTOR is the author of three previous novels, *The Death of Che Guevara, Krazy Kat,* and *Great Neck* as well as two books of essays, *The Space Between: Literature and Politics* and *On Giving Birth to One's Own Mother.* A MacArthur Prize Fellow, Cantor teaches at Tufts University and lives in Cambridge, Massachusetts, with his wife, Melinda Marble, and their daughter, Grace.

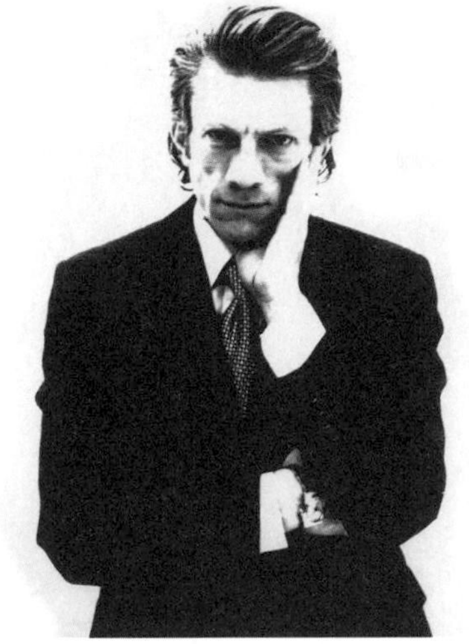
Photo by James Romberger

JAMES ROMBERGER collaborated with his wife Marguerite Van Cook and the late writer, artist and AIDS activist David Wojnarowicz on the critically acclaimed *Seven Miles A Second*; with Jamie Delano on *2020 Visions;* and with Peter Milligan on *The Bronx Kill*—all published by Vertigo. His drawings are in many private and public collections including the Metropolitan Museum of Art, Harvard University and the Library of Congress.